D1615251

Church and State
in Scotland
1660-1681

Church and State
in Scotland
1660-1681

JULIA BUCKROYD

JOHN DONALD PUBLISHERS LTD
EDINBURGH

For dearest B,
without whom not

ISBN 0 85976 042 1

Printed in Great Britain by Bell & Bain Ltd., Glasgow
Typeset by Wright Printers, Dundee

Acknowledgements

THIS book owes much to the teaching of Ronald Cant at St Andrews University. He it was who first aroused my curiosity in its subject when I was an undergraduate there. My thanks are due to him not only for the inspiration of his teaching but for the continuing interest he has taken in my work since then.

My warmest thanks are also due to Professor Gordon Rupp and Dr I. B. Cowan, of the Universities of Cambridge and Glasgow respectively, who supervised the work for this book in its earlier manifestation as a Ph.D. thesis. I owe a debt of thanks to the staffs of the manuscript libraries I have used for their generous assistance, particularly to the Department of Manuscripts of the National Library of Scotland.

I am indebted to the Principal and Fellows of Lady Margaret Hall, Oxford. The two years I spent in their company as Talbot Research Fellow provided me not only with time and leisure to complete this book, but also with the pleasant stimulus of their interest and encouragement.

Julia Buckroyd

Contents

1
Introduction

THIS book attempts to analyse the evolution of ecclesiastical policy in Scotland between 1660 and 1681. It seeks not only to discover the details of the way in which policy was evolved but also tries to discern what that policy was intended to achieve.

It attempts to answer what at first sight is a very puzzling question for the historian of the period of the Restoration in Scotland. Why was episcopacy re-imposed by the secular power on a country which in the preceding century had had limited experience of episcopacy and apparently even less liking for it? Given that Charles II was particularly anxious not to go on his travels again, why did he sanction a policy whose implementation was to cause the gravest difficulties for the forces of law and order? Further, given that the policy had given rise to such problems, were any attempts made to modify it during the period 1660-1681?

The period 1660-1681 has been chosen because it covers the years during which the second earl and first duke of Lauderdale was Secretary of State for Scotland; it was a period which was dominated by him and his contemporaries and colleagues. These men, who included the earls of Rothes, Tweeddale, Kincardine and Moray, and the former presbyterian minister James Sharp, archbishop of St Andrews, had all taken part in the covenanting revolution of the 1640s. They differed radically from the new generation of politicians of the 1680s who had grown up in the Restoration world, and who unlike the older generation of Lauderdale and his contemporaries had neither recollection of nor sympathy for the presbyterian heyday. The ecclesiastical policies of Lauderdale and his contemporaries can be seen as an era which was brought to an end by the murder of archbishop Sharp and the Battle of Bothwell Brig in 1679.

This book, then, begins with an attempt to answer the questions, how and why episcopacy was re-introduced into Scotland in the Restoration period. The Scottish Reformation had taken place in 1560. By 1660, therefore, the reformed church in Scotland was a century old. Attempts to characterise the nature of this church have provoked fierce academic debate. Until quite recently it was the accepted orthodoxy that its polity was fundamentally presbyterian. Even during the earliest period of the church's emergence in the 1560s, so the orthodoxy ran, before the development of a fully fledged presbyterian system under Andrew Melville's influence, the inchoate and temporary arrangements made in the wake of John Knox's revolution were implicity anti-hierarchical and proto-presbyterian. The period of episcopal church government during the reigns of James VI and Charles I, a period lasting from about 1610 until 1637, was, so this same argument ran, an aberration, whose destruction by the Scots in defiance of Charles I was readily understandable.

This orthodoxy was challenged most trenchantly by Professor Gordon Donaldson. He argues that the reformed episcopate was an admirable compromise between presbytery and episcopacy which brought peace to the Scottish church until that compromise was challenged by the growing radicalism of the Scottish presbyterian minority.

Most recently, however, the pendulum of historical interpretation has begun to swing the other way. Historians have questioned whether the Jacobean peace was quite so profound as Professor Donaldson has suggested. They have noted that the bishops of James's creation were sitting rather uneasily as royal appointees on top of a presbyterian pyramid and that it may after all be a closer approximation to the truth to say that the Scottish church between 1560 and 1660 was fundamentally presbyterian in its nature.

What is certain is that the abolition of episcopacy in 1637 had taken place amid a blaze of publicity and had been attended and followed up by a sustained propaganda campaign, which repeatedly detailed the defects of 'prelacy' and extolled the merits of presbytery as the only form of church government pleasing to God. Between 1637 and 1660 there does not appear to have been any attempt to revive an episcopal system in Scotland.

The transformation brought about in the wake of the Restoration was effected not by considerations of what form of church government might be best pleasing to God, but by political considerations.

The first of these considerations was the political implications of presbytery. The revolution of the 1640s had after all been carried out in the name of presbyterian church government. That association had been renewed by the treatment of the young Charles II in 1650 and 1651 during his stay in Scotland. Although the kirk had split into two factions - Resolutioner and Protester − in 1650 over this very issue, and although the royalist Resolutioner party thought of itself as the king's friends, it is evident that as far as Charles was concerned, and even more his chief adviser in exile Edward Hyde, later Earl of Clarendon, all presbyterians were tarred with the same subversive brush.

The practical result of this association of presbytery with rebellion was that all ministers including the leaders of the Resolutioner party were excluded from taking any part whatever in the making of ecclesiastical policy at the Restoration. Ecclesiastical policy was determined at that crucial moment by an entirely secular assembly.

The other major consideration in the formation of Scottish ecclesiastical policy was the political ambitions of those with power to make decisions. Most significant of these men at that moment was the earl of Middleton, Clarendon's protégé, who was fired with the desire to please his patron and make his name by destroying a presbyterian system under which he had suffered humiliation. By a mixture of threats and bribes Middleton succeeded in carrying with him a large majority of parliament and in stifling protest from the ministers.

Those who most probably would have led the resistance to this cynical manoeuvring were themselves pinioned by their political ambition, which dictated their conformity. Foremost among these was John Maitland, earl and later duke of Lauderdale. His family owed its rise to its service to the crown; however zealous Lauderdale's service to presbytery, his ultimate allegiance was to the crown and to his own survival as its servant. At the Restoration, therefore, he was not prepared to endanger his political career under the new regime for the sake of presbytery. If royal policy as engineered by Clarendon favoured an episcopalian settlement he would, however great his scruples, obey the royal will.

The principal negotiator among the ministers, James Sharp, was excluded from the circle of decision makers at an early date because of his clerical status. The abrupt decline in his influence led his fellow-presbyterians then, and many an historian since, to suppose that he had sold a presbyterian settlement for the sake of his own preferment as archbishop of St. Andrews. There is no clear evidence of Sharp's treachery, and a great deal to suggest that he was pressured to accept a settlement made by secular interests as the price of his continuing influence in ecclesiastical matters. As with Lauderdale, his desire for political survival induced him to conform with a settlement for which he had few sympathies.

But even if it is fairly clear how royal policy evolved and how the acquiescence of leading political figures was ensured, it still remains to explain how this policy found acceptance among the political nation in Scotland generally. It is clear there was no enthusiasm for an episcopal system. Only one synod produced a statement in favour of it and there was opposition to the Act of Revocation, rescinding laws in favour of presbytery passed during the 'troubles', at every stage of its progress through the Committee of the Articles and Parliament.

Conformity was induced by a mixture of threats and bribes. The events of the preceding twenty-five years had left very many Scots in a position where they were extremely vulnerable to pressure. Many were in grave financial trouble and dependent on royal favour for the recovery of their fortunes; most had supported what was now termed 'rebellion' and could be threatened with punishment. English occupation forces were still in Scotland, and Scotland's economic survival was in English hands. Few members of the political nation, therefore, were prepared to make a bold stand in favour of a system of church government which had in any case sometimes threatened the hegemony of the landed classes.

The restoration of episcopacy had been effected by the earl of Middleton, a mercenary soldier ennobled for his contribution to the royalist cause in the 1650s. He was ambitious, but no match for the political skills of the established nobility who, moreover, resented him as an upstart in their ranks. The challenge offered him by the earl of Lauderdale resulted in Middleton's downfall and disgrace by the end of 1662.

Middleton's fall, however, did not bring an end to the ecclesiastical settlement which he had created. The bishops whom he had created in the Scottish sees were, with the exception of James Sharp, doctrinaire prelatists or political appointees chosen by the king or Middleton. Moreover, the legislation establishing the episcopate implied erastian bishops living in the old prelatic manner, performing functions locally as royal, judicial and financial servants and in central government resuming their role as the first estate on which the king could rely absolutely. Additionally, legislation was passed to purge both administration and church of presbyterian dissenters.

Lauderdale, with Sharp as his main ally, had undoubtedly envisaged a far more moderate form of episcopacy, and clearly had considerable support among both ministers and nobility. The damage had, however, already been done by the end of 1662. It proved too difficult for Lauderdale to reverse policies and appointments which had met with royal approval. Neither he nor Sharp was prepared to hazard his new-found political eminence in the name of a return to presbytery. Nevertheless, there is considerable evidence to show that a very serious attempt was made to modify the rigour with which episcopal policy was put into action and enforced.

The modest hope that even if episcopal policies could not be reversed they could be implemented in a way that would be much less provocative than those espoused by Middleton and his allies, was likewise to be disappointed. Apparently under the influence of Gilbert Sheldon, archbishop of Canterbury, Sharp became progressively more committed to an episcopal system. Although his influence on the Church Commission seems to have been one of restraining moderation, he was less and less sympathetic to presbyterian non-conformity. At the same time active dissent burgeoned, encouraged by those members of the nobility, led by Hamilton, who were not prepared to co-operate with the bishops in the repression of non-conformity.

This move towards a more rigorous policy coincided with a period during which government policy weighed heavily on Scotland in various ways. Financial exactions and interference with trade were exacerbated by the uncontrolled behaviour of troops charged with the collection of fines and taxes. In an atmosphere of crisis and unrest the activities of the soldiery provoked the celebrated Pentland Rising in December 1666, an outbreak of disaffection that had been brewing for some time.

The effect of the Rising was to bring about a radical change in ecclesiastical policies. Lauderdale, as Secretary of State, had been in London for most of the time since Middleton's fall. It was therefore possible and convenient for him to make Sharp the scapegoat for a failure to maintain security that seriously threatened his own political position, and to inflict on him a disgrace that lasted until 1667 and a reduction in status not reversed until 1673.

Sharp and his ally the earl of Rothes were replaced in Lauderdale's confidence by Sir Robert Moray and the earls of Tweeddale and Kincardine. They enlisted the moderate Robert Leighton as their ally among the bishops. Then, with Lauderdale's support, they embarked on the policy, tentatively explored in 1663, of retaining an episcopal system but modifying its less acceptable features. In pursuit of this aim they sought various means of reconciling dissenters to the establishment by granting them some concessions.

These good intentions were modified from the beginning, however, by the political necessity of maintaining security in Scotland. Although concessions could be made to passive and peaceable dissenters, vigorous measures, it was agreed, had to be taken against active conventicling. The first Indulgence of 1669, which permitted forty-two dissenting ministers to function in parishes, with government approval, was proclaimed at the same time that legislation imposed ever harsher penalties for non-conformity.

These equivocal proceedings inevitably aroused deep distrust among the dissenters, while the failure of the Indulgence to satisfy them perfectly likewise aroused the apprehensions of Lauderdale and his allies. Nevertheless, Lauderdale was sufficiently committed to policies of moderation to crush the opposition of Sharp and the other bishops by the Act of Supremacy of 1669. Thus, ironically, the erastian nature of the whole Restoration settlement of the church was underlined. It was further demonstrated by the dismissal of Alexander Burnet, archbishop of Glasgow, whose compliance with the Indulgence it had proved impossible to secure.

These fundamentally contradictory policies of indulgence and repression had necessitated such violent measures with bishops and dissenters alike that their continuance was impossible. Further attempts were made to bring over the dissenters, culminating in the second Indulgence of 1672, but hopes for it were small when at the same time legislation against non-conformity was again made harsher. Even though it seems highly unlikely that these measures were ever put into effect and that they were designed to serve other political ends, yet the impression which they conveyed was not conducive to a lasting settlement of the church.

From about 1672 policies of moderation were progressively abandoned. This was not simply because they had proved less than totally successful: Lauderdale was under increasing political pressure to maintain security on England's northern border by repressing any illegal gatherings. Furthermore, the duke of Hamilton had allied with Lauderdale's enemies in London in an attempt to challenge his political pre-eminence in Scotland. Lauderdale, therefore, found it necessary to ally in both England and Scotland with those who stood for policies of harsh repression of dissent.

Lauderdale's increasing reliance on Sharp in Scotland was underlined by Sharp's skill in quelling a protest movement among orthodox, conformist ministers who felt that they had been ignored and who wished to air their grievances in a National Synod. This unrest was the more sinister from Lauderdale's point of view because it plainly enjoyed backing from Hamilton. Thus the wheel had come full circle since 1661; Lauderdale and Sharp were again allied for their respective political survival, but this time in the name of severity in the church rather than moderation.

Thus from 1674 government policy became progressively harsher towards dissent, now clearly identified with the political opposition, a development symptomised by the restoration of Alexander Burnet to the archbishopric of Glasgow from which he had been summarily dismissed five years previously. Legislation was made progressively more repressive and a number of violent and illegal incidents indicated the way things were going.

Matters culminated in 1679 in the murder of Sharp and the rising which ended with the battle of Bothwell Brig. The complete failure, therefore, of Lauderdale's policies in maintaining the all-important security of England's northern border was glaringly apparent. Furthermore, Lauderdale's ecclesiastical policies had left him open to attack in both England and Scotland so that, predictably, he eventually lost the support of the king in the autumn of 1679.

Lauderdale's political demise in 1680 appeared to open the way for a less exploitive approach to ecclesiastical affairs, but as in 1661 the patterns already established proved too strong. A brief interlude of moderation was followed by the arrival on the political scene of a new generation of Scots politicians who were likewise determined to retain royal favour by taking violent measures with those dissenters who continued to defy the government. These men lacked even that fundamental sympathy which had for so long tempered the activities of Lauderdale and his allies.

Ultimately, however, the worm turned and, at the Revolution, ecclesiastical affairs were removed from the centre of political conflict. The political ambition which support for episcopacy had thinly disguised in so many politicians found other modes of expression, and the discontents which dissent had voiced found secular manifestations.

In short, this book describes twenty years of the last era in Scotland when ecclesiastical policy was part of national politics, and when its evolution was largely dictated by issues of political expediency.

In what follows, where quotations are taken from unpublished sources, spelling and punctuation have been modernised. In quotations from published sources, contractions have been expanded.

2
Church and State in the Interregnum, 1649-1660

WHEN in the early months of 1660 it became gradually more certain that the upheavals of the previous months and years would culminate in the return of Charles Stuart to his father's dominions,[1] those with causes to plead in the settlement of Scotland, no less than of England, made it their business to represent their cases to the king.

During the 1650s the church in Scotland had split into two hostile factions: the Resolutioners and the Protesters.[2] In July 1650 the last united General Assembly of the kirk had met. Although united - relatively - its edicts were not published and have never been accepted as part of the corpus of church law. However, it had appointed, as usual, a Commission or standing committee to take care of 'the publick affairs of the Kirk'.[3] The Commission, in the months that followed, had concerned itself primarily with two issues: one, the military situation in Scotland and the other, the sincerity of Charles and his noble supporters.

By receiving Charles in Scotland in the summer of 1650[4] the Scots had caused Cromwell to come to the defence of the Commonwealth by sending an army into Scotland.[5] By the late summer of that year it was plain that his army had to be challenged.[6] However, it was also plain to the Commission that the motives and behaviour of the king and his entourage were secular rather than religious. So, for example, the Commission wrote to the Committee of Estates in August 1650 asking for a purging of the royal household:

> Wee do earnestlie exhort and obtest your Lordships, that yow will not onlie remove from the Kings familie and Court such persons as have not hitherto taken the Covenant and befriended the worke of Reformation, or have been active in councill or in armes against the same, or against whom this Kirk and Kingdome have just cause of exception or ground of jealousie; and such as are profane and scandalous in their conversation and cariage; but that yow will also take care with all possible diligence to constitut his Majesties familie and Court of such persons as are of knowen affection and approven integrity in the Covenant and Cause of God, and of a blamelesse and Christian conversation.[7]

The similar hesitation felt in the Commission about the employment, even after the Scottish defeat at Dunbar on 3 September, of those with worldly ambitions in an army which would fight in a righteous cause against Cromwell, came to a head over the matter of two letters sent to the Commission from the west of Scotland.[8]

These letters are known as the Remonstrance, and were concerned principally with the question of whether the Engagers, those who had taken part in the Engagement of 1647-8,[9] or who had otherwise disobeyed the kirk, should be allowed to fight, even if repentant. The authors argued that since

Engagers had been employed in September at Dunbar, where the army had in any case been beaten, the kirk would be better advised to put its trust in God and an army, however small, of sincere believers. [10] They feared, they said, that otherwise God would be provoked to further demonstrations of his anger with Scotland:

> If we in the tyme of this distresse shall sin yet more in the same way, and make a conjunction with such evill instruments once more, how can we escape the judgement vnto which we have sentenced ourselfes in the day of our vowes, even to be consumed vntill ther be no remnant nor escaping. [11]

There was no disagreement in the Commission about the matter of the Remonstrance. The members were all perfectly well aware of the shortcomings of the king and his supporters. They were also aware of the possibility that even those who repented of their former activities, particularly as Engagers, might be insincere. [12] The only difference lay in the members' view of what action should be taken on this issue. The differences were so severe and fundamental that they became the issue on which the ministry and church of Scotland split into two factions.

The split in the Commission came first of all because a public statement was forced from the Commission about the Remonstrance, when at least seven of forty-seven members would have preferred to keep the matter quiet. An attempt had been made by some members to delay discussion of the Remonstrance, presumably in the hope that the whole issue would fall to the ground if it were not publicly discussed. Thus although the first letter had been received from the Remonstrants on 9 October, the Commission did not express its judgment on the matter until 28 November. What is more, on 27 November an attempt was made to delay any further pronouncement:

> This day, after reading the Remonstrance, and free debate upon it, it being voted whither it wer not fitting to delay to give any sense upon it at this tyme . . . Resolved *Negative,* that they will not delay.

When the attempt at delay had failed, seven of those who had put it on foot protested 'for themselves and others that will adhere unto them . . . against the proceedings of the Commission to give their sense upon the said Remonstrance'. [13]

A second reason for the split was that a majority thought the Remonstrance dealt with matters beyond the competence of the authors, and explicitly feared that to agree with them must provoke divisions within the kirk. Although the Commission felt itself obliged to make a public statement, that statement was by no means sympathetic to the Remonstrants, although it acknowledged the truth of their claims:

> The Commission, having taken in consideration the said Remonstrance, Doe find, and acknowledge therein to be contained, many sad trueths in relation to sinnes charged upon the King, his familie, and the publict judicatories . . . We doe also find it our duetie to show that, in respect there seems to be therein entrincheing upon some conclusions and determinations of the General Assembly . . . We are dissatisfied therewith; and that we thinke it is apt to breid divisions in this Kirk and Kingdome. [14]

Thirdly, a majority feared that open agreement with the Remonstrance would lead to a breach with the Committee of Estates. They feared that that would in turn lead to disunity and consequent further military losses. In a letter sent to the Remonstrants with the Commission's statement, the hope was expressed that the Remonstrants would not lessen their military endeavours whatever their dissatisfactions:

> We are confident that nothing hither to passed in all these debates shall in any measure blunt your affection to the worke of God, or slacken and weaken your hands toward the zealous prosecution thereof, now especiallie, when the bleeding condition of our Kirk and Kingdome calles for action from all who tenders the well of religion, libertie, governement, or what els is pretious. [15]

Fourthly, a minority - twelve out of forty-seven - with backing from an army and ministers in the west, [16] was prepared to use this opportunity to seize control of the Commission and, by implication, the kingdom. Twelve of the forty-seven members declared their dissent from the Commission's statement and withdrew from all further meetings. They included James Guthrie, Samuel Rutherford and Andrew Cant, three of the most influential members of the Commission; it seems certain that they intended thereby to make the continuation of the Commission impossible and use the leverage they would gain by such a manoeuvre to impose their point of view on the other members. [17]

Although the Remonstrance had provided the occasion for the split, the division in the church was of very long standing. Underlying the conflict was a fundamental disagreement on the nature of relations between church and state. The minority Remonstrants were the backbone of the former theocratic party in Scotland; [18] the majority expressly dissociated themselves from any desire to meddle in civil affairs. The real issue lay in how much power the kirk should have in society and how much authority rightfully belonged to the civil government.

Once the split had been created it very soon became established. Naturally the majority who had favoured a less rigorous attitude towards the king's party and its deficiencies drew towards the secular government. The Commission, sitting without those members who supported the Remonstrance, [19] issued public resolutions or edicts for the instruction of ministers and people. Thus the 'Resolutioners', as the edicts' authors were afterwards termed, readmitted many Engagers to favour with the church, [20] and supported the Committee of Estates in calling a general levy of all fencible men, provided only that any 'malignants' first did penance. [21]

This development met with opposition from those ministers who supported the Remonstrance, who then became known as the 'Protesters'. [22] Messages of protest from one side [23] were matched by messages of support from the other. [24] Arrangements for meetings to discuss the differences [25] contributed only to the ever clearer definition of the two sides. The expression of opposing views, often in bitter terms, began, [26] and widened the differences. Not surprisingly the General Assemblies of 1651 and 1652 failed to resolve the debate, and their authority, challenged at the time by the Protesters, was never accepted.[27] The question of the lawfulness of these two Assemblies thus became a further matter for dispute and the occasion of the setting up of rival presbyteries, synods and Assemblies.[28]

By the time the Cromwellian armies had thoroughly conquered Scotland in 1652, therefore, the division in the church was well established. What must now be considered is the relations between the Cromwellian government and the two parties. The history of those relations clearly had a bearing on the subsequent relations between the Scottish ministers and the king at the Restoration.

It might have been expected that the Cromwellians would favour the Protester party above the Resolutioners. After all, the Protesters had rejected Charles Stuart and his supporters as perjured and insincere,[29] while the Resolutioners had identified themselves with the king's cause. Whatever the difficulties of their relationship, even Charles seems to have recognised that the Resolutioners were committed to him.[30] In fact, to begin with, the invaders seemed to have little sympathy for either faction. The basis of Cromwellian policy in Scotland was a committee which required loyalty to the government of the Commonwealth from the ministers, but forbade them to take any part in the direction of civil affairs.[31] Furthermore, the Cromwellians were determined to enforce toleration. Thus their edicts always provided for the existence of congregations independent of the Scottish church. Exclusion from civil affairs, erastian interference in the church, and toleration, were all equally detestable principles to the ministers, whether Resolutioner or Protester.[32] In addition, the Cromwellians thought of both parties as royalist,[33] and thus mistrusted them as enemies of the Commonwealth.

However, it is also true that the Cromwellians consistently favoured Protester candidates for the ministry and the universities,[34] and supporters of the Protesters for jobs in the civilian administration.[35] These policies did not win them the gratitude of the Protester party, who instead condemned erastian interference in the planting of the churches and universities[36] and were doubtful of the morality of supporting the Cromwellian system by operating its administration.[37] Thus, although to an outsider the Cromwellians were much closer to the Protesters than to the Resolutioners, in fact these scruples were enough to keep most ministers of both parties and the government of occupation at loggerheads for some considerable time.

In 1653, however, this deadlock was broken over the issue of the royalist rising which began in that year and was not finally defeated by the Cromwellian forces until the following autumn. The rising was supported by the Resolutioner ministers[38] who thereby influenced public opinion also to countenance it. Both the very real prospect that the royalists might defeat the Cromwellians, and the undisciplined conduct of the royalist troops, induced a number of the Protesters and their supporters in the west to dissociate themselves from the rising, and to make advances to the Cromwellian government. [39]

The Protester initiative met with an eager response and three of the ministers of that persuasion were thereupon invited to London. [40] It very soon emerged, however, that Cromwell had in mind negotiations with a more representative sample of all shades of opinion. Three others were invited to London, [41] and Cromwell announced that he wished to discuss plans for unity in the Scottish church. [42]

Unity in the church was clearly a very enticing proposition for Cromwell, and it is not difficult to see why. The help that a ministry disposed to support the occupation forces could give in administration, in the maintenance of law and order, and in the influencing of public opinion, was incalculable. It is clear from the requests for additional troops that the Cromwellian forces were severely stretched at the time of the rebellion. They were also, it seems from their edicts, aware of the power of grass roots support and sympathy. [43]

On the other hand, there were some men in both parties for whom unity was anything but an agreeable prospect. From the beginning the dispute had been a struggle for power in the church; unity implies compromise, and by definition excluded the possibility of a triumph by either side. The continuing negotiations for a union of the two parties throughout 1654 and 1655, [44] therefore, although supported by the Cromwellian administration, met with no success.

In the autumn of 1656, as a result of skilful manoeuvring by the President of the Council for Scotland, Lord Broghill, both parties were induced to submit their quarrel to Cromwell in London. [45] This had been the goal of Cromwellian policy since early in 1654. From this time until immediately before the Restoration in 1660 the dispute was thus carried on in London. Nothing was achieved during these final years of the Interregnum by either party, but the dispute was at least removed from the sphere of responsibility of the Cromwellian government in Scotland, and brought some respite to the Scottish church. [46]

If, therefore, some sort of tally were to be made to the end of 1659 of the respective merits of the two parties in the eyes of the king, the result could not be in doubt. The Protesters had impeded the king's military preparations; they had dropped him from their public prayers with indecent haste from the time of Worcester; they and their supporters had been preferred, however ungraciously and unwillingly, to posts in the ministry, the universities and the Cromwellian administration; they had failed to support the royalist rising, and, from 1653, they had flirted with the Interregnum government in an attempt to achieve supremacy in the church. Not all the Protesters were equally guilty, but as a party their record was poor.

As soon as it became evident that the king would be returned, the cause was finished, although it took some time before they recognised the fact. [47] When, therefore, we consider the application of the Scottish church to the king, we are considering the application only of the Resolutioners. The Protesters did not dare present themselves.

The man who was entrusted with the Resolutioner case in London and then on an embassy to Charles II at Breda was James Sharp, later archbishop of St Andrews. This man was to be so important in the ecclesiastical affairs of the Restoration that his career must first be reviewed[48] before the narrative can proceed further.

James Sharp was born in the castle of the town of Banff in 1618. He was the first child of William Sharp, the sheriff clerk of Banff, and of Isobel Lesley, the daughter of a laird.[49] He was thus born into a respectable middle class professional home and into the sphere of royalist sympathies, not only by virtue of his father's position as a royal servant, but also by being brought up in an area of Scotland traditionally and strongly royalist, as was to be demonstrated by the support for Charles I in the north east at the time of the Covenant.[50]

He proceeded from the local grammar school, where he is said to have acquitted himself well,[51] to the University of Aberdeen in 1633 at the age of fifteen, and embarked upon the four-year arts degree at King's College.[52] He was fortunate to attend King's, the older and pre-reformation university in Aberdeen, when both it and the other - post-reformation - university, Marischal College, were benefiting from the reforms introduced by Bishop Forbes.

Sharp completed his undergraduate degree in 1637[53] and then seems to have proceeded to post-graduate study of divinity under the two Professors of that subject, John Forbes, the bishop's son, and Robert Baron.[54] From them he would learn the principal elements of the thought of what came to be regarded as the school of the Aberdeen Doctors. The Doctors held that episcopal government was of the *melius esse* of the church, not of the *esse;* it was rather a matter to be dictated by the specific circumstances of the church.[55] This is the first important element in the thought of the Aberdeen Doctors to be of later significance to Sharp. The second is that the Doctors distinguished between things fundamental to the Christian faith, and things indifferent. Among the latter were observances or traditions within the church which might be desirable but which were in no way essential to the practice of the Christian faith.[56] Among such 'things indifferent' were, for example, the ritual observances laid down by the Five Articles of Perth which Forbes had been prepared to obey. By this means the Doctors conceded that the king might have authority within the church unless his desires could be shown to be contrary to the word of God - that is, unless he interfered with the 'fundamentals' of the Christian faith.[57] The Doctors had succeeded in reducing these 'fundamentals' to a far greater extent than their predecessors. Correspondingly they allowed the king a much larger authority within the church. This is the theological basis from which Sharp was later to develop his ideas on episcopacy.[58]

Sharp was thus early endowed with pro-royalist and pro-episcopal sympathies, at a time when these theories, unexceptional in protestant Scotland[59] since 1560, were being superseded by something altogether more radical and uncompromising. Sharp was from an early age a conservative, therefore, since the ideas with which he was imbued so thoroughly in Aberdeen were already out of date and out of favour.

In 1638 Aberdeen, led by the Catholic earl of Huntly and the Aberdeen Doctors, refused to lend support to the National Covenant,[60] a document which constituted an implicit criticism of every aspect - political, social and religious - of the government of Charles. A vigorous debate on the issue[61] ensued which provoked the attack on the town by the presbyterian party.[62] During this period of turmoil Sharp left Aberdeen.

There is a tradition that he went from Aberdeen to England, there to seek church preferment,[63] but it is not known, if he did so, with whom he associated or what influences acted upon him.[64] Certainly by 1642 he was working as a regent, or junior academic, in St Leonard's College of St Andrews University.[65] Although he had probably left Aberdeen without signing the Covenant, it seems most unlikely that he could have held his post at St Andrews without signing. A series of edicts of the General Assembly enforced the general signing of the Covenant. It was particularly required of divinity students, on pain of not being allowed to teach or preach, in August 1640. The very fact that Sharp was appointed, supposedly on the recommendation of Alexander Henderson, a leading Covenanter,[66] suggests that Sharp was prepared to put into practice the precepts of the Aberdeen Doctors which laid small importance on the form of church government, and much on the maintenance of peace in the church.

Sharp was at St Leonard's until early in 1648, when he was appointed minister of the Kirk at Crail.[67] There are rumours that Sharp's behaviour in St Andrews was scandalous, his list of vices including fornication and infanticide,[68] but we are entitled to dismiss these if we consider that as a regent he was living in a small community in which his every movement would be known, and where he was expected to set a good example to his pupils. It is inconceivable that had anything been found amiss in his conduct it could have escaped notice, or that he could have then been appointed minister of a parish.

As minister of Crail Sharp had a reputation for undue severity, a tradition which lingers in folk memory in Crail, but study of the Kirk Session Records[69] indicates a pattern of discipline probably no different from that exercised elsewhere in Scotland, and no doubt influenced more by the general atmosphere and morale within the church than by Sharp as an individual.

He was from the very beginning regarded by his fellow ministers as an intelligent man, capable of understanding and promoting the best interests of the church, for in April 1649, only a little more than a year after the start of his ministry at Crail, he was chosen by the provincial assembly of Fife as one of five ministers to attend the competition for a regent's place at his old college, St Leonard's.[70] In November 1649[71] and again in 1650 the ministers and baillies of Edinburgh thought so highly of Sharp's reputation that they petitioned to have him transferred to the capital to be one of their ministers. It appears that in 1650 the previously denied request of the baillies and ministers of Edinburgh was granted, but perhaps because of the unsettled nature of the times, Sharp does not seem to have moved. [72]

He took his place in the Presbytery of St Andrews, [73] the Synod of Fife [74] and the General Assembly, [75] and was a member of the executive committee of the kirk which met with the Committee of Estates at Alyth in August 1651 in an attempt to maintain some form of government during the Cromwellian invasion. On this occasion, along with the other members of the Committee, he was captured and sent prisoner to London. [76]

On his release within the year he returned to Scotland [77] and, far from diminishing them, increased his political activities [78] to such an extent that, when the dissensions within the church created the Resolutioner and Protester disagreement, Sharp was one of those named to take part in a Resolutioner-Protester conference, [79] and then the man chosen in August 1656 to represent the Resolutioner case before Cromwell in London. [80] It was at least partly owing to Sharp's efforts that Cromwell was gradually brought round to a more favourable view of the Resolutioners.

From August 1656 until the end of 1657 Sharp was in London, [81] and on his return to Edinburgh not only was he commended by his brethren there 'for his unwearied labours and diligence in his employment', [82] but he also brought with him a letter from the two English presbyterians, Calamy and Ashe, who had done what they could to help the Resolutioner cause, and who pointed out in warm terms how Sharp

> hath with much prudence courage and laboriousness unweariedly attended and managed the trust committed to him, yea, (as we believe) he hath secured your cause from sundry aspersions which otherwise might probably have reproached it, and he hath gained respect in the opinions of some in highest place by his wisdom and meekness in vindicating it from misrepresentation. [83]

In February 1659 Sharp was again prevailed upon to go to London as Resolutioner agent, [84] where he remained until June of that year, [85] when the ascendancy of the army and the expulsion of the Rump made it clear that there was no longer any point in his pursuing his mission. On his arrival in Edinburgh he

> was for his faithfulnes, diligence and prudence very thankfullie approven, and the Lord's name blessed and praised on his behalf. [86]

So by mid-1659 Sharp had acquired not only a very great deal of experience as a negotiator at the highest levels, but had also acquired a reputation for prudence and restraint in arguing a case against vehement opponents. Early experience in church courts in Scotland had doubtless stood him in good stead in acquiring this standing. It was on the strength of his previous experience that he was a third time commissioned as Resolutioner representative, this time to General Monck in February 1660,[87] when it became apparent that major political upheavals lay ahead.

Up to this point the efforts of the Resolutioners had been wholly directed to establishing their own supremacy over the Protesters. The terms of the instructions to James Sharp from the Edinburgh ministers who had taken upon themselves the leadership of the Resolutioner party indicated that as late as January 1660 the implications of Monck's march on London were by no means clear to them, and that they still thought in terms of the struggle against the Protesters and a government of occupation.[88] When, however, it seemed that Parliament would return the king on presbyterian terms,[89] the Resolutioners hurriedly formulated their desires in such an event.

The Solemn League and Covenant was initially fixed upon as the basis for any negotiation. The background to this choice requires some explanation. During the Interregnum the Protesters had allowed emphasis on the Covenant to fade. It is not difficult to see why. The Solemn League and Covenant committed its signatories to the defence of royalism and presbytery. The Protesters had in fact betrayed both causes between 1650 and 1660, the first by their conduct towards the king, and the second by their willingness to allow their candidates to become parish ministers without the approval of the established presbyterial machinery in such cases. In contrast, and in order to justify their own position, the Resolutioners had kept alive the memory of the Solemn League and Covenant.[90]

When, therefore, Monck declared for presbytery 'not rigid'[91] and Parliament ordered the reprinting of the Covenant,[92] both Sharp in London[93] and the ministers in Edinburgh[94] were encouraged to think in terms of the implementation at long last of the terms of the Covenant in all three kingdoms. What they wanted to see, as Sharp spelled out, was the return of the king on Covenant terms.[95] Very soon, however, Sharp began to be aware through his many political contacts that the king would be restored but that his implementation of the Covenant was extremely unlikely.[96] The Edinburgh ministers were much further from the hub of events and so clung on to their hopes much longer.[97] In April, however, Sharp reported to them that he had heard a rumour that the church in England would be settled by means of a synod of divines to take place after the restoration of the king.[98] The implications of such a rumour were quite clear: the Covenant would be discarded. The reaction of the Edinburgh ministers was understandably one of grief. They found themselves unable to understand why, when the English king and nation were pledged to uphold the Solemn League and Covenant, there should be thought to be any need for further discussion.[99] It was at this point that it began to dawn upon then that perhaps presbytery in Scotland was not quite as safe as they had assumed it would be.

The Covenant was, moreover, by no means the only matter for concern among the Resolutioner ministers. During the brief space of time that Sharp had been on his mission, from early February to late April, a whole host of problems had arisen. To begin with, the Protesters, although they recognised that their fate was sealed if the king should return, were by no means reconciled to that fate. Not only was Wariston pestering Sharp to use his influence; he was thought to be intriguing with the English sectaries and with Argyll. A meeting of Protester ministers had also been held in Edinburgh.[100] The Resolutioners were not sure exactly what was going on, but they could be sure that the Protesters would not be intriguing for the Resolutioners' benefit.

Then there was the question of the commissioners. Sharp and the Edinburgh ministers had agreed that it would be ideal for their purposes if Crawford and Lauderdale, their two noble supporters now released from prison but still obliged to stay in London, were made commissioners for the Kingdom of Scotland to do any negotiating in the coming 'great revolution of affairs'. This plan, however, had failed to get the necessary approval from Monck, with the result that commissioners unsympathetic to the Resolutioner cause had not only been appointed, but were on their way to London.[101]

Thirdly, there was the question of Scotland's independence. The occupation and unification of Scotland with England had, as has been seen, brought a complete stop to meetings of all Scottish institutions, including meetings of church courts from the General Assembly down. The Resolutioners feared that if Scotland were not restored to independence, the church would never be presbyterian again. Accordingly, they tried hard to get assurances that Scotland would be favourably treated in the coming settlement, and had done their best to prevent a renewal of administrative arrangements which underlined her subjection - but all without success.[102]

Fourthly, although Monck, the king, Crawford, Lauderdale and the Resolutioner ministers had all stressed the necessity for Scotland to keep absolutely quiet at a time of crisis, yet there were rumours of an association of the Scottish nobility, backed by Middleton, who had declared their readiness to rise for the king, and who had been sending letters to and fro to that effect. The Resolutioners were well aware that Middleton had no love for presbytery and feared that if it came to civil war the Resolutioner cause would be the loser.[103] It was this last threat which induced the Edinburgh ministers to suggest that Sharp should make his way to the king and there state the Resolutioner cause.[104]

The formal instructions to Sharp did not reach him until he had returned from Holland, but they were merely a more concise expression of what he had already discussed with the Edinburgh ministers. There was a letter for the king and a list of instructions for Sharp.[105] The letter, as might have been expected, consisted of congratulations on the king's good fortune, protestations of the loyalty and affection of the ministers, and an introduction for Sharp who had, it was explained, been sent 'to inform your Majesty more fully of the true state of the church'. The point of the letter did not come until the end. The ministers stated as boldly as they dared that the king had sworn to maintain the kirk in Scotland according to the Covenant, and that they hoped he would do the same in England:

So that we nothing doubt of your Majesty's constant resolution to protect this church in her established privileges, and are no less confident . . . that your Majesty . . . will also of your own royal inclination appear to settle the house of God according to his word, in all your dominions.[106]

To settle the church according to the word of God implied, of course, for the writers, a presbyterian system.

The formal instructions then spelled out clearly exactly what Sharp was to do. First of all he was to emphasise the constant loyalty of the Resolutioners to the king throughout the Interregnum.[107] Secondly, whatever the king decided for the settlement of religion in England, it was to be impressed on him that in Scotland the continuance of presbytery was emphatically desired. Thirdly, the king was to be urged to moderation in rewarding royalists who had complied with the Interregnum government, and to firmness in excluding Protesters from public office.[108] Finally, Sharp, when he spoke to the king about the settlement of religion in England, was to point out the demerits of episcopacy.

The bulk of these instructions consists of familiar Resolutioner attitudes. There is only one change. The implementation of the Solemn League and Covenant in all three kingdoms had regretfully been abandoned as an impossible dream. When the very continuance of presbytery in Scotland seemed a little insecure, its safety was bound to be the Resolutioners' principal concern.

Sharp, however, was not the only Scot to go to Breda, nor was the Resolutioners' the only interest to be represented there. John Maitland, earl and later duke of Lauderdale, also went.[109] Lauderdale had been born into the great political family of the Maitlands of Thirlestane.[110] William Maitland and his brother John had been advisers to Mary Queen of Scots and James VI. John's son was created first earl of Lauderdale in 1624.

The earls of Lauderdale were therefore by no means of the ancient Scottish nobility. They owed their position first of all to their own political ability and then to the crown. It is perhaps not surprising that the first earl in the troubles of the 1630s and 1640s remained a consistent if moderate supporter of the king.[111]

The National Covenant had met with very wide acceptance among the Scottish nobility, and the first earl of Lauderdale was among those who had signed it. He played his part in political affairs, therefore, as a moderate covenanter-royalist. He was elected as a moderate to the Committee of the Articles for the Parliament of 1639 and was a member of the royalist party loosely held together by the marquis of Hamilton, the king's Commissioner. In June 1644 he was elected President of the Parliament and re-elected in January 1645, honours that were no doubt a tribute to his status as a respected senior statesman. In the month of his re-election, however, he died and was succeeded to the title by his son, another John Maitland, whose political sympathies were initially at some distance from his father's.[112]

The second earl was born in 1616 and educated at St Andrews University, where he matriculated at St Leonard's College for the session 1630-1631.[113] He was, like James Sharp, fortunate to attend a Scottish university when the changes of the Reformation had taken effect, and yet before the upheavals of the National Covenant and its attendant disruptions.[114] There was little of the intellectual excitement of Aberdeen, but nevertheless the young Lauderdale seems to have received a thorough grounding in contemporary learning. As a diplomat, during his imprisonment in the 1650s, and even when Secretary of State, he seems to have found time for study.[115] The catalogue of his library at his death reveals a man of wide interests and considerable intellectual powers.[116]

Indeed the young man was obviously intelligent and it was not long before that intelligence brought him into public life. He first appears to history in 1640 as the protégé of Robert Baillie, and it is from Baillie that the young Lord Maitland is known to have acquired a reputation for piety and covenanting zeal.[117] He must certainly have signed the Covenant in 1638. Within two years he was well enough thought of to be allowed to go to London with the Scottish Commissioners to the Parliament of England.

In 1642 Maitland was involved as an elder in the meeting of the General Assembly at St Andrews where preliminary discussion of the document that became the Solemn League and Covenant took place, and then in 1643 he was one of the Commissioners to the Westminster Assembly. He was apparently considered as able in political as in religious matters and was appointed as one of the Scots commissioners to look after Scottish interests in England, and then to the Committee of both Kingdoms. The authority of this commission dated from July 1644 and was renewed in March 1647; consequently Lauderdale (as he was from January 1645) was closely involved in all the negotiations with the king which took place during that period.

It had been noted that while the king was the prisoner of the Scots at Newcastle, Lauderdale was the commissioner most sympathetic towards him. For that reason, when Cornet Joyce captured the king for the English army of independents, Lauderdale was sent to London to negotiate, ahead of the other commissioners.[118] Such was his anxiety for the king that he put forward plans and terms for the king's rescue for which he had no authority.[119] Moreover, when news of this scheming came to the ears of the army, Lauderdale was temporarily denied further access to Charles.[120] However, in October 1647 Lauderdale was again negotiating with the king at Hampton Court, and it was he who, with the earl of Lanark, tried to persuade the king to escape.[121] Soon afterwards the king did flee, but to the Isle of Wight rather than to Berwick as the two Scots had recommended.

Throughout all these negotiations Lauderdale had been principally concerned to induce the king to make concessions concerning religion: chiefly that the Solemn League and Covenant should be taken by the king and all his subjects, and presbyterian church government permanently established in England as well as in Scotland. By late 1647, so anxious was Lauderdale about the king's safety that he, with two other Scottish nobles Loudoun and Lanark, agreed to modify their demands. On the basis, therefore, of the simple confirmation of the Covenant in the English Parliament and the establishment of presbytery for an initial period of three years only, the compact known as the Engagement was signed.[122]

The Engagement had been concluded by the three Scots commissioners without the authority of either kirk or the parliament in Scotland, and yet it committed the Scots to rescuing the king from the English with an army, if that should prove necessary.[123] On the return of the commissioners to Scotland their conduct was approved by the Committee of Estates, and later by the Parliament of March 1648.[124] The kirk, however, was by no means satisfied.[125]

From that time Lauderdale's principal desire was to get the Scottish army into England as soon as possible. The implication of this determination, held in the face of the opposition of the kirk, must be that in the last analysis Lauderdale was a royalist more than he was a covenanter. In this he was very much the heir of his family traditions. Within five years he had come round to the moderate covenanting royalism which his father had represented in 1642.

Nevertheless, Lauderdale apparently felt quite sincerely that he had secured the best available settlement for the church.[126] Indeed, given that the Scots were not prepared to reject their king totally, he was probably right. It was because of this same inconvenient religious sincerity, not shared by Hamilton and others of the royalist party, that Lauderdale was sent abroad in August 1648 to negotiate with the Prince of Wales and various European powers for their assistance.[127]

While Lauderdale was thus occupied, the Engagement army was decisively beaten by Cromwell at Preston in late August. Then followed the *coup d'état* by the anti-Engagers, and the Treaty of Stirling of September 1648. This treaty required all forces in Scotland to lay down their arms, and promised that no harm would come to Engagers who accepted it.[128] Lauderdale did not.[129] By the Act of Classes, therefore, in January 1649, Lauderdale, as a leading promoter of the Engagement, was banned for life from holding office or from taking part in public affairs.[130]

At this time Lauderdale was still in Holland, but he was sent by the Prince of Wales, about to be king, to try and patch up relations with the kirk party. His return to Scotland was a complete fiasco. He refused to submit to the kirk's requirements for his repentance, he found himself excluded from public life by the Act of Classes and, threatened with arrest, he fled back to Holland.[131]

When, therefore, the kirk régime then began negotiations with the new king, Lauderdale was one of the Scottish nobility at the king's court in Holland. Naturally he acted as one of Charles's advisers, and as such he urged the king to come to terms with the kirk.[132] This advice was quite consistent with all his actions to this point.

In the end, after much delay, Charles did follow at least the form of Lauderdale's advice, and in May 1650 signed the agreement at Breda. Although Lauderdale then accompanied Charles to Scotland, the kirk party refused to let him remain in the royal entourage. [133] However, by May 1651 the growth of the king's influence and that of the Resolutioner ministers permitted his return to favour and his admission to the committee for the army. In June the Act of Classes was rescinded and Lauderdale was immediately appointed to the Committee of Estates. [134] Inevitably he then took part in the disastrous Worcester campaign of September 1651, and was taken prisoner.

By 1651, therefore, Lauderdale had acquired enormous influence and experience as a negotiator and diplomat at the highest levels. Although it was plain that he would continue the Maitland tradition of loyalty and service to the king, yet through all the vicissitudes of the decade of his public office he had behaved in a way that was consistently loyal also to the code of the moderate Covenanters. Their continuing esteem for him was demonstrated during the nine years of his imprisonment in England by the contacts maintained between him and Robert Baillie [135] and by the visits paid to him by Sharp in London. [136] Thus he and his fellow-prisoners were kept in touch with developments in the church.

When Sharp reached London in February 1660, therefore, the release of Lauderdale and those nobles still imprisoned with him, Crawford and Sinclair, was one of his first concerns. Their release does indeed seem to have been hastened by Sharp, but was probably not his work entirely. [137] From the time that they were freed, Sharp spent a lot of time with them, particularly with Lauderdale. [138] It is quite clear that Sharp and the Edinburgh ministers gauged that Crawford and Lauderdale at least would be prepared to act for the Resolutioner interest. [139] Accordingly, the ministers tried as best they could to secure the two noblemen official status in London as commissioners for the Kingdom of Scotland. [140]

Although this project was not successful, Lauderdale continued to associate with Sharp in London, and it seemed clear that he would be prepared to defend the interests of the Resolutioners and of Scottish presbytery to the king.

John Middleton was the major representative of the third group of supplicants to the king in 1660. [141] He was the son of a Scots laird, and like many another of his class became a professional soldier. He had fought abroad before returning to take part in the conflicts of the 1640s. During these years he fought for numerous causes and on different sides, so that it is difficult to see him as much more than a mercenary. Two circumstances, however, gave a more certain direction to his career in the 1650s. Firstly, in 1651 he was obliged to perform public penance of a particularly humiliating kind by James Guthrie, minister of Stirling, and a Protester. [142] Middleton led an abortive rising on behalf of the king as a protest against the treatment meted out by the ministers to Charles. The penance was his punishment, and it created in him a lifelong antagonism to presbytery. Secondly, he was taken prisoner at Worcester. He escaped, but was thus induced to identify himself firmly with the fortunes of the exiled king. [143]

In 1654 he took command of a royalist rising in Scotland. The rising was a failure, but Middleton thereby gained favour with the king, who created him an earl in 1656. He was then employed by Charles on various missions to raise money, support or troops, until the Restoration. During this period he was adopted into favour by Clarendon.[144] The contact with the anti-presbyterian Chancellor served to increase Middleton's existing antipathy to his one-time associates.

At the Restoration, therefore, Middleton could count on exerting a considerable influence with the king, both because of his services during the 1650s, which were more considerable than those of any other member of the Scottish nobility, and through his friendship with the now all-powerful Chancellor. This influence in ecclesiastical matters was certain to be anti-presbyterian.

These three men - Sharp, Lauderdale and Middleton - represented the three most powerful influences on the form the coming ecclesiastical settlement was likely to take. What must now be considered are the negotiations towards that end.

3

Presbytery and Episcopacy:
The Struggle for Ascendancy, 1660-1661

THE first round of the negotiations towards an ecclesiastical settlement in Scotland took place even before Charles had returned to England. On 4 May 1660 James Sharp set out for the court at Breda.[1] His intention was first to correct if possible any unfavourable view of the Resolutioners which the king might entertain, and to urge upon Charles the necessity of the continuation of presbytery in Scotland. He was also, however, charged by General Monck with taking advice and information relating to English affairs to the king. It was no doubt because of the urgency of this latter mission that a boat was provided for his passage across the Channel, and that immediately on the evening of his arrival at Breda he was given access to the king.

During the following few days Sharp enjoyed the privilege of no fewer than five interviews with Charles. This favour is partly to be explained by the king's close interest in Monck's activities which Sharp was called on to describe, but it was also the fruit of recommendations which Sharp had carried with him from Monck, Glencairn and Lauderdale. Even before he had left England Sharp had come to Chancellor Hyde's attention as a man who had defended the king's reputation against slurs cast upon it, and as one esteemed to be 'moderate'. Burnet later asserted that the favour shown to Sharp was extended because he was recommended to the king by the earl of Glencairn as the man able to establish episcopacy in Scotland. The letters in question still survive, however, and disclose that Glencairn in fact described Sharp as 'no severe Presbyterian'.

Although Sharp was well received at Breda, his own reports of his interviews with the king indicate that so far as ecclesiastical matters were concerned they were inconclusive. Scottish matters were certainly discussed: Sharp delivered a salvo against the Protesters, stressed the loyalty of the Resolutioners to the king, and in general represented the Resolutioner case according to the guidelines worked out in correspondence with Robert Douglas. The king for his part behaved pleasantly with Sharp and assured him of his goodwill towards the Resolutioners. Yet when Sharp attempted to press the further discussion of Scottish affairs, Charles would not be committed in any way and simply replied that 'he would reserve a full communing about that till his coming to England.' With that Sharp was obliged to be content until negotiations began once again in London. Although he moved with the court to the Hague and from there to England, no further significant meetings with the king took place for some time.

Lauderdale's part in the pre-Restoration manoeuvrings towards a church settlement were more complex. His background as a presbyterian, a royalist and a Resolutioner supporter has already been described. He had promoted Sharp in his visit to the king, and certainly in the estimation of the Resolutioner leaders was their unquestionable ally. So sure were they of his allegiance to their cause that they had written a series of letters in which they outlined the services they hoped he and his fellow prisoners, now all at liberty, would perform.[2] In return Lauderdale, Crawford and Sinclair had replied:

> if we shall be so happy as to have your advices . . . we shall be very ready to follow them as coming from so eminent servants to God.[3]

In May, therefore, the Resolutioners obliged by providing an outline of the issues they wished Lauderdale and his noble friends to present to the king concerning ecclesiastical affairs.[4] The implication which can apparently be drawn from this exchange is that Lauderdale could be expected to negotiate with the king entirely in the Resolutioner interest. It is doubtful whether this implication can be sustained.

In the first place Lauderdale's conduct with reference to church government while he was at the Hague was rather equivocal. There are two accounts of his behaviour on this occasion, though neither of them is very satisfactory because both were written by men who disliked the earl. Both, however, seem to make substantially the same point. One is the work of Clarendon,[5] who was, of course, a witness to the events he described. He asserted that Lauderdale had attempted to curry political favour at the Hague by making jokes about the Solemn League and Covenant. A second account of his behaviour comes from Gilbert Burnet, who maintained that he was told the story by Lauderdale himself.[6] He asserts that when Lauderdale first went to the Hague he had made known to the king his allegiance to presbytery. To this the king replied that presbytery 'was not a religion for gentlemen'. Lauderdale then attempted to persuade the king to maintain presbytery at least in Scotland as a long-term political safeguard against a future combination of the two countries against the king. His argument was that if one country was episcopal and one presbyterian, their antagonism would prevent their combination.

What both these stories seem to show is that while Lauderdale was very likely himself a presbyterian by conviction, yet he was aware that presbyterian church government and the Solemn League and Covenant were by no means to Charles' liking. Lauderdale had been imprisoned and thus excluded from political life for nine years. He was eager for power and favour. His solution to the problem, therefore, was to modify his religious stance. He was prepared to abandon the Solemn League and Covenant completely, and to make a case for the continuation of presbytery in Scotland as a matter of expediency and political convenience rather than as a matter of conviction or religious truth. Thus he hoped to safeguard both Scottish presbytery and his own career.

A number of additional pieces of evidence seem to support this interpretation of Lauderdale's position at this time. First, shortly after his release from prison, it came to Hyde's ears that Lauderdale 'takes pains to be thought no Presbyterian'. If this is so, remarks Hyde, the two of them have no further cause to quarrel.[7] It cannot have been accident that Lauderdale, the correspondent of the Resolutioner ministers, should have taken the trouble to let it be known in some quarters that his devotion to presbytery was not after all so great. The implication is that the connection between religious belief and future political advancement was clear to him before he went to the Hague.

Secondly, immediately after the Restoration Lauderdale was exploring two different possibilities of reconciling his presbyterian convictions and his political ambition. One was to support a scheme of moderate episcopacy in England. The hope was that such a scheme would prove acceptable to the king, as presbytery would not, but yet avoid the pitfalls of prelacy. The implementation of the Solemn League and Covenant was obviously out of the question. This scheme might offer a viable alternative.[8] The second scheme was to arrange for suitable Scottish agents to be sent to London to persuade the king of the general aversion of Scots to episcopacy.[9] This was a further attempt to persuade the king that to abolish presbyterian church government in Scotland was not politically expedient. All this material suggests that Lauderdale's eventual stance with regard to the ecclesiastical settlement would be modified by ambition and opportunism rather than be dictated by principle.

When Charles reached England at the end of May, his time was at first very fully occupied with crucial questions of security, and with a host of English business. The affairs of Scotland had to await his leisure. The first significant move in ecclesiastical matters was the exclusion of the Resolutioner ministers from the discussion.

When Sharp arrived back in London from the Hague he found waiting for him a pile of instructions from Robert Douglas and the Resolutioner leaders. These communications made it clear that it was their intention that Sharp should continue his task of representing the Resolutioner case to the king. But Sharp was tired of his mission. He therefore proposed to his colleagues that the king's permission should be sought for other Resolutioner ministers to come to London to see for themselves how matters stood, and to give their views on ecclesiastical affairs to the king. Although Sharp had had enough, it was clearly his intention also that there should continue to be Resolutioner ministers in London to advise with the king.[10]

On 14 June, about a fortnight after this resolve, Charles summoned Sharp to him. He assured Sharp once more of his intention 'to preserve to us [Scots] the discipline and government of our Church, as it is settled amongst us', and he promised that he would call a General Assembly. But, although these soothing assurances were given, the real reason for the summons was to tell Sharp to go home to Edinburgh, and to forbid his replacement by other ministers.[11]

Such was the trust of the Resolutioners in their king that this decision caused them no dismay. In August the king provided a letter for Sharp to take home with him which appeared to be an unequivocal royal guarantee of presbyterian church government. Sharp and the letter were received in Edinburgh in early September with great satisfaction and thanksgiving by the ministers, and thus their contentment and the quiet of the church were effortlessly secured.[12] Then, once the ministers were out of the way, the negotiating began in earnest.

The letter and the circumstances surrounding it have been the subject of much controversy.[13] As it stood, the missive undoubtedly provided a royal guarantee of presbyterian church government. Was Charles sincere, or was it, as was later alleged, a deliberate misleading of the Resolutioners in order to preserve calm for the moment? In view of Charles' behaviour at the conference on Scottish church government in December 1660, shortly to be discussed, it seems clear that in August the king had by no means made up his mind what should be done about Scottish church affairs. His personal preference was for episcopacy, but he was not sure how possible it would be to restore that system in Scotland. In these circumstances the letter was a way of maintaining the *status quo* and of avoiding any threat to the stability of the Restoration from Scotland. At the very best, however, the letter was a political device which might or might not have permanent effect. It cannot be construed as evidence of Charles' inner conviction of his commitment to the Covenant.

Disappointed presbyterians later alleged that Sharp had been the evil genius behind the letter. It was maintained that he had composed it to soothe the suspicions of his fellow ministers, knowing always that it was merely a temporary device soon to be supplanted.[14] There is no evidence anywhere that this was the case. Nor is there any evidence for another assertion from Burnet[15] that Middleton had taken Sharp into his confidence over his intention to restore episcopacy, and had employed him to help put the design under way.

Sharp was no fool. He realised from early in the Restoration that the Scottish nobility were prepared to bring in episcopacy. Like his fellow Resolutioners, however, he had a high opinion of the king's good will towards presbytery. It seems most likely that he took the letter at its face value. He warned his brethren on his return to Scotland of the danger from the nobility and stressed that they must avoid giving offence and thus strengthening the hand of the episcopal party.[16] This was not the action of a man trying to mislead, or pledged to assist in the introduction of episcopacy. Indeed it is extremely doubtful in the prevailing mood of anti-clericalism whether the nobility would have been prepared to trust a minister with their secret intentions.

Moreover, even if the charges against Sharp could be demonstrated, it would still be true that ministers were excluded from the circle of policy makers in London. The very fact that no ministers took part in the discussions on the form of church government which should prevail in Scotland was a clear indication of the secular spirit which governed them.

Since Monck had first left Scotland for London in January 1660, a procession of Scots had followed him south. Before Charles even landed in England the Noblemen and Gentlemen of the Shires - that is the Estate of

Barons - had sent a delegation to the capital.[17] Similarly the Commissioners of the Burghs sent an agent to the king.[18] By June, according to Sharp, London was full of importunate Scottish nobility.[19] The preoccupation of all was secular matters. A joint meeting of the noblemen and the representatives of the barons and burgesses was permitted by the king.[20] At this meeting a petition to the king was drawn up, embodying their common urgent desires. The form of church government did not appear in the petition, nor did any other reference to religion.[21]

The pressing interest of the nobility was the awarding of offices of state. The distribution was made during July and August, and made apparently without reference to the religious opinions of the beneficiaries.[22] Thus all indications pointed to a settlement of the church by the secular power without reference to the ministers, and with scant regard to the religious issues. This impression was strengthened by the behaviour of the Committee of Estates in Edinburgh.

The system of Commissioners by which Scotland was governed during the Interregnum was allowed to continue until August 1660. Towards the end of that month the Commissioners relinquished their authority to a Committee of Estates presided over by the earl of Glencairn, now Chancellor of Scotland.[23] Virtually as soon as it met, this body arrested a group of Protester ministers who had met to draw up a letter to the king. The letter was confiscated and proved to consist of a reminder to the king of his obligations under the terms of the Covenants, and a detailed statement of the form of church settlement that would be acceptable to the Protesters. This document was extremely distasteful to Glencairn and the Committee of Estates, and its authors were imprisoned. This action was followed by a proclamation 'against unlawful meetings and seditious papers'.[24]

The basis for the action taken against the Protesters by the Committee of Estates was the conviction of the members of the Committee that the Protesters offered a threat to public order.[25] The letter was described to the king as not a monitory but a minatory petition.[26] This view, and its underlying implication that the Protesters' views were incompatible with monarchical government, was heartily endorsed by Sharp from Edinburgh.[27] His intention was to underline the differences between Protesters and Resolutioners, and by implication to stress the loyalty of the Resolutioners. The Resolutioners had consistently claimed throughout the Interregnum and since, by their letters and addresses to the king, that they were always loyal to the Stuart monarchy. Their intention was to stress that there was no history of political antagonism between king and Resolutioner which would justify punitive action against their version of presbytery. The events of the next few months were to demonstrate that their conviction was not shared by all the nobility. The incompatibility of any form of presbyterian church government with monarchy was to be the cornerstone of the coming attack against it.

In December 1660 the time came for considering the instructions to be given to Middleton as Commissioner to the Scots Parliament, summoned to meet on

1 January 1661.[28] It seems that only at this late date were the first formal discussions held concerning the ecclesiastical settlement in Scotland.[29] On that occasion a number of circumstances ensured that the sense of the meeting would be against the continuance of presbytery.

The first of such circumstances was the presence at the meeting of Clarendon and his protégé, Middleton. Clarendon was himself fervently in favour of episcopacy and opposed to presbytery. It was no secret that he thought presbyterians and Covenanters to have been traitors to Charles I, and he entertained a particular antipathy to Scottish presbyterians. Clarendon did not reveal his part in the debate in his account of it. It is certain, however, that his enormous power and prestige at this juncture, as the successful architect of the Restoration, must have given his views more than ordinary weight. It is most probably his influence that can be seen behind the stance taken at the meeting by Middleton.

Middleton had his private reasons for antipathy to presbytery. In addition he was ambitious. Since Clarendon had condescended to favour him with his attention, he was unlikely to spurn this aid to his advancement by disagreeing with him on religious issues. He therefore opened the discussion with a request that he might be allowed 'for the Humiliation of the Preachers' to begin his legislation in the coming Parliament with the rescinding of the Covenant and the restoration of the bishops.

This suggestion met with general agreement except from Lauderdale. It is possible that the agreement was made the more readily as the result of a paper that may well have been before the meeting on this occasion.[30] Bishop Sydserf, the sole surviving bishop from the 1630s, had been among those who had made their way to London in the summer of 1660.[31] It was undoubtedly his intention to influence the nobility in the direction of episcopacy if he could, and it therefore seems likely that a brief, written by him and setting out the incompatibility of monarchy and presbytery, can be dated to this period.[32] Such a document was certainly well calculated to appeal to the prejudices of some of the Scottish nobility.

Only Lauderdale stood out in the general acquiescence. He was certainly not the ideal man to enter upon a defence of presbytery. His argument in its favour was a perilous display of tightrope walking. He began by asserting that the Covenant had been a 'wicked, traiterous Combination of Rebels against their lawful Sovereign' with which he repented ever having been involved. He then went on to say that Scotland could never 'be reduced to a perfect Submission and Obedience to the King, till the Episcopal Government was again established there'. The real issue, he maintained, was not in these two points at all, but in how to choose an appropriate moment for the introduction of episcopacy when so many Scots of influence were still supporters of the Covenant. He therefore suggested that any change should be delayed at least until after the first session of Parliament.

Thus Lauderdale, in his reluctance to compromise his political career by a defence of presbytery, had conceded the main point: that such a system of church government *was* incompatible with monarchy. He therefore had no defence when Middleton and others contradicted his estimate of public opinion in Scotland, and suggested that it should be left to the Commissioner to use his discretion in selecting the appropriate moment for the restoration of episcopacy.

The circumstance which finally confirmed the decision against presbytery was the king's agreement to the policy of giving Middleton a free hand. The king had no love for presbytery. That had been as clear in 1650 as it was in 1660 to all except presbyterian ministers: 'It was then taken for granted by those that knew not the mysteries and intrigues of court and estate policy, that it was to continue as when the King swore the covenants and took the oath of coronation at Scoone 1651.'[33] On the other hand, the Restoration was by no means firmly established. No risk could be run of unnecessary tumult in Scotland. This insecurity had, at least initially, made the king likely to take notice of Lauderdale's point of view. But when Middleton, the man among Scots to whom Charles owed the biggest debt of gratitude,[34] provided assurances that episcopacy would be restored without upset, Charles was bound to agree.

The basic premise of those members of the Scottish nobility who had argued for the restoration of episcopacy at the meeting in London in December had been that the politically significant members of the nation were in favour of it. That was certainly true of the major office holders present on that occasion: Glencairn, now Chancellor, Middleton, Commissioner to the Parliament, and Rothes, President of the Privy Council. Whether it was also true of the rest of the nobility and of the Estates of Barons and Burgesses remained to be seen.

The first few months of 1661, therefore, constituted a period of experiment and trial of public opinion. Measures were passed in Parliament and reactions to them carefully gauged before new moves were made. The inner circle of policy makers were sufficiently aware of the king's positive desire for calm in Scotland, and of the bearing of their success in maintaining it on their own political ambitions, to proceed with caution.

However, for those like James Wood, the Resolutioner leader,[35] who looked for signs and portents, the splendour and exuberance of the ceremonies for the reception of the Commissioner into Edinburgh, and the sitting of Parliament[36] were a clear indication of the arrogance of the nobility. For ten years Scotland's traditional rulers had been out of the saddle. There was small chance now that they would be willing to admit the pretensions of presbyterian ministers to power and influence.

On 1 January 1661 the Parliament assembled for the first time. The Rolls were called, and Middleton's commission and a letter from the king were read. Then an act was passed for the taking of the Oath of Allegiance.[37] This was the first measure which would test the temper of Parliament. The most controversial clause read, 'I acknowledge my said Soverane only Supream Governour of this Kingdome over all persons and in all causes.' It immediately harked back to the disputes of the previous twenty-five years over the role of the king in the church. How far was the new Parliament at the beginning of a new era prepared to trust the new king's interpretation of this expression?

The answer on 2 January, when members were required to take the oath, seemed to be that some Scots were not prepared to trust him very far. The earl of Cassillis,[38] supported by the earls of Crawford and Leven, Lords Cranston, Balmerino and Couper, and possibly others as well, asked for an official interpretation of the scope of the oath. Sir John Fletcher, King's Advocate and Middleton's ally, replied that the supremacy applied only to civil matters. This assurance was apparently frequently repeated thereafter. Cassillis then asked for this interpretation to be put on record and appended to the oath. The request was refused, presumably because of its implied slight on the king's honour. Cassillis therefore withdrew with a number of other members, while some who had taken the oath formally declared that they had taken it only in the sense given by the Commissioner.

This was a formidable chorus of opposition to have arisen on the very first day for the transaction of parliamentary business. Small wonder that Middleton attempted to quell the apprehensions created by assuring Sharp, now Royal Chaplain, that he had no intention of meddling with the church.[39] Similarly he found it desirable to slow down the pace of action against presbytery. At a meeting of the Articles on 9 January it was suggested that an act which 'would have all overturned since '38' should be passed. The Articles was the committee which prepared legislation for the approval of Parliament. What passed there could surely pass in Parliament. This suggested reform seems to have been the work of a group within the Committee which was eager for radical measures. Middleton, however, 'gave a very seasonable check unto the motion, and dashed the designe of the high party'.[40] Clearly the Commissioner was not yet confident of the reception radical legislation would provoke.

Not long after this, however, he was prepared to go a little further. On 16 January legislation was passed which declared the making of leagues, and treaties with foreign powers without royal permission, to be illegal.[41] These were edicts obviously directed against the Covenants but not yet mentioning them explicitly by name.[42] On 22 January an act was passed annulling the Convention of Estates of 1643.[43] This meeting had passed the Solemn League and Covenant, but again that document was not mentioned by name. On 25 January it was declared illegal to *renew* the Solemn League and Covenant without royal permission.[44]

These 'late brisk proceedings of the parliament' again raised apprehensions.[45] On this occasion the Resolutioner ministers seem to have been the ones to have protested most vigorously.[46] Robert Douglas and James Sharp submitted a paper on the subject to Middleton and Glencairn on 31 January.[47] The immediate reaction from them was a promise that, as the ministers had requested, an act would be passed 'for owning of the doctrin and disciplin of this church'.[48] To this concession were added other indications that

Middleton still feared to disregard signs of dissidence. A complaint from Sharp that the Resolutioners disliked the anti-clerical tone of the weekly Edinburgh newspaper *Mercurius Caledonius*[49] produced a promise from Middleton that it would be silenced.[50] Furthermore, Middleton again intervened in the Articles to prevent an increase in ministers' stipends, awarded by the Parliament of 1649, from being annulled along with other legislation of that Parliament.[51] Such an edict would have been clear evidence of the malice and hostility of the policy makers towards the ministers. This ill-will was already evident to observers such as Sharp and his brethren.[52] Plainly Middleton wished as yet to avoid any more obvious demonstration of it.

This cautious mode of proceeding was continued into the middle of February. At his meeting with the Resolutioners at the end of January, Middleton had asked the ministers to draw up a draft of the act they wanted for ratifying church government. This request had no doubt been a gesture to win time for the government, and to prevent the ministers losing all hope. Nevertheless, the ministers had taken the request seriously, and on 15 February the draft was duly presented to Middleton by Sharp.[53] Middleton accepted it. He was still not secure enough to dispense with such appeasing gestures.

But then there came a change. In the last week in February the project of rescinding all acts against episcopacy and for presbytery was again raised in the Articles. Once again it came to nothing for the moment, and had perhaps been suggested only as a joke. But this time,

> though they vaved the determining of it for the time, yet by vote of all the Committee saif 4 it was marked to be takin into consideration befor the rysing of this parliament.[54]

When Douglas and Dickson complained once more to Middleton and Glencairn, another conference was fixed, to be held between the administration and the Resolutioner leaders.[55] This conference was never held, but constantly postponed by the administration. The most that could be obtained by mid-March was a private assurance from Middleton to Sharp and Douglas that nothing would be determined until 'he received his returne from England'.[56] Such a promise was small comfort when it was rumoured in Edinburgh 'that upon his returne the parliament will rescind all standing acts for presbyterian government'.[57]

Plainly something had happened to induce Middleton to abandon his policy of caution and conciliation. One factor which argued the safety of proceeding rapidly was the continuing disunity of the ministers. When the Restoration was imminent, and again in the summer of 1660, there had been moves towards unity by the Protesters.[58] Their idea seems to have been to unite the ministry in face of the trials they felt sure were coming upon the church, fearing justly, as a critic noted, 'that his Majesty had an aversion from their principles'.[59] This interpretation of the Restoration was repellent to the Resolutioners, particularly as at that time they felt confident not only of the future of presbytery but also of the utter demise of the Protester party.[60] Consequently the divisions continued.

The failure to implement the Covenant in England, however, followed by the imprisonment of the Protester ministers, produced a temporary feeling of solidarity.[61] Baillie refrained from publishing his latest outpouring against the Protesters.[62] The Resolutioner leaders drew up overtures for a union.[63] Sharp tried to use his influence in favour of those imprisoned, especially Samuel Rutherford.[64]

These gestures not only failed to produce instant accord, but were overtaken by the legislation of the Parliament. Although there was caution on the part of the administration in the way the issue of church government was approached, there could be no doubt at all of the hostility of the Parliament towards the Covenanters and legislation of the past twenty-five years, and of their determination to find scapegoats from outside their own number.[65] On 1 January, Johnston of Wariston, one of the most conspicuous supporters of the Protesters, was declared fugitive and rebel.[66] On 16 January all those who had supported the Remonstrance were ordered to be expelled from Edinburgh.[67] In February Argyll, Guthrie and other Remonstrants were brought to answer for their behaviour before the Parliament.[68]

The reaction of the Resolutioners to these assaults was not to close ranks with those who were being attacked, but to dissociate themselves from the Protesters as far as possible.[69] No doubt they intended thereby to allow the hostility towards presbytery to fall upon the Protesters alone, while retaining favour themselves. So, for example, in the sermons preached before Parliament by Resolutioner ministers in the first three months of 1661, James Sharp, James Chambers, George Halyburton, William Colville, James Wood, David Fletcher, John Paterson, Archibald Turner, James Hamilton and John Menzies are all reported to have preached in ways that could only be construed as offensive to the Protesters, and highly critical of their past activities.[70]

The effect of this continuing animosity was to render any united opposition to government policies impossible from the ministers as a whole. Furthermore, the impression made on Middleton by the Resolutioners' strategy of dissociating themselves from the Protesters was not that the Resolutioners had thus earned the right to the continuation of presbyterian church government. Rather he took it to mean that they could be induced to accept episcopacy without undue trouble. He wrote to Clarendon to this effect as early as January 21.[71]

A second factor encouraging Middleton to abandon caution in implementing his policies for the church was public opinion. It seems certain from the indications that survive that there was a groundswell of opinion in the early months of 1661 against the presbyterian ministers and all that they represented. Baillie noted this change in temper:

Many of our people are hankering after Bishops, having forgot the evill they have done, and the nature of their office. An exceeding great profanitie and contempt both of the ministrie and religion itself, is everywhere prevalent; a young fry of ministers in Lothian, and Fife, and elsewhere, looks as if they intended some change, without any fear or reverence to the elder ministers, who latelie put them in their places.[72]

There was a spirit of malice and the desire for revenge on ministers among those who had suffered during the past twenty-five years. Sharp noted its presence in Parliament:

> The drift of the most of this parliament is to bring the ministerie under beggary and the extremity of contempt.[73]

This spirit was also evident to Kirkton.[74]

The effect on the administration of this demonstration of hostility to the ministers can only have been to reassure them that the presbyterians and their supporters could safely be overruled without their case inspiring much sympathy or support.

The most important factor, however, in encouraging Middleton to proceed with his ecclesiastical policies was the disintegration of the parliamentary opposition. Events at the time of the taking of the Oath of Allegiance had indicated that Cassillis and Crawford were the most senior and most influential members of the opposition. Cassillis was a respected member of the generation that had been involved in the covenanting revolution since the beginning. His letters[75] suggest that he was well aware of Middleton's antagonism to the church and had intended to use his position in Parliament to further a 'project' - most likely the defence of presbytery. He was therefore a potentially powerful leader of a presbyterian party. But he was old. Furthermore, although he wrote to Lauderdale asking for support in his stance against the Oath, and reminding Lauderdale that he too had hoped for the success of the 'project', he received no reply. His explanations of his apparent defiance over the matter of the Oath of Allegiance which he sent to the king were again met with silence. He seems then to have lost heart. He left Parliament after the first few days of its sitting and did not return.[76] In April he and Cranston, lately made Viscount Oxenford, both forfeited their places as Lords of Session because of their continued refusal to take the Oath of Allegiance as it stood.[77] Cassillis' place went to Middleton.[78] Thus Cassillis was effectively without influence from the very first few days of the Parliament's sitting.

The other, more realistic possibility for the leader of an opposition was Crawford. He too was one of the original Covenanters, about the same age as Cassillis, and he enjoyed a formidable reputation among presbyterians. On his release from imprisonment with Lauderdale he too had made his way to the Hague, but had earlier demonstrated to one of Hyde's agents that he would be less pliant than Lauderdale in his attitude to presbytery in England.[79] He was received with enthusiasm in Edinburgh when he returned there in December 1660, and he seemed to have support as leader of the presbyterian party.[80] His opposition to the Oath of Allegiance had not disqualified him from attendance in Parliament or from office, as that of Cassillis had done. He was therefore able to take his place in the Articles by virtue of his re-appointment to the office of Treasurer which he had held before the Interregnum. The opportunity was thus open to him to have some influence on policy-making.

By the end of February, however, it had become clear that there was no party for him to lead, and that in the Articles he was virtually an isolated figure. The story that the project to pass a Rescissory Act was first suggested at that time 'by way of ralliery with Crafurd'[81] suggests that his principles were so out of step with those of the other members of the Committee that they had become a joke and a byword. On that occasion only four, of more than forty members, were willing to register any objection whatever to such a suggestion. The other three, Sir John Gilmour, Sir Peter Wedderburn, and another unknown,[82] were the only ones found to be bold enough to join Crawford.

It is possible that the representatives of the Estate of Barons had been selected for their readiness to agree to whatever was proposed.[83] Alternatively, they may simply have been frightened of possible reprisals should they offer any opposition to the policies of the administration, as Kirkton suggested:

> Loyalty was so on horseback amongst them, and withall they were so much under fear for their late actings, which were all reputed treasonable, that their actings were very faint.[84]

Whatever the reason for the unanimity, Middleton was surely justified in writing very soon after this meeting of the Articles to Clarendon, assuring him that the Parliament would gladly pass an Act Rescissory, and asking for further instructions. Glencairn seconded this with the view that generally public opinion was in favour of restoring episcopacy.[85]

The receipt of these letters provoked much controversy in London. A meeting of Charles, the Duke of York, Ormonde, Lauderdale and Clarendon discussed the matter. Lauderdale maintained his former argument that there was insufficient support for the restoration of the bishops. Similarly, the king had hesitations as before about the timing of the move. Clarendon supported the idea of an Act Rescissory as an appropriate way of rewriting the past, yet he too felt that if the automatic effect of such an act were to be the suppression of presbytery, then it would be better to wait till support from the ministers was certain.[86]

Clarendon's caution may well have been due to his concern with English ecclesiastical affairs at this moment, and to his unwillingness to offend the English presbyterians about to attend the Savoy Conference.[87] It is clear, however, that Crawford and the ministers had managed to convey to those in London their dislike of the proceedings in Edinburgh. Middleton and Glencairn were therefore instructed to confer with those who had objected, and to present their views to the king.[88]

Before this letter, dated 26 March, can have reached Edinburgh, however, Middleton had already acted. On 28 March the Act Rescinding and Annulling the pretendit Parliaments in the years 1640, 1641, etc., was passed, and it was immediately followed by the Act Concerning Religion and Church Government.[89] The first rescinded all legal guarantees of presbytery while the second declared that

as to the Government of the Church his Maiestie will make it his care to satle and secure the
same in such a frame as shall be most agreeable to the word of God most suteable to
monarchical Government, and most complying with the publict peace and quyet of the
Kingdome.

There were considerable objections to the passing of a Rescissory Act, as had
been recognised when the matter was discussed in London. The difficulties
were also recognised at meetings of the Articles in Edinburgh,[90] where
Middleton was advised by Primrose to act with caution, but they had not
prevented the members of that committee from requiring Primrose, the Clerk
Register, to draw up a draft of the act which was duly passed.[91] The Act
Concerning Religion and Church Government, then, served two purposes. It
suspended for the moment the effect of the Rescissory Act on church
government, and it placed the final decision on that issue in the king's hands.

Middleton and his allies had acted in this way without authorisation from
the king.[92] Why? Middleton was confident that he had support for a
Rescissory Act. Moreover, he was already engaged in a struggle for power with
Lauderdale. If, as he had assured the king in December, he could repeal the
laws establishing presbytery without fuss or protest, then he would have won a
considerable political victory over Lauderdale who had urged caution. His
letter asking for instructions and advice had been sent by express on 4 March,
and yet by 28 March, more than three weeks later, he had heard nothing. The
silence itself was negative, and it is not impossible that one of Middleton's
busy agents, perhaps Mungo Murray, had already heard enough to know what
advice would eventually be sent.[93] To proceed without permission, but to
reserve the final decision for the king, must have seemed an excellent way for
Middleton to hedge his bets. He could hardly be accused of taking the law into
his hands if the final decision was left to the king, and yet if he succeeded in his
plan the victory and the praise would be his.

The storm of opposition that the two Acts aroused proved, however, that
Middleton had made a miscalculation. Crawford and Hamilton, supported by
perhaps as many as forty others, dissented from the Rescissory Act in
Parliament.[94] Baillie wrote to Lauderdale condemning the measures, and
Lauderdale's supposed part in them, in the strongest terms.[95] Hutcheson's
sentiments matched those of Baillie.[96] Wood is said to have threatened
Middleton with the mob if the Act were passed.[97] The presbytery of
Edinburgh attempted to petition Middleton.[98] The general opinion in the
church proved so hostile that it was found necessary to interfere with meetings
of synods to prevent them making their discontent public.[99] Tweeddale was so
dismayed by the adverse reaction that he wrote to Lauderdale suggesting that it
might after all be possible to retain an appropriately regulated form of
presbytery, as Middleton's second act had in theory allowed for:

And for all is yet done I shall be hopeful, though the way of settling the church government
here doth displease, yet without changing the form (which we are so much engaged to) being
regulated as shall be found necessary and expedient, it may be resettled by the king's
majesty's own appointment.[100]

News of the failure of Middleton's *coup* soon reached London, where it was used against him by Lauderdale.[101] At the Restoration a feud had grown up between Middleton and Lauderdale, as the result of their common desire for power. Despite Clarendon's opposition, Lauderdale had secured the position of Secretary of State which ensured his presence at the centre of things in London.[102] He had therefore been content that Middleton, Clarendon's protégé, should be Commissioner to the Parliament, especially since it was not a permanent appointment,[103] and because a Commissioner's instructions usually allowed him very little freedom of manoeuvre.

Almost as soon as the Parliament began sitting, however, the struggle between the two had begun. Middleton's success in putting through legislation enhancing the royal prerogative and enacting the king's views of the events of the past twenty-five years made him a potentially dangerous rival. Apparently in order to disarm Lauderdale, assurances were given from Edinburgh that Middleton was well disposed to Lauderdale.[104] Petitioners began to realise, however, that one could be played off against the other,[105] and a more sinister note sounded when Lauderdale was warned to beware that his rival did not ruin him.[106]

Furthermore, by taking action over the Act Rescissory without official permission, Middleton was demonstrating that even in his position as Commissioner his powers were not limited by his instructions, and he was thereby showing himself as a more formidable opponent than ever. The vocal opposition to the Rescissory Act was thus a heaven-sent opportunity for Lauderdale to recover lost ground. Middleton recognised his danger well enough and wrote to Lauderdale himself, professing friendship.[107] However, on the same day that the letter was written, Rothes and Glencairn were sent to court[108] to defend Middleton's actions to the king until he should have dissolved Parliament and gone to London himself. The policy-making and the fate of the Scottish church thus moved back to London.

In the hiatus thus created in decisions on the church's future, there was still some hope that churchmen might be able to influence events. Accordingly James Sharp also made his way to London as the official chaplain to accompany Glencairn and Rothes. Sharp's role in events at this stage is extremely obscure. In the first weeks of the Parliament's sitting he had co-operated with the Resolutioner leaders in representing their case to the government and had clearly retained their trust. During this period he had, however, been the subject of rumour, beginning in London, perhaps with Lauderdale, perhaps with English presbyterians there, that he had been involved in the plans to introduce episcopacy. Sharp had tried to rebut these insinuations in a very convincing series of letters.[109] The case against him, however, was given weight by the fact that he had undoubtedly attempted to prevent any general and public protest against the tendency of legislation. In retrospect, when the legislation against presbytery and the Covenants had been passed, that policy seemed to the leading Resolutioners to have been unduly timid.[110] Sharp's urging of it began to look like complicity. The fact remains, though, that there is no known evidence that Sharp was anything but loyal to the Resolutioners up to the time of the Act Rescissory.

What is more difficult to assess is the nature of his relationship with Middleton. Lauderdale clearly had suspected that Sharp had deserted him in favour of Middleton some time in the first three months of 1661. Sharp then went to some trouble to deny this in the letters already mentioned, but it is certain that he was very intimate with Middleton during that period. His journey to London[111] strongly suggests a liaison with the Commissioner. The simplest solution to the conundrum is to suppose that Sharp was trying to keep a foot in both camps, so that whoever won the contest between Lauderdale and Middleton, Sharp would find himself on the winning side. Something of the kind was clearly suspected by the Resolutioners by the end of March,[112] and he had no commission from them for his journey.[113]

Although self-preservation undoubtedly played a part in Sharp's motivations, he had a perfectly clear and explicit idea of how the church might benefit from an alliance between Lauderdale and Middleton. These ideas he expounded to Lauderdale.[114] In a lengthy and complex letter he recalled that he had tried to prevent the Rescissory Act but had failed: 'I saw it was not in my power, nor of any else here to oppose that headstrong resolution.' The Act had passed, and thus, Sharp went on to say, his predictions of 'a general dissatisfaction amongst the best of the ministers and people' had been proved correct. In this situation, he continued, the only ray of light was that the fate of the church now rested in the king's power: 'The only reserve we have is in the king's favour and graciousness towards the state of this poor church.' At such a juncture, Sharp stressed, Lauderdale could play a vital role in the defence of presbytery. Moreover it was not only in Lauderdale's power to use 'an opportunity to oblige and gratify this poor church', but by doing so he could help himself. It was, Sharp said, an opportunity 'to fix your interest here [in Scotland] which cannot be shaken'. This could be accomplished, Sharp went on, by Lauderdale and Middleton making friends, which Middleton would be glad to do: 'I should think it were his interest to do it.' Together they should then agree to do nothing further for the moment in the matter of church government until by conference they might arrange a compromise:

> If there could be a demur for some time, both upon your lordship's part, and upon [the part of] those who are here of making any further step in reference to the Rescissory Act, and endeavours used in the [mean] while for preparing towards a coalescing betwixt your lordship and the Earl of Middleton, then you might by joint concurring fall upon the best expedient for preventing the evils which else will rush upon us. This were the only way in my poor apprehension for an effectual preventing of a change.

A final compelling reason for Lauderdale to co-operate was given. It was clear, Sharp said, that the whole issue of church government was merely part of a political game: 'The disposing of our church matters is intended in subserviency to another interest.' Lauderdale could be expected to realise whose 'interest' was intended.

This scheme must also have been expounded by Sharp to Middleton. Middleton found himself in sudden acute and unexpected political difficulties. It was likely to appeal to him, and who better for an agent of reconciliation than Sharp himself? Possibly the whole idea had been discussed with some of the Resolutioners, for Baillie seemed to know why Sharp was off to London[115] and Sharp met Wood immediately before he went, and corresponded with him from London.[116] What had perhaps led to a break with the leaders was Sharp's views on what the desired compromise in church government might be.

In a letter written in March, Sharp had expressed the view that if 'erastianism of the worst form' were to be avoided in the Scottish church, then some compromise with the civil power over the form of church government would have to be made: 'We must fall upon constant commissionars, moderators, or Bishops.'[117] As early as the Synod of Fife of October 1660 Sharp had argued that moderate episcopacy was not necessarily incompatible with the Covenant.[118] His views in the spring of 1661 were an extension of that premise, and may have been influenced by the Worcester House Declaration of October 1660.[119] That document had appeared to offer to English dissenters the possibility of a moderate limited episcopacy.[120] It may well have appealed to Sharp as a tolerable compromise. He probably went to London hoping to preserve presbytery, but with the possibility at the back of his mind of offering some concessions.

The whole notion of churchmen having any influence in the resolution of the issue of church government, however, depended on two assumptions: that Middleton would be in political disgrace because of his miscalculations over the Rescissory Act, and therefore would be willing to abandon his ruthless imposition of episcopacy, and that the king would be sufficiently well disposed to the Resolutioners to look favourably on their desires for the continuance of presbytery, or at worst some moderate alternative. Both of these calculations proved to be mistaken.

The protests in the synods against the Act Rescissory were seen not as evidence that Middleton had misjudged the moment and acted beyond his authority, but as disaffection which ought to be suppressed.[121] This aggression in turn derived from the successes of the episcopal party in England. The presbyterians there were thoroughly demoralised and their opposition to the course of events had withered away.[122] To those at court it now seemed certain that the same tactics could be pursued in Scotland: that opposition could be disregarded and episcopacy imposed.[123]

When Sharp arrived in London on 6 May he was therefore not received as a presbyterian whose views must now be carefully considered but as a suitable subject for bullying. It was Clarendon's job to bend Sharp to an appropriate frame of mind. First of all it was represented to him that he owed his reputation at court to Middleton.[124] The implication was that he should now repay that debt by supporting Middleton and the episcopalians rather than Lauderdale and the presbyterians. It was further impressed on him that the king was in favour of episcopacy, and not, as Sharp had been so certain, in

favour of presbytery and the Resolutioners.[125] Lastly it was conveyed to him
that unless Scotland submitted to episcopal government, the English garrisons
would remain in Scotland. In mid-January these had amounted to 3,000 foot
and 100 horse.[126] What was being threatened, therefore, was the continued
presence and expense of an alien army of occupation. This threat was not new
to Sharp; he had heard it rumoured in March,[127] but its confirmation at the
highest level must have been extremely disturbing.

Faced with all this, Sharp was prepared to capitulate over presbytery. It was
clear that some form of episcopacy would be imposed, but he must still have
hoped to influence the form of it.[128] His capitulation was doubtless made easier
by this consideration, and also by his growing conviction that if the
Resolutioners were made to see, as he had been, that the restoration of
episcopacy was the king's expressed will and quite unavoidable, then they too
would capitulate. This he expressed in his assurances to those in London that it
would be possible to introduce episcopacy.[129]

At the same time he continued his policy of maintaining good relations with
both Middleton and Lauderdale. A particularly sycophantic letter to
Middleton written from London in mid-May welcomed the prevailing climate
for episcopacy and looked forward to the time when Middleton should arrive
in London himself to put the finishing touches to the scheme for the
restoration of bishops.[130] It was seen by Osmund Airy as proof positive of
Sharp's perjury.[131] It seems more likely that by this means Sharp reassured
Middleton in Edinburgh that no secret plotting against him and his policies
was taking place in London, and at the same time reserved for himself a
measure of influence when Middleton should indeed appear on the scene. Such
an interpretation is reinforced by Sharp's collaboration with Lauderdale in the
drawing up of a proclamation of 10 June which repeated the Act of 28 March
in leaving the final decision on church government to the king, meanwhile
allowing the continuation of kirk sessions, presbyteries and synods.[132] Thus
Sharp avoided a break with either of the two rivals.

The measures which had been taken to persuade Sharp that he must
abandon presbytery were merely the preliminary salvos in the battle still to be
fought between Middleton and Lauderdale. Cassillis and Crawford had been
subjected to the same strong treatment because of their presbyterian
sympathies. Cassillis had ventured up to London to explain his conduct over
the Oath of Allegiance to the king, but his suit had not met with favour.[133]
Crawford had similarly tried to explain his attitude to the Oath. In a letter
written by his son, Crawford's loyalty had been stressed, and an attempt had
been made to enlist Lauderdale's help in representing his case to the king.[134]
Despite this he too had met with a hostile reception at court.[135] By the time that
Middleton arrived in London, therefore, the defenders of presbytery were in
disarray.

Lauderdale himself was similarly under considerable pressure. On the one
hand the Resolutioners were urging him in the most earnest tones to ensure
that leading ministers and synods should be consulted before any decision were
made on church government. They assured him

that to our best observation and knowledge the generality of the church judicatories are against a change of government.[136]

Crawford, Cassillis and Sharp undoubtedly looked to him as the chief spokesman for their cause. On the other hand Lauderdale as before was concerned for his political future, and reluctant to sacrifice it for the defence of presbytery. His circumstances at that particular juncture were especially critical since Middleton, whom he had hoped to destroy over the issue of church government, was returning to London, not in disgrace but in triumph,[137] ready and willing to press his unexpected advantage against him. Lauderdale had found it possible earlier in the case of England to support the idea of a moderate form of episcopacy as a means of avoiding prelacy, and an acceptable alternative to presbytery. It is likely that at this time he was coming closer to accepting the possibility of such a compromise also for Scotland.

Matters came to a head at the meeting of the Scottish Council summoned on Middleton's return from the Parliament in Edinburgh in mid-June.[138] There Middleton formally proposed the restoration of episcopacy. Lauderdale then pressed for delay in order to allow time for consultations with churchmen, on the basis that public opinion was not sufficiently in favour to warrant going straight ahead. This was the defence for presbytery that he had offered before: that it should be retained as a matter of expediency for the moment in order to preserve stability in Scotland. The changed circumstances in England made it a much less powerful defence than it had been in December 1660. Although he was supported by Hamilton and Robert Moray, this argument was as before attacked by Middleton and his allies. On this occasion Middleton, supported by Glencairn, replied firstly that 'they need not fear opposition'. The evidence he produced for this assertion was the lone petition in favour of episcopacy from the Synod of Aberdeen, but it sufficed. He went on to say that the opinion of the ministers, which Lauderdale had suggested was important, was neither significant nor important. Such a rejoinder was quite in character with Middleton's activities to that point, and agreeable to the anti-clerical bias of the administration. For good measure Glencairn and Rothes went on to repeat the old argument that presbytery was incompatible with civil obedience and monarchy. The implication was that the disagreement with government policies of presbyterian ministers was only to be expected and simply proved their culpable disaffection.

Crawford was the only man present to declare himself unequivocally in favour of presbytery. He asserted that the vast majority of Scots thought as he did, and he went on to excuse past excesses committed in the name of presbytery. He then asserted that, contrary to Middleton's claim that the Act Rescissory had in effect rescinded presbytery and re-established episcopacy, presbytery was still established by acts of the General Assembly which had been ratified by royal authority. Hamilton then added that had this not been generally supposed to be the case, then the Act Rescissory would not have passed.

These assertions were particularly unwelcome to an administration hyper-sensitive to any suggestion of the power of the ministers. Clarendon's response was an attack on Crawford's claim for the independent force of General Assembly legislation. His influence was decisive in producing a majority in favour of episcopacy, and with that the meeting was over and the matter closed. A proclamation dated 14 August was prepared and sent down to Edinburgh with Glencairn.[139] A last-minute protest by Tweeddale was ignored.

Once again the debate had been conducted in entirely secular terms. The questions at issue were still those of the relations between presbytery and monarchy, and the political expediency of a change of church government. The agreement of a large majority of Parliament and of nearly all the most important members of the administration had been secured for a change in church government on grounds which took no account whatsoever of the religious issues involved. Their acquiescence requires some explanation beyond that of simple malice and revenge on the ministers.

It seems likely that the agreement of a good many had been secured by a mixture of threats and bribes. The issue of the garrisons and the prospect of the continuing occupation of Scotland by English forces had been used to bend Sharp. It is probable that it had been used more generally as a threat by Middleton and as a means of forcing through his measures.[140] A petition from the Parliament in June had asked for the removal of the garrisons specifically as a reward for its own good behaviour.[141] Secondly, the promised Act of Indemnity for Scots for their activities since 1651 had been deliberately delayed. Fear of royal reprisals for past misdemeanours had undoubtedly made the Parliament more pliant than it would otherwise have been.[142] Lastly, after the final agreement of the Scottish Council had been secured, the king exempted Scotland from the effects of the English Navigation Act and thus gave her some of the commercial benefits she so urgently desired in her trade with England.[143] The timimg of this measure is unlikely to have been co-incidental.

Agreement having been secured by whatever means, the Proclamation of 14 August declared that, according to the power put in the king's hands by the Act Concerning Religion and Church Government of 28 March, Charles now wished to restore bishops as they had been 'before the late troubles'. The rents of bishoprics and deaneries were to be restored and no more synods were to meet until royal pleasure. Thus Middleton's ascendancy, the humiliation of the ministers and the secular control of the church were all secured. What remained to be seen was the precise form the episcopacy would take.

4

Lauderdale and the Policies of Moderation, 1661-1664

IN the struggle for power between Lauderdale and Middleton, Lauderdale had undoubtedly lost over presbytery. Neither he nor Sharp was yet defeated, however. During the rest of 1661 they worked together in an attempt to control the selection of the candidates for the episcopate, and thus indirectly to determine the nature of the episcopal regime. In this more limited aim they were similarly to be defeated.

Their original intention in the autumn of 1661 was to recruit the Resolutioner leaders as bishops.[1] Douglas was provisionally selected for St Andrews,[2] Sharp was offered a see, and plans were made for him to offer bishoprics to the most eminent of his party. Such a move was not only the work of Lauderdale and his allies, however. It was approved by the king who owed a debt of gratitude to the Resolutioner ministers for their support of him throughout the Interregnum. It may well also have commanded the assent of a number among the nobility who had supported a change of church government. Men such as Glencairn and Rothes had associated closely with the ministers in question and very likely respected them as individuals.[3] Their true rancour had always been reserved for the Protesters.

Lauderdale clearly had misgivings about whether the Resolutioner leaders could be persuaded to co-operate in taking bishoprics. In late August, therefore, he wrote to Dickson, Douglas, Hamilton, Smith, Garven and Hutcheson[4] in reply to their earlier letter urging him to represent their case to the king. His message was that their desire that a General Assembly or synods or individual ministers should be consulted before any decision were made on church government, had been submitted to the king. He told them that they must accept what could not be altered. He went on to explain that it had been thought undesirable for any opportunity to be created for public criticism of what had already been enacted by Parliament in the Act Rescissory, and accordingly their request had been refused. He then added his personal opinion that the decision for episcopacy had been taken largely because of the king's view of 'the great miscarriages in the exercise of our church government these twenty years'. He consoled them with the king's promise to 'use all tenderness and command great moderation to be used toward such of a contrary judgment who shall not wilfully oppose his Majesty', but at the same time he warned them that any overt opposition would be interpreted in the most unfavourable way:

D

> Give me leave to tell you, any opposition will be construed to have a worse design at bottom; and if I have any skill in the constitution of affairs, the resolution of settling episcopacy is unalterable, and there is no way to preserve peace . . . but by a complying with the resolution.

The implications of what Lauderdale conveyed by this letter were brutally clear: the decision to implement episcopacy was fixed and could not be altered. No open opposition to it would be allowed, and therefore the Resolutioners need not hope to make any public gesture of dissent. If they did not wish to be mute or to be considered disloyal, they must co-operate in the change. This letter was then sent to Edinburgh with Sharp, who was given instructions to offer bishoprics to Douglas, Wood, Baillie and Hutcheson at least,[5] and very likely to others also.

Sharp himself seems to have felt genuinely hopeful that the letter would have the desired effect and that at least some of the Resolutioner leaders might accept. Even after Douglas had rejected the offer, with a curse as he later claimed,[6] Sharp still felt reasonably sanguine of the others.[7] By the end of September, however, it was plain that the Resolutioner leaders would not accept bishoprics. By October, when Sharp returned from his recruiting in Scotland to London, only two ministers, Alexander Fairfoul and James Hamilton, had been persuaded to accompany him,[8] and neither of them was anything like the first rank among Resolutioners.

It is almost impossible to tell how these two were recruited. Perhaps they had been on a list of second-choice candidates from among the ministry. James Hamilton, minister of Cambusnethan, had been minister of that parish since his induction to it in 1635.[9] He had certainly taken no prominent part in the church politics of the preceding twenty-five years. Similarly Alexander Fairfoul had played no very conspicuous part in the history of that era.[10] Their qualifications as Resolutioners were therefore not strong for any sort of preferment.

There are indications, rather, that both these men were chosen not by Sharp as Resolutioner candidates, but by Middleton in default of such candidates. James Hamilton had been one of those selected to preach before the Parliament. Baillie thought that the necessary qualification for this honour was to be sympathetic to a change of church government.[11] It seems likely that Hamilton was known of old to have episcopal sympathies.[12] His sermon preached on 10 March attracted the favourable attention of Sydserf, editor of *Mercurius Caledonius*. He reported that Hamilton 'preached up both the King's Authority and the churches right to Tyths'.[13] The man who could preach such a sermon at such a time was much more likely to appeal to Middleton as a candidate for the episcopate than to Sharp or Lauderdale. Similarly there are grounds for supposing that Fairfoul was not a Resolutioner candidate. He had been a strong supporter of Charles I and the Engagement in 1648[14] in contrast to the ministers generally. It was said that he had preached before Charles II in 1650 to the king's satisfaction and that this was now the basis for his selection as a bishop by the king.[15] He had been chaplain to Rothes, one of Middleton's allies.[16] The fact that he too had preached before the Parliament[17] suggests a means whereby he might have attracted renewed attention.

The only other man who was recruited at this stage was Robert Leighton, and it seems virtually certain that he was not a Resolutioner appointment either. Leighton was a man who had taken no part whatever in the Resolutioner - Protester schism, but had confined himself to his pastoral duties in Newbattle.[18] During the Interregnum he had been appointed Principal of Edinburgh University. This position he had filled with much attention to the welfare of his students and little to the party politics raging in all other Scottish universities for control by Resolutioners or Protesters.[19] Burnet's story was that Leighton had been appointed through his brother Elisha's influence at court. Elisha Leighton apparently thought that to have a brother who was a bishop would shed a little reflected glory on him.[20] There may, however, have been another reason for his appointment. During the Interregnum Leighton had made at least one journey to Charles's court as the agent of the earl of Lothian.[21] Charles must therefore have known him. His appointment as bishop much against his own inclinations[22] looks very much like the intervention of the king once more.

Although these three men were certainly not the first choice of Lauderdale and his party for the new bishops, it is not impossible that they were compromise candidates selected with a view to their moderation. That is a possible interpretation of a number of pieces of evidence which together suggest that Sharp and Lauderdale still envisaged an episcopacy which would avoid prelacy. At the consecration of the first four bishops held in December 1661 in London, Sharp, who had not been episcopally ordained, objected - at least initially - to his reordination by a bishop, on the grounds that his presbyterial ordination was perfectly valid.[23] Such a position would certainly be characteristic of the episcopacy envisaged in the Worcester Declaration. Furthermore, Leighton's personal reasons for accepting the bishopric were principally his desire to be an agent of reconciliation and moderation in church affairs in Scotland.[24] In addition, Andrew Fairfoul went out of his way to convey his intentions to maintain good relations with Baillie as soon as he arrived back in Scotland.[25] Hamilton had apparently co-operated with a Declaration drawn up in the Synod of Glasgow at the time of the Act Rescissory which could be interpreted as condoning moderate episcopacy.[26]

Nevertheless, although these first appointments might indicate that moderation was still the aim of Lauderdale and Sharp, it was becoming increasingly clear that once again they would be defeated by Middleton's contrary aims. In the first place, the scheme to recruit the Resolutioner leaders had been a complete failure, with the single exception of Sharp. The initiative had thereby passed to Middleton. The appointment of the rest of the bishops indicated that the desires of Middleton and his allies had dictated the choice.

Three of those who had been members of the pre-Covenant church were selected for bishoprics. The first of these was Thomas Sydserf, the one surviving bishop. He was rewarded for his longevity, his devotion to episcopacy, and his contribution to the debate on church government, with the bishopric of Orkney,[27] second richest after St Andrews of all fourteen Scottish bishoprics.[28] The other two were David Mitchell, now to become bishop of Aberdeen, and George Wishart, bishop of Edinburgh.[29] Both these men had been deposed by the General Assembly for 'heresy', that is their refusal to sign the Covenant. Rather than conform, they had gone to England and ministered to congregations there. Wishart had also the very valuable qualification of having been chaplain to Montrose. These three appointments were therefore not of Resolutioners, who because the times were evil would reluctantly put up with a moderate episcopacy, but men who for their adherence had been deprived of their livelihood. The possibility of their acting as the agents of peace and reconciliation within the Scottish church was small.

Two further appointments were from the Synod of Aberdeen. Aberdeen had been extremely hostile to the Covenant, and had fostered long-standing episcopal sympathies deriving from the Aberdeen Doctors. After the Act Rescissory the Synod had been the only one to express its satisfaction with the imminent change of church government. Two of the men now preferred, John Paterson, bishop of Ross, and Patrick Forbes, bishop of Caithness,[30] were associated with the document expressing satisfaction at the reintroduction of episcopacy.[31] Paterson had also been one of those who had preached before the Parliament. His sermon on 17 April was sufficiently to the administration's liking to be published.[32] In it, besides bewailing much of the history of the previous twenty-five years, Paterson made a particular attack on the intervention of ministers in politics, and a plea for 'the regulation of Church-Government by Civil Authority'. He made it clear that although the supreme civil authority had no right to interfere in purely spiritual matters, such as the administration of the sacraments, yet it had an obligation to create 'such a chain of regulation as may lay a restraint upon the ministers'. It would not have required much imagination to see this as a plea for episcopacy. There was no doubt that it was a plea for erastian control of the church. Patrick Forbes was similarly strongly identified with the episcopal cause. He was the nephew of the famous Patrick Forbes, bishop of Aberdeen.[33] Thus two more appointments had been made of men unacceptable to the broad majority in the Scottish church.

All of the remaining five appointments seem to have been made as the result of patronage by the king or Middleton and his allies. George Haliburton, bishop of Dunkeld, had been minister at Perth when in 1650 he gave an ovation to Charles II on his entry to the city. Haliburton then successfully supplicated the king for compensation to the city for losses suffered under Cromwell.[34] In addition Haliburton had brought himself to the attention of the administration more recently by his sermon to Parliament on 20 January. The attitude of the Resolutioner ministers to what he said could be gauged by Row's comment:

> In the afternoon, Mr George Haliburton preached most wickedly. He downright condemned the League and Covenant, advising the Parliament to enjoin a day of humiliation for making such an unlawful covenant.[35]

On the other hand the very different sentiments of the administration could be gauged from the report in *Mercurius Caledonius*. Haliburton, it was reported, preached

> to such an excellent purpose, that if the most pernicious Rumper had been present, he would have made him in love with Loyalty; for with unanswerable Arguments he confounded that Apocryphal allegiance which is built upon conditional Oaths.[36]

Here was a man who had attracted the king's favourable attention years before and had now compounded his good reputation by preaching the new orthodoxy.

Robert Wallace, bishop of the Isles, had been minister of Barnweil in the Presbytery of Ayr.[37] His activities as a Resolutioner had been confined to contests with the Protesters within his presbytery and synod.[38] He was, however, a relation of the Chancellor Glencairn,[39] Middleton's strongest ally, and it was no doubt for that reason that he was favoured.

Murdo Mackenzie, bishop of Moray, had been minister of Elgin and another middle-rank Resolutioner.[40] In his case he probably benefited from his relationship to the earls of Seaforth.[41] In 1660 and 1661 the earls of Seaforth and Moray were engaged in a dispute over the sheriffdoms of Ross and Inverness, in which Moray was befriended by Lauderdale and Seaforth by Middleton.[42] In March 1662 Seaforth won his case before the Privy Council.[43] His presence in Edinburgh and the favour of the administration made it more likely that he could request favours in turn for his family.

David Strachan, bishop of Brechin, was certainly the beneficiary of Middleton's favour. As another middle-rank Resolutioner[44] he owed his preferment to the fact that he was minister of Fettercairn, where Middleton's home was.[45]

Finally David Fletcher, minister at Melrose,[46] was the brother of Sir John Fletcher, Lord Advocate,[47] another of Middleton's strongest allies. He was consecrated, last of all, bishop of Argyll.[48]

Including the four initial appointments, there had thus been created an episcopate composed of six convinced supporters of episcopacy, and eight men chosen for their past reputation as royalists or their present connection with Middleton and his party. With the sole exception of Sharp, they had played no distinguished part in the history of the church since 1638. They were second-rate men as far as their power of leadership and authority were concerned, and no doubt they had been chosen very largely for that reason. Their function was to disseminate the nature of the social and political order as perceived by the administration.

Just as it had taken some time for the recruitment of the bishops, so it took some time for the intentions of the administration as to the functions and status of the episcopate to become clear. Here too there was evidence of a continuing struggle between Lauderdale and Middleton, in which the initiative at first seemed to lie with Middleton. After the initial letter to the Privy

Council announcing the establishment of episcopacy, no further decrees were issued until December. By that time it was clear that the Resolutioner leaders would not be brought over, and that there was little hope of a moderate episcopacy. From that time it was gradually made clearer that what was envisaged was an episcopate living in the old prelatic manner, performing functions locally as royal, judicial and financial servants, and in central government resuming its role as the first estate of fourteen votes on which the king could rely absolutely.[49] Furthermore, it was to be an erastian church in which the functions of religion were performed as and because the king allowed them. An episcopacy such as this would have been utterly unthinkable had the bishops been the Resolutioner leaders. Their failure to co-operate once again gave the episcopal party at court the initiative.

The first two proclamations on 12 December and 9 January set the tone by declaring that presentations to parishes and the meetings of church courts were to cease forthwith until permitted to recommence by the bishop.[50] Thus the cherished presbyterian principle that church courts existed by right and not by permission was at a blow removed, and with it any claim to the independence of church from state. In February a series of instructions to Middleton for the coming session of Parliament which met in May 1662 indicated very clearly that the status of the new bishops was to be that of royal servants and prelates.[51] The instructions prescribed the restitution of their 'accustomed dignities, privileges and jurisdictions', including their fiscal and legal functions, and the complete restoration of their 'rights, superiorities, rents, possessions and privileges', particularly the financial endowments of the bishoprics.

It was anticipated that there would be opposition to this settlement. The authoritarian character of the regime was therefore emphasised by the series of instructions relating to provisions for dealing with dissent. Preaching against episcopacy and failure to submit to the bishops' authority in church assemblies were both to be punished. Furthermore, all ministers who had entered their parishes since the abolition of patronage in 1649 were required to obtain presentations to their parishes in order to be allowed to continue to collect their stipends.

These instructions were enacted in the Parliament which duly met in May.[52] The major alteration to the instructions was a requirement that ministers admitted since 1649 should obtain not only presentation from the patron but also collation (or confirmation of the presentation) from the bishop. The impression that this was the work of Middleton and designed simply to rub the noses of the ministers in the fact of episcopal government, was strengthened by the manner of Middleton's later enforcement of the requirement.

At the same time a further apparently provocative act was passed 'for keiping the anniversarie thanksgiving for the King's Majesties birth and restauration'.[53] Ministers were required to commemorate this day on pain of loss of benefice. The celebration of particular occasions by ministers at the behest of the civil power was a notoriously sensitive point with ministers. To impose such observation and to condemn those who found it undesirable to keep it as 'desperat and uncorrigible enemies to the present Government of Church and State' bore all the marks of deliberate provocation. [54]

This legislation was accompanied by an act intended by Middleton to get rid of any presbyterians still surviving within the administration, and aimed in particular at Crawford and Lauderdale. [55] The act required all persons in positions of public trust to swear an oath declaring that the Covenants 'wer unlawfull and seditious'. [56] Lauderdale had come too far to be caught by any such manoeuvre, and he signed the declaration. [57] Crawford was a much more straightforward man, and allowed himself by this means to be removed from office as Treasurer, as well as from Parliament. [58]

When the Parliament rose Middleton, confident no doubt that the presbyterian party was completely crushed, made his way to the west with the Privy Council in the month of October 1662. There he demonstrated to the full his hatred of presbyterians in general and Protesters in particular by forbidding those ministers who had not yet obtained presentation and collation to exercise their ministry, and thereby created over the next few months about two hundred vacant parishes. [59]

It seems extremely likely that his action was modelled on the similar mass eviction of English nonconformists from their parishes on St. Bartholomew's Day, 24 August, that same year. No doubt a similar bloodless victory was anticipated as a further demonstration of Middleton's masterful control of the Scottish church.

It would be hard to find a programme of legislation that demonstrated a more autocratic or ambitious spirit. Nevertheless, Middleton's attitude and behaviour, since the final decision to restore episcopacy had been taken in August 1661, had not received anything like unanimous support. There had been opposition from all directions. There had been a number of indications that Lauderdale still had influence at court, and that Middleton's activities did not meet with unqualified approval in that quarter. The earliest demonstration of that fact had come over the case of the Earl of Tweeddale.

Tweeddale had been a supporter of Lauderdale in the lining up of parties after the Restoration. [60] During the debates in London on Scottish church government in the summer of 1661, Tweeddale had supported Lauderdale's suggestion that consultations with the synods should precede any decision. Tweeddale himself was thought to be indifferent on matters of church government, [61] and his suggestion seems to have been made with a view to preserving the king's honour among his subjects. Nevertheless this mild opposition to Middleton, together with Tweeddale's family connection with Lauderdale, were thought to have aroused Middleton's anger. [62] The opportunity was therefore taken by Middleton to accuse Tweeddale to the king of treason, when during the trial of the Protester minister, Guthrie, he argued against imposing the death penalty. Tweeddale was ordered by the king to be imprisoned in Edinburgh Castle, and then placed under house arrest. He then wrote to the king and to Lauderdale, explaining his action and protesting his loyalty. Through Lauderdale's intercession he was set at liberty in May 1662, after having been under arrest since September 1661.[63]

Although it was a demonstration of Middleton's power and malice to be able to imprison an earl for more than eight months on entirely groundless charges, it was also a demonstration of Lauderdale's influence and Charles's basic good sense that suspected presbyterian sympathies were still not enough to condemn a man.

The indication that Middleton's hostility towards presbyterians was not matched at court was further demonstrated over the Act of Indemnity and the fines. The Act of Indemnity was so designed that many would only be eligible for indemnity from past crimes after the payment of a fine. According to instructions given to Middleton by the king, the fines were payable by those

> who joynd in arms or opposition to the Engagement for our Royall fathers delivery in the year 1648: or who were most guilty in the usurpations and unworthie acts and actings that issued thereupon: or who had any accession to the Western Remonstrance, or to any base complyance with the late usurpers: or who sold their Levies in the year 1648 or thereafter.[64]

Clearly many ministers, especially those of the Protester party, were liable for fines under one or more of these heads. Middleton was given considerable freedom to fix the amounts.

When the list of fines was drawn up and passed in Parliament in September 1662, however,[65] no ministers' names appeared on it. It seems that they had first been included, but later had been withdrawn, perhaps on the king's orders.[66] Middleton was certainly fully capable of fining ministers, and their omission from the list was a further indication that his behaviour towards the church continued to meet with opposition.

Not only were there signs of disagreement in the matter of the appropriate treatment of presbyterians; there were also indications that the episcopate was seen by some in rather less erastian terms than those Middleton espoused. In particular, provision had been made in the legislation passed in the Parliament for consultation between the king and the bishops in 'the externall Government and policie of the Church', and for the exercise of the bishops' functions in consultation with members of the lower clergy. These provisions had not appeared in Middleton's original instructions, and the suspicion must be that they had been decided upon under Lauderdale's influence after Middleton left for Scotland.

Even in Scotland itself there was opposition from the administration to the tenor of the ecclesiastical regime. In January 1662, for example, the Privy Council protested against the proclamation which suspended ecclesiastical courts until their re-authorisation by the bishops, on the grounds that thus all ecclesiastical jurisdiction and discipline was brought to a halt.[67]

Similarly, from one or two of the bishops there were demonstrations that the regime envisaged by Middleton and his supporters was not the regime envisaged by them. Sharp and Leighton were the most conspicuous examples. Although Sharp had conducted the service of consecration of six bishops at

Edinburgh immediately before the Parliament of May 1662 with ceremonial that was bound to be felt by presbyterians to be offensive,[68] yet there had been no re-ordination of those concerned.[69] He and Leighton had been forced by Sheldon to submit to high-flying notions on episcopal orders and to be re-ordained when they were consecrated in London,[70] but Sharp would not impose them on others. Clearly he envisaged something more moderate than English prelacy.

Furthermore, although a prelatic form was being imposed on the church by legislation, and an episcopate had been recruited some of whom at least were willing to justify episcopacy in the most exalted terms, Sharp did not as yet share in this prevailing trend. In a sermon preached in St Andrews on 20 April[71] he had attempted to justify his support of the change in church government. His justification had been pragmatic and moderate. He maintained, in the tradition of the Aberdeen Doctors who had educated him, that the form of church government was not 'a fundamental point of religion', and that episcopacy had a long and honourable history in the church. He asserted that for the moment episcopacy was a political necessity: 'that which is most convenient and necessary for Scotland as it stands now stated'. He accepted that his views were not those of every man, but argued that the need for peace and unity should induce Scots to conform at least with what could not be altered.

It is true that this message was surrounded by a froth of rhetoric which repeated the administration's views of recent history, but beneath the padding was no doctrinaire divine-right episcopacy, but a dispassionate argument from necessity. During the Parliament's sitting Sharp had made plain to Lauderdale his dissatisfaction with the endless criticism of the Covenants:

> yesterday by an act passed unanimously the Covenants were condemned . . . This act is sent to your lordship; and I hope the obligation of them being thus nulled we shall have no more severe proceedings against them.[72]

This differed radically from Middleton's view of the legislation as a way to get rid of presbyterians, and argues a continuing desire for moderation.

Furthermore, in his role of archbishop, Sharp exhibited a desire, in contrast to Middleton, that the change in the church should go through with the minimum of disturbance and rancour. He asked Lauderdale to attempt once more to win over the Resolutioner leaders:

> It will contribute much . . . if your lordship by a letter to Mr Robert Douglas and another to Mr David Frost, to be communicated to the rest, would be pleased to advise them for their own and the church's good, and evidencing their respect to his Majesty's authority, to comport their carriage in obedience to the laws.

He also hoped that after a decent interval of time most ministers would find it possible to obtain collation:

> Some ministers in Fife, Lothian and generally in the west were shy of making application to us [bishops]. I know not if they will see it fit for them to relent after the law is settled, and some time to make their retreat with credit.

In the Synod of Fife of October 1662 Sharp tried to convince the ministers there 'that he was to innovate nothing', and to persuade them to obey the law in deference to the king's wishes.[73]

Sharp had also disapproved of Middleton's violent action in creating so many vacant parishes in the west.[74] When the folly of that course of action became apparent, Sharp was requested with Fairfoul to advise what should be done.[75] Their solution was an extension of the time limit for obtaining presentation and collation until the end of February 1663.[76]

Not only had Fairfoul collaborated with Sharp in modifying the penalties imposed; he refrained from reporting to the Privy Council those ministers absent from the Synod in October 1662.[77] The story that it was he who had egged on Middleton to eject ministers wholesale[78] seems quite inconsistent with what is otherwise known of both Fairfoul and Middleton.

Leighton too gave public demonstration of his dissatisfaction with the trend of church affairs. He had absented himself from the ceremonial reception of the bishops into Edinburgh, from the consecration which followed, and from the subsequent restoration of the First Estate of Parliament.[79] When he did appear in Parliament it was to defend dissident ministers.[80]

During 1662, therefore, although Middleton's legislation had been extremely rigorous it had by no means met with unqualified support. It was in an attempt to eliminate all such objections and render his own power absolute that Middleton attempted during the Parliament of 1662 to ruin Lauderdale and his friends by excepting them completely from the Act of Indemnity.[81] It was a clever idea, perhaps the brainchild of Clarendon, who had been involved in the English precedent.[82] By a simple vote of each member of Parliament a list should be compiled of the twelve men with most votes to be excepted. It had the supreme advantage that the vote was anonymous and nothing need be proved against any of those excepted. The scheme won the agreement of the king, however, apparently only because it had not occurred to him that office-bearers might be thus excepted. When, however, the list of excepted members was found to include Crawford and Lauderdale,[83] it lost the support of the king. It also lost Middleton the support of Clarendon, perhaps because he now saw that such a device could be used against himself,[84] or more probably because he saw that the scheme had misfired. By the end of 1662 it was clear that Middleton would be ruined by his miscalculation. Although it took until the end of 1663 for Lauderdale to consolidate his victory, a victory it was.

His method was to challenge Middleton in the king's presence of mismanagement of his role as Commissioner, and in particular of exceeding his authority. Middleton attempted to reply to these challenges, but in this sophisticated political game Lauderdale was undoubtedly his master.[85] The first round was played out in the spring of 1663. The king was then sufficiently persuaded to allow Lauderdale to go to Scotland in the autumn of that year to investigate Middleton's conduct. Middleton was deprived of his post as Commissioner and it was given instead to Lauderdale's ally, Rothes. Then, armed with much evidence against Middleton, Lauderdale returned to court in

October 1663 to present it to the king. His skill in so doing obliged Middleton to tender the resignation of his position as Captain General, in January 1664,[86] and effectively removed him from any further influence in Scottish affairs.

It seemed possible, therefore, that the way was being made open for a return to presbytery, or at least to moderate episcopacy.[87] Yet within six months Lauderdale had gone out of his way to pledge his support for prelacy, and Middleton's establishment had been confirmed. What had brought about this development?

First of all, although Middleton was obliged to retire from political life, there were relatively few other casualties as a result of his fall. His allies retained their places. Glencairn, perhaps Middleton's strongest supporter, was favoured with a personal letter from the king in which he assured Glencairn, 'my kindness to you and my confidence in you is not at all lessened in this change'.[88] This came despite Lauderdale's rather cool feelings towards Glencairn.[89] Mackenzie of Tarbet, who had been the chief messenger and spokesman for Middleton at court in the Billeting Affair,[90] lost his place as a Lord of Session for his deep complicity in Middleton's plans. Sir John Fletcher, the Lord Advocate, another strong ally of Middleton,[91] similarly lost his position,[92] but there were no other major casualties.

There was nothing very surprising in most of the Scottish administration retaining their positions. After all, the parliaments of 1661 and 1662 had undoubtedly promoted the king's power and prerogative to undreamt of heights. Middleton had overstepped the mark, but his achievement was too much in the king's interest for his fall to destroy all his allies. On the other hand the presbyterian nobility who had been hustled out of public life by Middleton — Cassillis, Cranston, Balmerino and Crawford — were not reinstated. Two advocates who refused to sign the Declaration against the Covenants, Lords Stair and Arniston, were removed from their places as Senators of the College of Justice.[93] In other words, most of those who had supported Middleton retained their places. Those who had opposed him were not restored. This in itself rendered a reversal of his church policies unlikely.

Nevertheless, although it was clear that Middleton's policies were unlikely to be reversed, the opportunity was still there for Lauderdale to impose the settlement with restraint and moderation. The events of 1663, particularly the Parliamentary and Privy Council legislation against nonconformity, lend themselves most readily to a conventional interpretation of the increasing pressure on nonconformists. A number of factors, however, seem to render this interpretation unlikely. Lauderdale, so far as can be discerned, had spent his time since the Restoration in opposing extreme policies in the church. His prime concern as Secretary of State was the maintenance of peace and order in Scotland, objectives unlikely to be secured by policies of confrontation. The actual working out of policies in the church in 1664 in the wake of apparently punitive legislation suggests a deliberate policy of restraint and moderation. What, then, can the purpose have been in the legislation of autumn 1663? It seems likely that these apparently severe measures were intended to disarm the political opposition to Lauderdale in Scotland, led since Middleton's demise by Glencairn, and to placate those bishops who had been putting pressure on Sharp for severer measures against nonconformity.

During 1663 Lauderdale became aware that Middleton's policies had been handed on and taken up by Glencairn. The terms of the Declaration which gave the ministers outed by Middleton an extension of time for obtaining presentation and collation suggested that already by December 1662 the change in church government was giving rise to irregular behaviour in the west of Scotland. Reference was made to 'meitings in families upon pretence of religious exercises' and to

> the disorderly cariag of some ministers [which] hath occasioned that diverse of the people with whom they have interest doe withdraw from the worship of God in their oune paroch kirkes.[94]

In February ministers who had not obtained presentation and collation were continuing to act illegally as ministers in Galloway.[95] By March the number of 'conventicles', by which was meant unauthorised religious exercises, had grown to such an extent that the Privy Council in the absence of Lauderdale and his supporters began to consider the use of military force.[96] Sir James Turner, a professional soldier, was given instructions to take a hundred foot from the soldiers stationed at Glasgow and to quarter on conventiclers. He was ordered to arrest ministers who held conventicles, and with the advice and assistance of the bishop to exact the penalties already laid down for failure to observe the law, 'without noticing the moderation of any minister or others that shall intercede for them'.[97]

These were policies designed to provoke a confrontation between the government and the presbyterians, and understandably it was not long before that purpose was achieved. The clash came over the appointment to the parishes made vacant by recent legislation of new ministers or, as they were called, 'curates'. In April the heritors of Neilson near Paisley objected to the admission of a 'curate',[98] and shortly afterwards, at the beginning of May, there was fighting in both Kirkcudbright and Irongray over the admission of ministers.[99] The earl of Linlithgow and others were therefore ordered to use soldiers to deal with the unrest.[100]

It seems, however, that from the first this scuffle, which amounted to very little, was exaggerated.[101] William Sharp, Lauderdale's personal secretary in Scotland, tried to convey this to his master when the first report was sent out by Rothes, now Treasurer in succession to Crawford. Sharp warned Lauderdale:

> Strange stories will be made of this, but in truth there are many ways to break an egg without a hammer, and a little time may discover that this design will not serve to all intents and purposes.[102]

Further confirmation of the provocative intentions of the policies of Glencairn and his followers was given in the Parliament of 1663.

Glencairn, with his ally Dumfries, drew up a paper suggesting that all heritors and ministers should be obliged to take the Declaration against the Covenants.[103] At the time Lauderdale recognised this suggestion for what it was, a piece of deliberate provocation, and would have nothing to do with it.[104] The aim of the paper, and of this party's policies in general, was to alienate certain Scots from the government of church and state, and by provoking them to overt opposition, to create opportunities for profit for Glencairn and his allies. By the raising of troops and the fining of dissenters they seem to have intended to restore their fortunes at the expense of the presbyterians. Thus Lauderdale discovered that the troops raised earlier that year had been raised without royal permission[105] and irregularly financed. Two troops of horse and six companies of foot had been paid out of Scottish revenue, without royal warrant, and at far higher cost 'than ever Scotland knew'. By this means Middleton, and his ally the earl of Newburgh, Captain of the King's Life Guard, had profited handsomely from the alleged necessity to deal firmly with nonconformists.[106]

Somehow Lauderdale had to find a way to deal with this group, and to prevent them from provoking open conflict in Scotland. At the same time it had become necessary also to take measures to placate opposition among the bishops to Sharp's desire to side with Lauderdale and espouse policies of moderation.

In October 1662, at a meeting of the bishops, some among them had pressed, possibly at Clarendon's urging, that a letter should be written to the king expressing the bishops' 'gratitude for all Middleton had done for the church'.[107] This was an interpretation of Middleton's activities unlikely to appeal to Sharp or to such as Leighton who were apprehensive of difficulties ahead. In addition it was extremely awkward for Sharp to be associated with such a letter when he had endeavoured not to take sides in the dispute. He had felt obliged to excuse himself to Lauderdale and remarked that he had ensured by the bearer that Lauderdale did not find himself presenting such a letter to the king in his capacity as Secetary of State because

> I thought your lordship would have taken it to be no courtesy done you to have sent a letter to be presented by your hand bearing testimony to the Earl of Middleton.

A further meeting of the bishops in February 1663[108] had again put pressure on Sharp, this time for the immediate implementation of the penalties against nonconformists. Sharp and Fairfoul had just arranged for the extension of the time limit for obtaining collation and presentation. Despite this the majority of the bishops clearly favoured rigour. A petition from them was presented to the Privy Council, asking for the acts against recusant ministers to be put into force.[109] Lauderdale's response to these pressures, both from the political opposition and from the bishops, was to pass legislation which would satisfy these groups. At the same time he used the opportunity to protest his loyalty to episcopacy, and thus demonstrated for the benefit of the king his steadfastness to the ecclesiastical settlement.

In the Scottish Parliament of 1663 an Act against Conventicles,[110] modelled on the English act passed at the same time,[111] made public the king's approval of what had been done concerning church government in the two previous sessions of Parliament. By implication it expressed also Lauderdale's support for those policies. It went on to declare that nonconformity would be interpreted as treason:

> So his Maiestie Doth Declare that he will and doth account a withdrawing from and not keeping and joyning in [the ordinary meitings of divine worship] . . . To be siditious and of dangerous example and consequence.

This was precisely the interpretation of nonconformity that had been favoured by Middleton.

Lauderdale then made it his business to make an explicit declaration of support for the church settlement generally.[112] His reasons for so doing he explained to the king:

> that other calumny of my opposition to your declared pleasure in church government did stick with divers, so that I thought it fit for me, and in some measure necessary for your service that I should make once a public declaration.

Then at some length Lauderdale described what he had said. He had emphasised to the Parliament the king's fixed intention to maintain episcopacy because of 'former miscarriages'. He stressed his 'hearty concurrence in, and obedience to', those laws, and urged the compliance of Parliament to them. He went on to recall that he had 'cheerfully' signed the Declaration against the Covenants, and explained to the Parliament that he heartily regretted his original signing of them. As Lauderdale himself added to the king:

> if any shall hereafter slander me as an opposer of bishops, they must at the same time declare me a very fool.

Thus, although Lauderdale's primary intention in attending the Parliament was to get to the bottom of the Billeting Affair,[113] he had seemed to make it clear that Middleton's policies for the church would continue as before.

The passing of the Act in the Privy Council on 11 August prescribed additional penalties for nonconformity.[114] Nonconformist ministers were required to move from their parishes on pain of being regarded as 'movers of sedition'. Those who supported them were threatened that they would be 'proceided against accordeing to law'. Ministers who failed to attend ecclesiastical meetings were 'to be proceeded against as contemners of his Majesteis authority'.

Lauderdale in Parliament and also in the Privy Council had thus enacted a body of legislation which laid down severe penalties for nonconformity, but which did far more. First of all it disarmed Glencairn and his party. From this time until his death at the end of May 1664 Glencairn made repeated efforts to resume good relations with Lauderdale.[115] Secondly it assured the king that Lauderdale was taking firm measures with nonconformists and that the peace would be kept.[116] Thirdly it relieved Lauderdale of the political embarrassment of being regarded as the potential leader of a presbyterian opposition.

This programme was succeeded by the appointment of Alexander Burnet as archbishop of Glasgow, and by the establishment of the Church Commission in the winter of 1663-64. The conventional interpretation of these events is that the Lauderdale party were consolidating the repressive policies enacted in the autumn of 1663, and thereby setting the scene for the repression which eventually provoked the Pentland Rising of 1666. An alternative explanation may be that, having disarmed the opposition, established his credibility as an episcopalian and disowned the presbyterians, Lauderdale now sought the help of Sharp and Rothes in establishing a body which could put moderate policies into effect by by-passing the Privy Council. At the same time Lauderdale approved the appointment of an apparent moderate as an ally and fellow-archbishop for Sharp in the shape of Alexander Burnet.

Gilbert Burnet asserted that the Church Commission was Sharp's project alone, and put through against Lauderdale's will.[117] This would be extremely unlikely at a time when Lauderdale was in absolute control of Scottish affairs. What is much more probable is that it was devised as a means whereby the Lauderdale party could control church business without interference from Glencairn and his party.[118]

The Church Commission had a quorum of only five members, of whom one had to be a bishop.[119] By this means, it seems, the Lauderdale party intended to control the administration of the ecclesiastical laws without having to do so in the Privy Council whose quorum was much larger and, as had already been demonstrated, would be far more difficult to manage.[120] The restraint of the Commission, shortly to be discussed, together with an appreciation of the fact that passing legislation is not the same thing as putting it into effect, must be the basis of the assertion that Lauderdale's legislation in 1663 was politically motivated and did not represent his true intentions. To this can be added other fragments which reinforce the impression that moderation was Lauderdale's intention.

In July 1663, at the very time that legislation against dissenters was being conceived, Lauderdale was maintaining what seems to have been a close friendship with Crawford,[121] who was certainly the most eminent and most outspoken of the dissenting nobility. He similarly maintained a friendship with Lothian, who had refused to sign the Declaration.[122]

In December 1663 the earl of Kellie thought it worth applying to Lauderdale for clemency towards a minister who had been prohibited from exercising his ministry by Sharp. He also thought it not inappropriate to let Lauderdale know that other local ministers equally guilty had not been silenced. Had Kellie thought that Lauderdale was the doctrinaire episcopalian his recent legislation might suggest, he would hardly have applied to him in this manner.[123]

During 1664 Lauderdale was petitioned on more than one occasion, and at least once with success, to suspend fines imposed on quite ordinary people in the west for failure to attend church.[124] Again these applications would never have been made had the petitioners not been convinced of Lauderdale's sympathy for their cause.

In January 1664 specific instructions were given to Sir James Turner that the earl of Cassillis and his family were not to be harrassed over their apparent refusal to comply with the law in ecclesiastical matters.[125] Certainly this was probably a good deed done by Lauderdale to a former ally, but it is also a demonstration of an unwillingness to provoke antagonism and disturbance in the name of uniformity. In fact events made Lauderdale's attempts to deal with the Glencairn party even more successful than could have been hoped.

The discovery by Alexander Burnet in February 1664 that there had been peculation of vacant stipends by the Glencairn party[126] was yet another mark against them. It was probably this charge which induced Glencairn himself to offer to Sharp his apologies for the 'occasions of jealousies' he had given in the matters of the church, and to make renewed offers of friendship with Lauderdale, a scene repeated about the same time, in early March, with Alexander Burnet.[127] His death at the end of May[128] left his supporters without an effective leader.

It seemed, then, that by the spring of 1664 the troubles in establishing the church settlement were over. The opposition to Lauderdale had been disarmed. The policies of moderation could survive. Unfortunately the situation was not quite so simple. Over the next three years tensions within the church forced the evolution of new and not altogether successful strategies.

5
The Failure of Laissez Faire, 1663-1666

THE man on whose shoulders fell the job of putting Lauderdale's policies into effect was Sharp. It is extremely hard to determine how far Sharp had been in Lauderdale's confidence after the failure to recruit the Resolutioner ministers in 1661. During the Billeting Affair and thereafter until early in 1663 he had tried to hedge his bets and avoid committing himself. It is difficult to know whether Sharp was aware, as Lauderdale had been made aware, that the Glencairn party was fomenting trouble in the spring of 1663. The sincerity of Lauderdale's commitment to episcopacy and a rigorous treatment of nonconformists is made doubtful by both his former opinions and the political advantages of the stance he took. Where does Sharp stand on these issues?

In the later months of 1662 Sharp had opposed severity towards dissenters. Not only does such an attitude indicate the moderation that a former Resolutioner leader might be expected to show; it also indicates a desire that conformity might be achieved with the minimum of fuss and dislocation. Thus such policies demonstrate in Sharp a continuing desire for power and political influence. In the simplest terms he wanted to keep his job. It was this desire which in 1663 can be seen to be beginning to act upon him in a rather different way.

In the winter and spring of 1663 Sharp had been in London.[1] At that time Sheldon and the high church party had finally consolidated their rise to power by making it impossible to pass an Indulgence for dissenters which had been under consideration since late 1662.[2] That development had coincided with Clarendon's increasing intolerance of dissent.[3] Sharp therefore witnessed in England among the most powerful figures in the church a move away from the moderation which had seemed a real possibility throughout 1660, 1661 and much of 1662. His reaction seems to have been to move with them. Although Sheldon was the man who insisted on Sharp's reordination in episcopal orders in December 1661, yet after Sharp's return to Scotland in June 1663 he began a correspondence with Sheldon which lasted for years, and in which he virtually never failed to make violent attacks on Scottish dissenters.[4] These letters were private, and although they were clearly what Sheldon wanted to hear, their relative frequency and informality argue that they represent not only what it was politically convenient for Sharp to be seen to believe, but in fact what he did believe. That is to say that from the spring of 1663 Sharp began to undergo a further transformation in his flight from presbytery. Like his former changes of emphasis, this was precipitated by elements of self-interest, and yet bears the mark of genuine conversion. Whereas Lauderdale had altered his policies for political advantage and in a spirit of cynical detachment, Sharp seems to have come to make a virtue of necessity.

E

During the Parliament the measures taken against the nonconformists were taken on the advice of an apparently re-united body of bishops. The legislation was of their devising,[5] undoubtedly with Sharp's concurrence, and Lauderdale's speech on episcopacy won from them a tribute of thanks.[6] Again the committee of the Privy Council appointed to consider what should be done about nonconformist ministers included Sharp. Thus he had associated himself closely with the new legislation. Similarly the Church Commission was instituted while Sharp was in London in November 1663 and therefore inevitably associated with him.

Nevertheless, just as Lauderdale's abandonment of any overt or public sympathy for the dissenters had been accompanied by gestures indicating a continuing spirit of moderation, so Sharp's apparently much more profound shift in attitude was accompanied by behaviour that argued a more liberal spirit. Sharp's candidate for the archbishopric of Glasgow may perhaps be seen as evidence of such moderation.

Alexander Burnet, bishop of Aberdeen, was a candidate apparently unsatisfactory to the other bishops.[7] It might be argued that Burnet was not a moderate choice, but a reactionary, and that the opposition of the bishops to him was very proper. Who the bishops had in mind instead is not known, but two factors suggest that Burnet was indeed selected by Sharp as a moderate: one, his success as bishop of Aberdeen, and the other Sharp's candidates for the bishopric of Aberdeen thus vacated.

Alexander Burnet turned out to be an unwise appointment in a church urgently in need of moderate bishops. It seems, however, that that could hardly have been anticipated in 1663. Burnet was a Scot, the son of a minister. He had been educated at Edinburgh University, and became a minister just as the covenanting movement was getting under way in the 1630s. Like his father he had strong episcopal sympathies and so left Scotland to become rector of a living in Kent until 1650. He was then removed for his episcopal beliefs and spent the next decade loosely attached to the court in exile. At the Restoration he became chaplain to the governor of Dunkirk, then briefly rector of another English living, before his appointment in 1663 to Aberdeen.[8] Here was a man whose background, like that of so many of the bishops appointed at the Restoration, was fundamentally unsympathetic to the past twenty-five years of Scottish history. However, he had been appointed to the diocese of Aberdeen, the only one of the fourteen to show any enthusiasm for episcopacy. It would seem extremely likely, therefore, that his brief stay there had been peaceful and successful. In other words, although his background might have given rise for caution, his record as a bishop in Scotland was so far unimpeachable. He could with some reason have been thought to be a moderate choice for archbishop. Even Row admitted that Burnet was 'thought by some to be of a mild and moderate temper'.[9]

The likelihood that his appointment was so intended is increased by the information available on Sharp's candidates for his replacement in Aberdeen, and the replacement of the recently dead Sydserf of Orkney. A short list of four drawn up early in 1664 with Sharp's approbation consisted of Harry Guthrie, Andrew Honeyman, Patrick Scougall and James Wood.[10] That Sharp was even considering Wood, a former Resolutioner leader, at this late date is an indication of faithfulness to at least some of his original intentions.

Inevitably Sharp was the major influence in the Commission for Church Affairs. A number of accounts of its actions indicate that Sharp exercised a moderating influence on its deliberations. The records of the Commission, which lasted only two years, have been lost. The opportunity has therefore been taken to assume that its activities were extravagant and repressive.[11] It happens, however, that Lauderdale had required Sir William Purves, later Solicitor General, to send accounts of the meetings of the Church Commission to him. These survive and, supplemented by other accounts from those present, demonstrate that from March 1664 when the Commission first met, and throughout the summer of that year, the Commission behaved with great restraint.

The most important case to come before the Commission in the first months of its existence was that of James Wood's death-bed declaration. Wood had apparently drawn up a paper just as he was dying in which he protested his conviction that presbytery was a worthy cause for martyrdom.[12] This paper was then circulated. As the testament of one of the former Resolutioner leaders it was clearly an explosive document likely to encourage resistance to the episcopal establishment. The case was therefore brought before the Commission on 15 April, at its second meeting, where the possibility of fining those who had witnessed the paper was discussed.[13] It was Sharp's opinion, and that of others, that Wood had not been of sound mind when he subscribed this testament, and that the witnesses, particularly John Carstairs, a former Protester, had compiled it themselves. The paper was burned by order of the Commission, but all the witnesses to it but Carstairs were dismissed.[14] Carstairs had been in trouble for nonconformity before, and so was cited to appear before the Privy Council,[15] but he does not seem to have done so. Whether or not he penned the paper, it is hard to see that the Commission's action was unduly severe.

In a case brought before the Commission in July, four ministers were accused of celebrating communion in an irregular way. On this occasion Sharp pressed for a milder penalty than deposition, which was favoured by the majority, and instead they were confined to their parishes and ordered to forfeit part of their stipend.[16] Again, a laird brought before the Commission was fined for refusal to take the Oath of Allegiance, but given time to reconsider and take the oath before the local bishop, in which case his fine would be remitted.[17] Similarly, when the Laird of Earlston was brought before the Privy Council for attending conventicles, Sharp was in favour of a milder sentence than that of one month's banishment which was passed on him.[18]

When the Commission began to meet in March, Sharp was already aware of the difficulties facing it in the control of nonconformity. He took the opportunity therefore to analyse these problems for Lauderdale's benefit. He recognised that dissent had been allowed to appear ever since the scuffles over the admission of curates twelve months previously. He suggested that brisk steps should be taken to deal with the ringleaders to arrest what would otherwise be an increasingly difficult problem:

> Discerning men think that if at first they fall briskly to work with some ringleaders, there will be the less to do afterwards. Else, if dissatisfaction which appears to authority be noticed with that remissness and coldness which we have found these twelve month past, it is the apprehension of sober men that this leaven will spread into a fermentation which will prove in a little time mischievous and remedyless.[19]

It was clear that any such policy would require the co-operation of the nobility as a whole. They represented authority in their own localities. The enforcement of policy depended on their vigilance over their own lands and tenants. Sharp also recognised, however, that this co-operation was unlikely to be forthcoming. The majority of the nobility had supported the establishment of episcopacy from selfish motives. When they discovered that their ambitions could not be satisfied by means of the bishops, they would retaliate by withdrawing their support for their policies. The Glencairn party had been virtually destroyed, but it was being replaced by an opposition of passive resistance:

> Your lop. may conjecture how some who for their own ends did co-operate for the restitution of our order, having found that their expectations hold not in the promising way as they projected, do now think it is fit for them to appear cold, and secretly to come [?] to a contempt and opposition of us.[20]

Nevertheless Sharp relied on much assistance from Rothes,[21] and clearly hoped that despite difficulties the church could be ordered peacefully.

It soon became apparent to both Sharp and Burnet that these hopes were illusory. The original core of Middleton's former allies was joined by people whose opposition took the form of refusal to co-operate with the bishops in the Commission. One group seems to have consisted of those doubtful of the legality of the proceedings. Although Sir John Gilmour, President of the Court of Session and a supposed ally of Lauderdale,[22] had told Sharp that he would support the Commission, on the first day it met there were legal quibbles raised: 'great men contending for nice formalities of law'.[23] Their arguments have not survived but presumably they were questioning the legal scope and powers of a court set up simply by royal proclamation. It was probable that these questions continued to be raised, since both Sharp and Burnet urged the appointment of the Lord Advocate to the Commission.[24] Here the Lauderdale party was caught in its own trap, for the Lord Advocate was Sir John Fletcher, Middleton's ally, and not included in the list of members of the Commission.

Furthermore those supporters of presbytery whose voices had been stilled by Middleton's legislation now began to emerge once more. Hamilton had opposed the re-introduction of episcopacy. Although the Lauderdale party had made repeated attempts to secure him for their interest by making promises of favours in return for his involvement in the affairs of the archdiocese of Glasgow,[25] yet they had been disappointed. Early in March a translation of Buchanan's *De Iure Regni* was known to be circulating in the west. The author was identified, and it was anticipated that Hamilton would have him arrested. In fact he was not apprehended, and Burnet at least seemed to think that this was deliberate negligence: 'if diligence had beene used the author might have been taken.'[26]

By the end of May the effects of this alteration in the opposition began to be apparent. The work of the Commission and the enforcement of the ecclesiastical settlement was becoming impossible. Sharp could rely on Rothes, Lauderdale's brother Hatton, the Lord Provost Sir Robert Murray,[27] Lord Rosslyn,[28] and apparently very few others for support. Otherwise he was met with non-cooperation:

> I find that those who formerly valued themselves upon the account of their actings and affection for the settlement of the Church are now very cool and more than indifferent, that confusions and opposition to us may grow.[29]

It was clear that the situation was becoming very difficult for Sharp. He was responsible for the maintenance of order in the Scottish church. The excesses of Glencairn and his party had been avoided by humbling Glencairn and discrediting his party, yet the policies of moderation with which Sharp had attempted to replace provocation were now being challenged by the passive resistance of other members of the nobility. Provocation was likely to create unrest, and had been avoided. Now that complete licence for dissenters was the threat, how could it be overcome?

Sharp's initial solution was to express his fears to Lauderdale.[30] He had some reason to think this was appropriate. After all he, Rothes and Lauderdale had together evolved policy; it was reasonable to think that new initiatives might be evolved in renewed consultations. In addition he and Burnet wrote frequently to Sheldon expressing their apprehensions for the church. They did so in the conviction that Lauderdale was on good terms with the archbishop and the high church party and presumably in the hope that between them Lauderdale and Sheldon might work out some solution for Scottish problems.

In fact Sharp had made a serious miscalculation. Lauderdale's power at court depended on the preservation of the illusion that everything in Scotland was going perfectly. Not only had both Sharp and Burnet threatened that illusion by writing letters to Lauderdale which it would be difficult for him to keep from the king; they had given an opportunity to his political rivals to discredit his management of Scotland. The alliance between Lauderdale and Sheldon could not be relied upon to take precedence over the far more stable and self-interested alliance of Sheldon and Clarendon.

Sharp's complaints, therefore, were met by a very chilly reception from Lauderdale, who laid the problem squarely back in Sharp's lap and invited him to find the solution:

For till I know more particularly the causes of the disease, with those remedies which your Grace thinkes still easie, I know neither what to say or doe. [31]

It seems in fact that Lauderdale suspected Sharp of deliberately making trouble for him, although Sharp protested that there was no 'design' in his complaints. [32]

It was at this point that the differences of attitude between Sharp and Lauderdale began to be apparent. Once the policies of Glencairn had been defeated, Lauderdale was content to let well alone and hope that dissent would simply disappear. Sharp, on the other hand, and Burnet, who now began to show his true colours, were committed to the extirpation of dissent. Sharp had learned his lesson from Sheldon extremely well.

Lauderdale appears to have disbelieved Sharp's version of events in Scotland, but sufficient pressure was put on him by the public nature of the complaints made by Sharp and Burnet to oblige him to agree to a meeting in London. [33] This was made more necessary by rumours of a breach between Sharp and Lauderdale.

Burnet three times wrote to Lauderdale begging him to remain on good terms with Sharp and Rothes, and in their conference together in London to work for a solution of the church's problems:

Let me therefore intreat your lop. . . . to study to strengthen and increase that firm friendship and correspondence with him [Sharp] and my Lord Treasurer [Rothes] which is necessary for his Majesty's service and the security and tranquillity of our all. [34]

By September rumours of a rift between Lauderdale and Sharp were apparently common knowledge. Sir James Dalrymple wrote to Lauderdale conveying this information and cautioning against it:

People talk also of jealousies between your Lordship and the Lord Primat. I believe yow will both be so wyse as to put a stope to such apprehensiones. [35]

It was clear what these men feared: that a rift in the triumvirate which governed the country would give an opportunity for the hopes of nonconformists to be translated into reality, and that in the confusion the dearly bought stability of Scotland would once again be destroyed. As Burnet wrote to Sheldon:

not a person whom we have yett questioned for disobedience to our ecclesiastical laws and constitutions that will endure the oath of allegiance, and how enclinable these people are to new tumults and commotions your Grace will heare. [36]

During the conference in London new initiatives in the church were evolved, but the central problem of the non-cooperation of the nobility and the measures to be taken against nonconformity were left untackled.

The National Synod was scheduled to meet in May 1665 with Rothes as Royal Commissioner to it. [37] The intention behind this was almost certainly to demonstrate royal support for episcopacy. The constitution of the Synod passed by Lauderdale in the Parliament of 1663, with its royal control of the agenda, [38] made it most unlikely that nonconformists would get any sympathetic hearing. The Synod was not designed to solve problems of the ecclesiastical settlement; rather, it was designed to confirm the settlement.

Secondly Rothes was given command of the forces in Scotland.[39] This move underlined the true anxieties of the triumvirate that their power would be challenged, especially at a time when war between England and Holland was expected.[40]

Thirdly the Chancellor's post, for which Sharp had angled,[41] was left vacant although Rothes was empowered to do the business of the office.[42] This was the strongest indication that Lauderdale was not prepared to trust Sharp.

Fourthly the Commission for Church Affairs was renewed for another year,[43] no doubt as before with the intention of keeping the affairs of the church out of the hands of the Privy Council.

This series of new policies had at least for the moment the intended effect. Burnet wrote a letter of thanks for Lauderdale's care of the church.[44] The duke of Hamilton, who had been named as remiss in his duty for the settling of the church, found himself obliged to write a letter defending his behaviour.[45]

The real tenor of Lauderdale's policy was revealed, however, in his new alliance with Tweeddale,[46] no friend to Rothes,[47] and no ally of the archbishops.[48]

Moreover, for all the renewed initiatives of the triumvirate, nothing had in fact been done to prevent the continuing opposition to them. At a meeting of the renewed Church Commission in late November, Sir John Gilmour and the new Lord Advocate, John Nisbet,[49] again challenged the legal scope and power of the Commission's authority.[50]

What the year 1664 had demonstrated was that the close friendship between Sharp and Lauderdale and Rothes was breaking up. Lauderdale was suspicious of Sharp's motives in retailing the troubles in the church of Scotland to London. He was prepared to make certain concessions to these fears, but no real action. Meanwhile Lauderdale began to transfer his affections to Tweeddale.

The implications for Sharp were equally clear. He and Burnet were to be required to manage the church as best they could, and with the minimum of fuss. They would, of course, be held responsible for their success or failure by Lauderdale, as Burnet recognised:

> I am afraid if any misfortune doe befall us we will beare too much of the blame.[51]

Sharp's reaction to this situation was to evolve his own policies for the church and to try to achieve a measure of independent action.

The first step in this policy was the postponement of the meeting of the National Synod. The country was in such a state of unrest that it seemed too dangerous to Sharp to risk holding such a public assembly:

> That which weighed much with us [bishops] also was the observations we make of the temper of the people which by the fines and other exactions and buzzings about the engagement in war with the Dutch, we find to be so [alert?] and discomposed that we cannot presage that compliance and respect to be paid to the Acts of that Assembly which will be necessary for owning of its authority.[52]

The Synod did not meet at the end of August 1665 as Sharp originally proposed, or at all.

Secondly the Commission and the Privy Council, with Rothes' encouragement, seem to have taken much more vigorous action against nonconformists.[53] It is impossible to be sure whether there was any objective increase in rigour, but there certainly was a change of attitude. In 1664 the Commission and Council had at Sharp's instance made their punishments mild in the hopes of reconciliation. Now the punishments were to be severe in the hope of repression of dissent. The nonconformists were assuming their later character as enemies of the established government.

Sharp and Burnet, in co-operation with Rothes, tried to moderate the effects of the exploitive policies of Lauderdale and Charles II carried out in Scotland in 1665. For some time they had been convinced that nonconformity was simply a means of expressing discontent with the government.[54] It was therefore in their interest and that of the episcopal settlement to minimise occasions of discontent. Thus objections were made by them to the raising of money for the Dutch war by a Convention;[55] the exaction of the fines fixed by Middleton;[56] the demands for back taxation;[57] the order to disarm the west;[58] the establishment of a garrison in Shetland at Scottish expense;[59] the enforced stoppage of Scottish trade during the Dutch war;[60] and the mode of raising taxation in Scotland.[61]

Next Sharp tried to retain control of the prior nomination of candidates for vacant bishoprics. This right had been granted to him by the king in June 1663. In May 1665 Sharp discovered that application was being made to Lauderdale for vacancies. In an attempt to avoid this precedent becoming established, Sharp complained to Lauderdale.[62] This boldness produced an immediate widening of the breach between them.[63] Correspondingly it was Burnet who made his way to London in July to seek renewed consultation over nonconformity, and to try once more to have Sharp made Chancellor.[64]

All these manoeuvres could not disguise the fact that there was no effective policy for dealing with the nonconformists, and that dissent was enjoying virtual toleration.[65] Even Wodrow was extremely hard put to it in this period to find evidence of action taken against presbyterians. Between June 1664 and December 1665 there was virtually no action taken against what appears to have been continuing nonconformity.[66]

Burnet's recitation of the church's troubles in Scotland, which he was able to make to the king despite the intense displeasure and opposition of Lauderdale, produced a great string of instructions to the Privy Council.[67] These seem to have been ignored, and conventicles continued as before.[68] Burnet wrote to Lauderdale in October reporting such occasions:

> Mr Cruikshanks . . . and some other outed ministers have of late drawn great multitudes of people together to their seditious meetings, and baptized at some places twenty, at others more, of the children of such as live within the parishes of orderly and obedient ministers, and not any sheriff or other subordinate officer . . . hath so much as offered to interrupt them or to seize or apprehend the ring-leaders that seduce and deceive the well-meaning multitude.[69]

It seems likely, however, that when a change of policy eventually came about it was prompted not by continuing conventicles so much as by England's ill-fortune in the Anglo-Dutch war and the alliance of France with Holland against England in January 1666.[70]

When the bishops met in convocation in February 1666 their customary reports to London of continuing nonconformity were lent new force by the references included to England's foreign policy:

> It is too manifest that as his Majesty's difficulties grow with forraigners abroad, so our discontents rise higher at home.[71]

Force was also lent by the renewed suggestion that England's embarrassment might be increased by the Scottish nonconformists' opportunity:

> If the warre with ffrance and Holland goe on it will be necessary to provide for the peace and security of this kingdome, for at present we may possibly prevent domestike disorders and insurrections, but the least commotion in England or Ireland, or encouragement from forraigners, would certainly engage us in a new rebellion.[72]

These arguments had been raised before, but early in 1666 in the aftermath of the plague and an unsuccessful year's campaign against the Dutch, now joined by the French, they were bound to carry a great deal more weight.

In March, therefore, soldiers were sent to the west by Rothes to repress nonconformity.[73] This measure was opposed by members of the nobility who represented to Lauderdale that nonconformity was not the problem the bishops had represented it to be,[74] but the continuing fear of Dutch victory gave added force to the argument for using troops.[75]

Sharp went up to London and there succeeded in persuading the king that security dictated the raising of more troops. At the same time he made himself even more enemies among the nobility by persuading the king that the troops should be paid for out of the fines imposed by Middleton and since collected.[76]

During August and September 1666 these troops were duly levied,[77] and disposed round the country.[78] In October, however, after the danger from the Dutch was over for the season, Rothes sent the forces to the west to crush nonconformity once and for all.[79] This policy was strengthened by a proclamation from the king making landlords, heads of families and magistrates responsible for the attendance at church of their dependents.[80]

The combination of this massive assault on nonconformity, together with the unrest caused by the Dutch war, the disarming of the west and the harsh financial policies of the government from 1664 on provoked the celebrated Pentland Rising.[81]

About 12 November, 1666 a scuffle in the village of Dalry in the south-west resulted in the overpowering of a small detachment of three or four soldiers who were stationed there to exact fines for nonconformity. On 13 November a similar fracas in nearby Balmaclellan succeeded in taking captive about sixteen more soldiers.

On the 14th a local rendezvous gathered perhaps about 200 rebels who the following day marched to Dumfries and took hostage the local garrison commander, Sir James Turner. From that Thursday till the following Monday, 19 November, the insurgents marched towards Glasgow apparently intending to enter the town, and gathering reinforcements on the way.

On the 19th, however, they heard that the government forces under General Dalyell were in Glasgow, and so instead the rebels turned south to Ayr, again collecting reinforcements. Then they began to march towards Edinburgh and reached Colinton on the outskirts of the city on 27 November.

By this time their numbers, which at their height had reached about 1,100, had been depleted by the appalling conditions of the march to about 900 men. Recognising that their position was hopeless, the rebels attempted to retreat from Edinburgh but were intercepted by Dalyell at Rullion Green in the Pentlands and defeated.[82] Fifty were killed during the battle and about eighty taken prisoner. During December trials and executions in Edinburgh and the west resulted in the deaths of thirty-six of the rebels. Including those who died of their wounds and those killed in battle, about 100 men had died in the expedition.

The only really coherent account of the origins of the rising is that given by the various dissenting diarists and biographers who sympathised with the rebels. Their accounts unanimously allege that the rising occurred spontaneously after the initial incident in Dalry. A party of three or four soldiers led by Corporal George Deanes were busy in the parish collecting fines for failure to attend church. In the absence of one offender, a farmer named Grier, the soldiers were confiscating his corn before he was taken prisoner.

The soldiers threatened to torture him, and the threat reached John MacLellan of Barscobe, a laird who was himself on the run from the soldiers. He, with three companions, happened to be in Dalry and decided to teach his oppressors a lesson. The soldiers were taken prisoner, one being wounded in the process, and although they managed to escape, news of the exploit reached nearby Balmaclellan and inspired a similar action there. From that point, according to the diarists, the country rose to join this spontaneous reaction to a programme of brutality and extortion that had been going on since 1663.

The major flaw in this account is that it explains only the initial moves in the neighbourhood of Dumfries; it fails to explain adequately the very rapid assembly of the first 200 men, the subsequent appearance of leaders of the expedition from outside the area, and the recruitment within a week of a further 900 men.

When the rising had been put down and the government looked for someone to blame, they hit on Sir James Turner. He was accused of having provoked the rising by the conduct of his troops. Turner was prepared to admit that not everything had been as it should, but he added that with only 70 troops at his command he failed to see how he could be held responsible for unrest leading to a rising over much of the western shires. Turner's reasoning seems sound, although it did not save him from official displeasure. Plainly there was much more to the rising than one instance of outrageous behaviour by two or three of his men.

At the time there were strong suspicions on the government side of conspiracy with foreign enemies — always a convenient explanation in the case of rebellion. It is clear, however, that the rising in the form it actually took was not the result of a conspiracy. Its obvious lack of planning, sudden changes of plan, incapacity to offer any adequate explanation of its intentions to the government, and lack of basic equipment including arms, all argue an expedition that was indeed spontaneous.

Nevertheless it seems almost certain that some sort of plotting and planning had been going on, particularly in 1666. The Dutch authorities, who had much to gain from creating a diversion in the north, were certainly in correspondence with presbyterians both in England and Scotland. Moreover, conventicle ministers had for some months been urging their audiences to be ready for an uprising.

Scattered circumstances at the time of the fracas at Dalry suggest that something was afoot. It was for instance rather odd that Barscobe and his companions should have emerged from hiding at that particular moment. It was stranger still that an unknown, Captain Grey, should appear from nowhere and with alleged external authority take command of the expedition in preference to the local lairds, only to abandon it once more as soon as it got under way. It was also uncanny coincidence that a professional soldier of some ability, Wallace, should be on hand to direct the strategy. Indeed Wallace was effective enough to offer a real challenge to the government forces at Rullion Green despite Dalyell's superior numbers.

It seems likely that a rising had been tentatively planned, on the promise of Dutch assistance. It is possible that such a rising had already been arranged once or even twice before in 1666, and likely that a third attempt was anticipated. Whether Dutch help would have materialised is another matter — probably the Dutch preferred to let the presbyterians take their chestnuts out of the fire.

There was a community of Scots presbyterian exiles in Holland, and it is likely that they had encouraged the Dutch to think in these terms. They were a sufficiently sinister group for the king to exert pressure on the Dutch, when peace was finally made, to have them removed from their haven in Holland.

Probably the little fracas at Dalry between Barscobe and the soldiers sparked off action that had been promised for some time but for which no definite date had been fixed. Such an explanation would account for the mixture of organisation and spontaneity that characterised the rising.

But whatever its origins, the results of the rising are clear. At a stroke the whole of Lauderdale's policies, both political and ecclesiastical, had been rendered void. The peace had not been kept, and the basic requirement of security had not been met. The dissenters had been repressed, and those involved in the rebellion harshly treated. The whole framework of the ecclesiastical settlement was in ruins and would have to be completely rebuilt.

6

In Search of a Policy, 1667-1669

IN 1667 Lauderdale embarked on the policy that was to serve him until about 1674. It involved the repudiation of his former allies in favour of a new set of men, and the recognition of the unwelcome fact that nonconformists in Scotland were there to stay. Over the next seven years or so Tweeddale, Sir Robert Moray and their supporters were to suggest a variety of policies whereby some sort of official recognition might be extended to dissenters from the established church. It had been proved impossible up to 1666 to comprehend, ignore or repress dissent. Now a much more positive and coherent approach would be tried. Their first and most pressing duty, however, was to ensure that there was no repetition of the rising, and to establish once more the peace and security of Scotland.

Needless to say, there had to be scapegoats for the Pentland Rising. The first of these was Sharp. Since the death of Glencairn in May 1664 and Sharp's consequent bid for the Chancellorship, Lauderdale had clearly felt threatened by Sharp. His fears were not altogether unrealistic. Sharp would certainly have liked to enjoy supreme power in Scotland.[1] Moreover, his public complaints about the situation in the church and his repeated criticisms of Lauderdale's other policies in Scotland marked him as an enemy to be reckoned with.

At the end of 1665 the Church Commission came to an end. The only coherent explanation for this move is as a reduction of Sharp's influence.[2] It was not enough, however, to subdue Sharp or to reassure Lauderdale. In 1666 Lauderdale's spy Bellenden informed his master that Sharp was trying to wean Rothes from Lauderdale and make an alliance with Middleton.[3] The message for Lauderdale was clear: that Sharp's intrigues must be ended once and for all.

The considerations which led to Sharp's fall were therefore political rather than ecclesiastical. It seems possible that Sharp's analysis of nonconformity in 1664, and his suggestion that prompt action with the ringleaders would deal with the problem most effectively, was correct. Certainly the policy of laissez-faire had in the end necessitated the use of force in a way that neither Sharp nor Lauderdale had ever anticipated. Since Sharp was publicly associated with the use of troops from early in 1666, his disgrace in the popular imagination was attributed to his ecclesiastical severities.[4] Sharp himself understood perfectly well that his fault was political.[5] For most of 1667 he took no part in public affairs.[6] Only in December 1667, when he was thought to be sufficiently humbled to be co-operative, was he officially pardoned and restored to favour.[7]

Rothes too was removed from power although not from office. Much against his will, he was obliged to take the Chancellorship.[8] In this position he remained an ineffective figurehead who took no part in decision-making. His disgrace, too, was political. He had been unwise enough to dabble briefly in the possibility of an alliance with Sharp and Middleton in 1666.[9] Although he tried to dissociate himself from the intrigue,[10] he had created the basis for mistrust in Lauderdale.[11]

In addition Rothes seems to have been a violent man who could summon up real hatred for dissenters.[12] His decisions to use troops under Turner in 1666, and then to send the whole army to the west, had been miscalculations made possible only by his willingness to use extreme measures. Such a man was not appropriate for the implementation of policies of moderation now in favour.

It was probably considered unwise to disgrace both archbishops at once, since the episcopal establishment was to continue. To subject both to public disesteem would be to suggest to infinitely suggestible observers that episcopacy itself was disesteemed. This consideration had saved Sharp from even harsher treatment.[13] More subtle measures were therefore taken with Alexander Burnet. Over the next three years he was subjected to a campaign whose object was to find an excuse for his dismissal. Eventually in 1669 a suitable occasion was found and Burnet was removed from the archbishopric.[14] His fault, too, was political. From his appointment to Glasgow he had written a constant stream of letters to London making public his analysis of the state of the Scottish church. The change of policy in 1667 did not silence him. Eventually therefore this threat to Lauderdale's position in London had to be silenced.

In place of these three former allies Lauderdale attached himself principally to Tweeddale and Sir Robert Moray.[15] The friendship with Tweeddale had been growing for some considerable time. He had been made a Lord of Session in June 1664,[16] and in late 1666 the growing intimacy between them was sealed by the marriage of Tweeddale's son to Lauderdale's daughter.[17] Tweeddale had acquired a reputation for moderation by his conduct over episcopacy and during the trial of Guthrie in Middleton's time. In 1665 he had apparently made his objections to severity in church affairs well known.[18] He was therefore the perfect man to initiate official policies of moderation towards dissenters.

Sir Robert Moray[19] had like many another member of the lesser nobility in Scotland spent his early life as a mercenary soldier on the Continent. In 1645 he returned to Britain and immediately became involved in the negotiations over presbytery between the Scots and Charles I. In this capacity he got to know Lauderdale, then one of the Scottish Commissioners, and supported the Engagement. He took part in the royalist rising in Scotland of 1652 to 1655, but was on poor terms with both Glencairn and Middleton.

At the Restoration, therefore, Moray was not from the ranks of the Covenanters and presbyterians, like so many of his fellow Scots. He was a former soldier, like Middleton, but with cultured and urbane tastes developed during the last five years of the Interregnum, which he spent in Italy.

In 1660 Moray was involved with Lauderdale in a scheme to make public Charles's steadfastness to Protestantism. His alliance with Lauderdale was to persist, and involved him also in the attempt condoned by Lauderdale to get moderate episcopacy accepted in England. Until 1667 Moray was very much a courtier and stayed in London, but during that time he sided with Lauderdale against the restoration of episcopacy. His reward was to be one of those billeted by Middleton, but thus in 1663 he emerged on the winning side. His advice in ecclesiastical affairs was, like Tweeddale's, for moderation,[20] and so in 1667 he was an obvious man to help with initiating the new policies.

With Tweeddale and Moray was associated a third member of the nobility, Kincardine. He had been a friend of Moray since before the Restoration, and shared not only his religious sympathies[21] but also his interest in science and manufacturing.[22] His inclusion in the circle of those entrusted with new initiatives in the church illustrates, moreover, the degree to which Sharp was now out of favour. In 1665 Sharp had accused Kincardine to the king of failing to support the royal policies for the church in Scotland. In particular he accused him of having attended an irregularly conducted communion service.[23] The accusations seem to have been true, but since Kincardine had such well-placed friends at court they were able to force Sharp, if not to contradict his own charges, then at least to moderate them.[24] It could hardly be supposed, however, that future relations between the two would be good. Lauderdale's intention was plainly to put his new policies into practice without reference to Sharp's opinion.

That point was further illustrated by the choice of an ally among the bishops, Robert Leighton.[25] Since his consecration Leighton had given a number of indications of his alienation from the other bishops. His defence in Parliament of the six ministers unwilling to take the Oath of Allegiance had by its timing and manner irritated Sharp.[26] He had taken no part in the ceremonial reception into Edinburgh of the bishops consecrated in London, nor in the consecration of the six bishops there, nor in the formal introduction of the bishops into Parliament. He had already by 1663 become so alienated from the rest of the bishops that he was the only one, apart from the three northern bishops, omitted from membership of the Church Commission. In 1665 he made his dissent plain and public by complaining to the king about the conduct of church affairs in Scotland.[27] Who better, therefore, than Leighton for the new favourites to adopt?

From June 1667 Tweeddale and Moray virtually took over the running of Scotland. Until about 1670 or a little later these two with Lauderdale formed a triumvirate which changed around between London and Edinburgh but kept control of Scottish business. Rothes was moved from the Treasury which was put in Commission.[28] Moray, a member of the Privy Council in theory since 1661, took his place in Edinburgh.[29] The withdrawal of Rothes' office of Royal Commissioner in October[30] consolidated the power of the new men. Peace with both Holland and France was achieved by a treaty signed in July,[31] and it was then thought possible to reduce the number of troops in Scotland.[32] The stage was thus set for new initiatives in ecclesiastical policy.

The first step was to enlist Sharp on the side of the new regime. Tweeddale and Moray had recognised that Sharp was potentially extremely useful to them by virtue of his ability to keep the bishops in order. [33] They recognised also that he was so eager to retain power that he would be prepared to co-operate with policies of which neither he nor the other bishops approved. He was thus restored to favour with Lauderdale only that he might be used. [34]

At this stage a round of negotiations with the dissenters took place. The plan was evidently originally Leighton's. As early as his consecration in 1661 Leighton had been considering Archbishop Ussher's 'Reduction' as a possible model for the restored episcopate in Scotland. [35] Some time before 1667 he had prepared two papers in manuscript which had apparently been intended as a basis for discussion between presbyterians and episcopalians. [36] The first of these argued that English presbyterians had in 1661 thought that presbytery and moderate episcopacy were compatible, and that moderate episcopacy was compatible with the Solemn League and Covenant. The second paper drew up a pattern for moderate episcopacy which envisaged 'Bishops governing in conjunction with Presbyters in Presbyteries and Synods'. It then went on to stress that such a fixed presidency was not the 'prelacy' against which the Covenant had been sworn, and was compatible with the Covenant.

The arguments were plainly addressed to presbyterians. It was clear that Leighton's scheme proposed their incorporation within the established church in return for concessions to be made by the bishops. Leighton certainly did not have the support of the bishops, [37] and his intention at this point seems only to have been to take advantage of government backing to introduce changes within his own diocese. [38] The reason for such a scheme, and for government support of it, was the recognition that there already existed in Scotland the basis for a schism. Six ministers were brought to a conference in Edinburgh in August 1667 by Leighton, all from his diocese, all Resolutioners and all 'licensed'. That is to say that all six had been allowed to continue their ministerial functions by the bishop despite not having fulfilled the letter of the law on conformity. This situation existed in other dioceses, including Glasgow [39] and St Andrews. [40] The six were accompanied by the former Resolutioner leader, George Hutcheson. A series of meetings between three or four of them and members of the Privy Council was disappointingly fruitless.

Tweeddale and Sir Robert Moray were not very satisfied with this situation. They both felt that too many concessions were being made. [41] They had allowed Leighton to initiate discussions, but at this date they saw their role simply as keeping matters on an even keel in Scotland.

Since the Pentland Rising all sorts of regroupings had been taking place among the Scottish nobility which had made it evident that even to maintain a policy of moderate treatment of dissenters would require skilful management by the Lauderdale party.

The raising of troops and their use against the Pentland Rising in December 1666 had given power, money and employment to a considerable number of Scots, both nobility and professional soldiers. These benefits they were unwilling to relinquish. The strategy of Argyll and Hamilton, therefore, had been to press for severe measures against the dissenters which would by implication require the maintenance of troops to enforce them.[42] Secondly Hamilton and Rothes had allied in an attempt to force the upkeep of a standing army by raising the spectre of renewed rebellion:

> They talk of nothing more than imminent and unavoidable insurrections in the west. To this they add assurances of an universall disposition in the whole kingdom to shake off Episcopall governement, and withall represent the spreading of discontents and ill humours every where upon severall accounts, intending thereby to evince the absolute necessity of having a constant great military force to prevent, curb, and suppress all insurrections and rebellions.[43]

A paper was prepared some time in the first six months of 1667 which went so far as to represent the desire to reduce the number of forces in Scotland as a plot concerted by enemies of the state who, once the army was removed, would effect the overthrow of civil and ecclesiastical government.[44]

The professional soldiers Drummond and Dalyell were sent to London to represent this point of view and to give it extra weight by their professional judgments of the military situation.[45]

Tweeddale's attitude to these manoeuvres, which he conveyed to Lauderdale, was that the zeal of the military men was self-interested, and that peace would be quite satisfactorily maintained by the use of ordinary moderation:

> It uill appear nether ther [the bishops'] establishment nor the good and peac of the country is sought, bot mens ouen interests and ends by upholding ane unlimitted pour bakid by the sword, over a poor nation that I dar say uold fayn live in qwiet if free of extremity of Arbitrarines and opressione.[46]

At the same time as these men were pressing for continued military action, Alexander Burnet was pressing his case to Sheldon, the archbishop of Canterbury. He too had made a friend of the professional soldiers and entrusted Drummond with conveying his opinion of the need for continued severity towards dissenters.[47] He then made a journey to London where in May he plotted with Sheldon and Clarendon to discredit Lauderdale's handling of the ecclesiastical situation. He went so far as to propose in a meeting with the king that the Oath of Allegiance 'and disclaiming of the rebellion's principles' should be made tests to be taken by all ministers. Lauderdale frankly gave his view that such a course of action would simply provoke more dissent:

> I told the king that I should be sorry to see such orders given to comprehend all who were not right for bishops, for that would list too many against us.[48]

He was fortunate on this occasion that both Clarendon and the king agreed with him. The danger he was in from such plotting was, however, very clear. Burnet then tried to enrol Sheldon in an attempt to thwart any official favour being extended to Leighton and his schemes.

Lauderdale's solution to the military problem was to propose the retention of a few of the standing forces and the raising of a militia[49] after the signing of the peace with Holland and France. This, it was thought, would satisfy the desire for military commands among the nobility, without incurring the excessive cost of a standing force, or risking its arbitrary behaviour. With this project Moray and Tweeddale agreed,[50] and it was enthusiastically supported by Sharp.[51] The wisdom of restoring Sharp to favour now became apparent, for he was able to induce all the bishops but Burnet to agree to a reduction in the number of troops.[52]

Lauderdale's method of dealing with Burnet was even more skilful. First he wrote to Sheldon in September protesting his devotion to the king's interests:

> You may indeed be assured . . . of the sincerity of my professed kindness and concernement for the ecclesiastical government as now settled. I have no end but the king's service, his honour and greatness, and the peace of the church and kingdom with the maintenance of episcopal government.

When they next met Sheldon began to retail to Lauderdale alarms about the church in Scotland conveyed to him by Burnet, and Lauderdale showed him a letter from Burnet which took much of the significance from his earlier letter to Sheldon. Sheldon had been made to look a fool, and the danger from that quarter was for the moment over.[53]

Then Sharp again showed his usefulness in bringing Burnet himself into line. Burnet had decided to force a general statement from all the bishops of dissatisfaction with the new moderate tendencies towards dissent.[54] In September Sharp instead manoeuvred the bishops into agreeing to an innocuous expression of concern for the church and trust in the care of Lauderdale and the king for its welfare.[55] Burnet had thus for the moment been isolated and subdued.

When the combined forces of the malcontents had finally and most unwillingly been induced to sign in the same week an indemnity for all those involved in the rising,[56] the way stood open once more for positive action. Sir Robert Moray wrote to Lauderdale urging him to take the opportunity offered to pursue the course of moderation that he had desired to see followed since 1660:

> Nobody can make the King suspect your loyalty, your integrity, your affection to him, nor the candor of your professions as to things Ecclesiasticall as well as Civil.[57]

In October, therefore, Lauderdale wrote to Sharp thanking him for the bishops' letter and telling him that leniency to dissenters was now to be the order of the day:

> In my humble opinion it will not be unfit for your Lops. of the Clergie to endeavor to moderate Severities as much as may consist with the Peace and order of the Church, that as wilfull opposers and Contemners must be severlie punished, So peaceable dissenters may be endeavoured to be reclaimed.[58]

F

There can be no doubt that Lauderdale's supreme concern was the continued security of Scotland. His hopes that dissent would simply disappear had proved false. His analysis of the situation in the second half of 1667 was that peaceful dissenters could benefit from concession, but that more active dissent should be severely punished. These instructions were conveyed to Moray in October:

> for the Lord's sake be vigilant over that perverse incorrigible fanatic party . . . Let them rather go to America than plot the trouble of Scotland. [59]

In conformity with them the Act of Indemnity was passed, [60] but open resistance to church authority was to be brought to the notice of the civil authorities. [61]

It was then agreed that no new initiatives should be taken until the following year. [62] In the meantime plans were made to discredit Burnet entirely, [63] and to try Turner for his severities during 1666. [64] This last would prove an indirect means of rehabilitating Sharp, who was now on intimate terms with Moray and Tweeddale [65] and had made his peace with Lauderdale [66] and Sheldon. [67] A letter from the king to Sharp [68] was the copestone of his restoration.

During 1668 ecclesiastical policy thus took three lines. The episcopal settlement was to be retained, but without the use of force. Those dissenters who were prepared to defy the law were to be firmly dealt with. Passive and peaceable dissent was to receive some measure of official recognition. It was characteristic, however, of the fundamentally political motivations of these policies that the first two should be pursued, while the third was given no legal expression until 1669.

In January the Privy Council were given orders from the king to make checks on those involved in the rebellion to ensure that any who had not sworn to keep the peace should be dealt with. In addition they were required to put an end to conventicles, but not by the use of undue force. The royal disfavour for the policies used in 1666 was expressed by the recall of the commissions to the generals of the troops. At the same time the opportunity was taken to impress upon the Council that any hints of leniency should not be misinterpreted as any lessening of the king's commitment to episcopacy:

> Above all we doe most especially recommend to yow to use all possible means and indevoures for preserving and setleing the publick peace under our authority and with speciall care to countenance and mantain Episcopall government, which all the kingdom must know we will most inviolably protect and defend. [69]

The assurances of the continuance of episcopacy served to reassure Sharp and to commit him ever more firmly to co-operating with Lauderdale's policies, and to give him additional authority over the bishops:

> Now having received so clear and abundant testimony and assurance that all jealousies and displeasure are discharged . . . nothing can . . . oblige [me] to a greater tie of gratitude and care that my actions may be ordered in the way pleasing and acceptable to your lordship . . . Neither do I doubt but that all my brethren will with one accord . . . make oblation of their prayers affection and service for your prospering in advancing the king's interest with the good of church and state. [70]

The intention implicit in these policies was to take steps towards the recognition of dissent only when the demands of national security had been met. Nonconformists could expect recognition only when conventicling had been rendered insignificant. Despite episcopal co-operation there were, however, a number of difficulties in the way of achieving these preliminary requirements.

First of all conventicling continued if anything at an increased rate. There are suggestions that there were as before exaggerations of the size of the disturbance,[71] but conventicles had certainly spread to Fife[72] and there were enough accounts to induce Lauderdale to encourage Tweeddale and Moray in their policies of positive action against dissent.[73]

Secondly, in this atmosphere an opportunity was created for Hamilton to complain that the exclusion of the western shires from the recruiting for the militia deprived him of his legitimate right to military positions.[74] In themselves these complaints were of no importance, but they illustrated that Hamilton was left unmoved by the requirements of national security when they conflicted with his self-interest. As such they demonstrated that Hamilton was still a political danger and a possible focus for renewed opposition to Lauderdale.

Thirdly, despite a continuing underground campaign by Lauderdale, Moray and Tweeddale to discredit Burnet with the king,[75] he continued as before to make public his anxieties about the church in Scotland. This posed a continuing threat to Lauderdale's political status at court.

At the end of May Lauderdale's hand was forced by revelations from Scotland that even the most moderate of the outed ministers had evolved a plan whereby ministers should preach in private homes where the parishes were vacant. Robert Douglas was reported already to have begun.[76] The importance of this development was clear. Lauderdale's plans for moderation and reconciliation hinged on the distinction among nonconformists between moderates and irreconcilables. If the most influential of the moderates, Robert Douglas, had taken deliberate steps to active nonconformity, the distinction was becoming very unclear. Thus Lauderdale was running the grave risk of using severity on all dissenters, and courting the dire results that policy had produced in 1666. A means had to be found, therefore, of reconciling moderate dissenters to the government.

It was obviously impossible to allow preaching in private homes, because there was no means of controlling what went on. The alternative was to allow some to preach in selected parishes without conforming to episcopacy. In that way their activities would be public and could be controlled. Tweeddale was therefore instructed early in June to confer with Sharp and the leading moderate dissenters about the form this arrangement should take.[77]

Consultations began immediately and continued into July.[78] By 9 or 10 July it looked as though Douglas and Hutcheson would reluctantly be brought to preach, and Sharp as reluctantly induced to allow it.[79] Nothing had been settled and no-one was very satisfied, least of all Tweeddale who foresaw the establishment of a schismatic church.[80] These negotiations were brought to an abrupt halt by the attempted assassination of Sharp in Edinburgh on 11 July.[81]

Once more, therefore, the ecclesiastical policy was in total disarray. Tweeddale expressed something like despair in an appeal for some new initiative:

> I must tell you I was never so put to it to know what is best, for neither lenity will work with this people, nor severity be suffered by them, and without they be divided there is no ordering them. For God sake therefore think of all ways to do it. [82]

Lauderdale's solution before July was out was to try once more to admit peaceable outed ministers. [83] The difficulty of finding dissenters prepared to accept such conditions had already been demonstrated to Tweeddale, [84] and Sharp was no longer prepared to support such a plan. [85] In an attempt to solve the dilemma Sharp made a journey to London to consult with Lauderdale. [86] This journey was completely fruitless and resulted only in Lauderdale's urging Tweeddale to find a solution while he was on the spot in Edinburgh. [87]

In Sharp's absence, however, a new approach to the whole problem had begun to develop, probably as a result of Tweeddale's discussions with Douglas and Hutcheson. The blame for the popularity of dissent was ascribed to the corruption in the established church. [88] Burnet was accused of exacerbating the situation further by suspending and deposing 'men otherwise quiet and peaceable'. [89] Tweeddale therefore set about trying to remove the causes of complaint. One move was to propose changes in the ministry of Edinburgh in order to introduce men more fitted for such important charges. [90] A second was to propose a special visitation of the diocese of Glasgow. [91] In October the idea of a 'western visitation' was still current. [92] The implications behind the proposal were too much of a slight on the bishops for it to be a welcome proposal and it dropped from sight.

Early in the new year this theme was again pursued by Tweeddale. Sharp was required to use his influence to force Burnet to change his tactics in his diocese. What Tweeddale wanted was simple enough: a purge of clergy in the west:

> to tourn out insufficient and scandalous ministers would be very acceptable to the people and to give them better. [93]

The trouble was that Burnet favoured those who conformed above all others. He had, Tweeddale claimed,

> espoused the interest of and countenanced only the most insolent and headstrong whom the people would never be reconciled to, besides that too many of them were scandalous, or at least imprudent. [94]

The blame for dissent was thus being shifted on to the established church, and Sharp was being made responsible for its deficiencies. Moreover Tweeddale appointed agents, one of whom was Gilbert Burnet, to send him reports on events in the west. These reports were highly critical of Alexander Burnet, archbishop of Glasgow, and his management of affairs, and suggested that with a little effort and goodwill the situation would be much improved and many dissenters reclaimed. [95] Probably as a result of them it was suggested in the Privy Council in February not only that more rigorous punishments should be imposed for failure to attend church, but also that a committee of the Council should be sent to take action against dissent. [96]

In March Nathaniel Fife and others sent to the west to impose civil penalties for ecclesiastical offence and to observe the situation,[97] found they had no power to deal with corruption, and Fife was hindered in carrying out his duties by Alexander Burnet.

The need for action within the established church was made yet more obvious by a paper drawn up by Gilbert Burnet entitled 'The Constitution and present condition of the Church of Scotland'.[98] It gave at length the presbyterian objections to joining in synods and presbyteries with the bishop, and complained both of Alexander Burnet's highhandedness and the continuing corruption among the episcopal ministry:

> no ecclesiastical remedy hath been used by turning out insufficient and scandalous ministers, which are more complained of in the west country than anywhere else, and putting in better in their room.

The solution suggested to this state of affairs was a Commission to investigate thoroughly the lives, morals, education and qualifications for the ministry of the established clergy in the province of Glasgow. The Commission should consist of Leighton, if a bishop was thought to be necessary, members of the legal profession including Lord Lee and Lord Stair, and five ministers including Gilbert Burnet.

Next it was suggested once more that certain nonconformist ministers should be readmitted to their former parishes, but that they should be required to attend meetings of presbyteries and synods on pain of being confined to their parishes.

Tweeddale then supplied his thoughts on this paper and submitted them to Lauderdale.[99] The scheme of admitting outed ministers was examined, and various conditions and limitations were placed upon its being put into practice. Tweeddale was summoned to London to consult on the issue.[100] The probability was that it would be thought worth trying again, despite the coolness of the former Resolutioner leaders to a similar scheme in the summer of 1668. For one thing, since then an approach had been made to the government by presbyterians. In February 1669 a paper had been drawn up and submitted to Tweeddale. His reaction was cool:

> I am weller pleased with the apology nor justification part of it. I think it justifies too much and acknowledges little or nothing, and promises far less for the future, and is much too long for the goodness it is of.[101]

Its principal suggestion seems to have been the indulgence of all outed ministers, which Lauderdale was not prepared to condone. Nevertheless the paper could, possibly, serve as an indication of their willingness to negotiate, doubtful though Lauderdale was of the outcome:

> I shall not easily, nay, I think never, consent to a general admission of all outed, and by their paper no less will serve; but if putting in the gravest soberest would do good, much might be said, but that would not quiet, but render them more insolent.[102]

In April, just as Tweeddale had left for London, a further presbyterian initiative gave even more hope for negotiation. A delegation of ministers, probably Hutcheson and Douglas, perhaps supported by others, expressed their desire for an Indulgence, the earnest desires and expectations of very many, both ministers and people, that an Indulgence to preach the Gospel may be granted by his Majesty.[103]

Again what they seemed to want was the indulgence of all outed ministers, but the fact that they had thought it worthwhile to present their petition to Tweeddale before he left for London was perhaps an indication that their desire was urgent enough to allow of negotiation.

Now that a concrete proposal had been framed by Gilbert Burnet, the presbyterian initiatives could possibly be exploited. Above all Lauderdale needed a policy, and for the moment indulgence was the most realistic possibility.

The implications of these developments were profound. The policy rejected in the summer of 1668 by Sharp for the admission of outed ministers had now been re-stated by a junior member of the church, with the apparent support of Leighton. Leighton's alienation from the episcopal establishment has already been described. Gilbert Burnet was no less unsympathetic to the establishment. Burnet was the son of a minister whose episcopal sympathies had prevented him from signing the Covenants.[104] These sympathies had descended to Gilbert who, after attending Aberdeen University, had been ordained into the episcopal church in 1665.[105] As a very young man of twenty-one he had expressed to Sharp his disapproval of the institution of the Church Commission in 1664. In 1666 he had carried his objections much further by making public his views on the episcopate and the running of the church.[106] As a result he was in disgrace for two years. These were the two men backed up by presbyterians whom Tweeddale now chose to support, without reference to Sharp or Alexander Burnet.

Initially Lauderdale was more cautious than Tweeddale and eager to win Sharp's support for the policy of indulging outed ministers.[107] Whether or not that consent could be obtained, the policy would still be passed. In July the Indulgence[108] was proclaimed, and during the following nine months forty-two ministers were admitted.[109]

Nevertheless, despite his determination to keep the dissenters in two camps, Lauderdale was not so rash as to wish to discredit the established church. The proposals for a commission raised by Gilbert Burnet were attractive to Tweeddale. He suggested that it should be convened when the Indulgence was proclaimed,[110] but Lauderdale, fearing that it would encourage dissent and lower the morale of the established church too far, suggested that instead it should be delayed until the following March,[111] to which Tweeddale agreed.[112]

Since the attempted assassination of Sharp in July 1668, the danger that divisions among the dissenters would disappear had thus been avoided by the policy of indulgence of the leading moderates. Lauderdale had, however, been obliged to espouse that policy before the prerequisite of a decline in active dissent had been met. The political dangers which he thereby courted were all too evident to him,[113] and for that reason, during the year between the attempted assassination of Sharp and the Indulgence, he repeatedly urged Tweeddale in Scotland to take stern measures with the extremists 'till the cursed Remonstrators be crushed'.[114] In 1668/69 rumours of an Indulgence in England and Ireland spread to Scotland and encouraged dissenters further.[115] Thus Lauderdale redoubled his exhortations.[116] The result was further legislation against nonconformity, continuing right through the year. The attempt on Sharp in July 1668 had raised the spectre of armed revolt once more. Sharp gave the clearest expression of this fear in a letter to Lauderdale:

> It is without all peradventure that the design was against me, and that, some time before, it was laid and contrived by a combination of those who influenced and acted in the late rebellion.[117]

Edinburgh had been searched and the magistrates made responsible for its peace.[118] Scanty standing forces were put in readiness.[119] The arrangements for raising the militia, still not complete, were also hastened.[120] The would-be assassin was lucky to remain free for the moment, for he was undoubtedly intended as a scapegoat and an excuse for further severities:

> let all that is possible be done for the catching that murderous villain. If he were taken it may be he would tell news.[121]

Because a conspiracy among dissenters was suspected, all those who had been involved in the Pentland Rising and had not yet fulfilled the terms of the indemnity were to be sought out and punished.[122] Illegal association was particularly suspect at this time, and consequently particular attention was urged to be paid to conventicle keepers.[123]

In February 1669 the problem of conventicles was again felt to be a serious enough reason to warrant yet further action.[124] Fines were therefore laid down for those who abandoned the parishes' churches or sought baptism for their children or communion from unauthorised persons. The sheriffs of the western shires and the militia were exhorted to see that these regulations were put into effect.[125]

In April, when conventicles still continued, the heritors (or landowners) in the west were made responsible for conventicles held on their property on pain of fining.[126] Despite this, unrest continued so that on 3 August, the very day when a group of ministers was licensed to preach under the terms of the Indulgence, a further proclamation against conventicles was published. It made heritors responsible for informing about conventicles held on their lands, and expressed the royal intention that all previous legislation against dissent would continue to be put into force:

> Lykas wee will that all our good subjects be hereby advertised that wee are resolved in the futur to putt our lawes, acts, statuts and proclamations vigorously in execution against withdrawers from the publick worship in their oune paroch churches.[127]

The government policy had thus been made absolutely clear. Active dissent would be punished, passive and peaceful dissent would be indulged. The only question that remained was, would it work?

7
In Search of a Policy, 1669-1670

DURING the time that had elapsed since Rullion Green, Lauderdale and his associates Tweeddale and Moray had evolved a policy in the church which, by dividing the dissenters, effected their political aim of maintaining peace in Scotland. There was good reason to suppose, however, that this solution would prove imperfect.

From the beginning the bishops had been opposed to the whole idea, presumably because the ministers, although required to attend church courts and thus implicitly to recognise the episcopal church government, were not required to obtain collation from a bishop. They were thus exempted from any direct personal acknowledgement of episcopacy, although the way was left open in the Indulgence for any ministers who wished to conform completely by accepting collation at this late date to do so. The incentive was the freedom to collect the stipend. Those who would not take collation were to be paid out of the vacant stipends disbursed through a government collector.

The two archbishops proceeded to make their opposition quite plain. In general terms they disliked the wording of the Indulgence and felt it would make their own task more difficult. In this they were supported by the bishops.[1] It was possible for Tweeddale to overrule these objections and force the bishops to agree to the passing of the Indulgence. Sharp, however, was not to be dealt with quite so simply. The process of actually admitting the indulged ministers had very much upset him. He saw the whole process as an assault on episcopal powers:

> The primate was yisternight as far out of tune as ever and the grudge is still that thes matters have bein transacted without him, implying that whatsoever the King does order in Church matters without the concurance of the clergy is illegal.[2]

Sharp's ideas on this subject were derived from the Act for the Restitution and Re-establishment of the Ancient Government of the Church by Archbishops and Bishops, passed in the Parliament of 1662.[3] This act provided for consultation on church policy between the king and the bishops:

> It is heirby Declared that whatever shall be determined by his Majestie with advice of the Archbishops and Bishops . . . in the externall Government and policie of the Church . . . shall be valeid and effectuall.

Since the Indulgence had been passed against the will of the bishops, Sharp had a very good case for saying it was illegal.[4]

The authors of the Indulgence thus found themselves in a very awkward situation. Their difficulty could only be resolved by a change in the law. It was that solution that was immediately proposed by Tweeddale:

> Yow [Lauderdale] may see what necessity ther is of explaining acts of parliament and aserting the King's autority mor fully.[5]

Sharp in the meantime had recognised that it was hopeless to oppose the Indulgence, at least if he wished to retain his power and position, and expressed his reluctant concurrence with the policy:

> though I have upon many reasons been under many perplexed thoughts, yet resolved to put no obstacle to the way proposed, and choose rather to be carried into an implicit belief of the good may ensue upon the right management of the king's orders in that so extraordinary a case (albeit in the sense of most, the gap to most dangerous distractions appears to be opened) than to make any doubt of the assurances your lordship was given to prescribe inviolably the government of the church as now settled by law.[6]

Lauderdale was certainly relieved that Sharp had seen fit to submit to the royal will,[7] but the issue of legality he had raised was not allowed to drop. Bishops in the first place had been created as royal servants. They were intended to be the king's creatures and to carry out his will. The idea that law might be cited by the primate in defence of his opposition to official government policy was a threat to the whole erastian nature of the Restoration settlement, as well as to current ecclesiastical policy.

In late July, Robert Moray, who was then in London and had therefore no doubt consulted on the matter with Lauderdale, drew up an outline of possible contents for an Act of Supremacy[8] to be passed in the Parliament summoned to meet in October that year.[9] The paper first of all cited three acts which suggested that the king had power by virtue of his royal prerogative to dispose of the external government and policy of the church. Then it turned to the Act for Restitution of the Bishops. Two points were made that the Act implied the king's power to act on his own, and then six more followed in which amendments to the wording were suggested to make clear the subordination of the clergy to the king's will.

Tweeddale and Kincardine and the Lord Advocate were astounded by the sweeping terms of Moray's suggestions. They warned him that it might be dangerous to pass an act so obviously directed against the bishops at a time when they were already so low in public esteem. Such a measure could only increase the hopes of dissenters.[10]

Lauderdale initially let Tweeddale know that apart from some minor stylistic changes he was satisfied with Moray's draft,[11] but then suggested changes sent from Tweeddale persuaded him to make some alterations before the final draft should be submitted to the king.[12] Tweeddale's main concern was to negotiate safely between the Scylla of denigrating the bishops and the Charybdis of exalting the dissenters. He therefore suggested that there should be two acts: one an Act of Supremacy to put the bishops in their places, but expressed in general terms; and another designed to discourage active dissent:

and between both, I believe a settlement would please all sober persons, and terminate the foolish hopes and needless fears of others.[13]

In October, when the Parliament began its sitting with Lauderdale as Commissioner, Sharp began to fight against the threat to episcopal independence implied in the draft Act of Supremacy. In a sermon preached before Parliament he took the opportunity not only to condemn the Indulgence, but also to analyse the nature of the royal supremacy, concluding that it was extremely limited. Tweeddale and Lauderdale heard this with outrage. Lauderdale forced Sharp to retract his obvious meaning, and made him promise to preach on the following Sunday to the opposite effect.[14]

Sharp's next resource was to prevent the passing of the Act in the committee appointed to draft it, but he was completely overridden by Hamilton, Kincardine and Tweeddale.[15] He then approached Lauderdale privately and promised co-operation on condition that a small change should be made in the wording of the Act. To the phrase

the ordering and disposall of the Externall Government and policie of the Church both propperlie belong to his Maiestie

Sharp asked that the phrase 'as it is settled by law' should be added.[16] This of course would have had the effect of rendering the whole Act superfluous, since from the beginning it had been designed to override the existing settlement. Needless to say Lauderdale understood perfectly the import of the addition and would not allow it.

The next stage was the submission of the draft to the Committee of the Articles. Here Sharp tried to express his opposition in such a way that it would not reflect on his loyalty to the king. His argument was thus theological. He asserted that episcopacy was *iure divino* and that consequently the Act of Supremacy which implied that the king had the authority to change the form of church government was misleading and undesirable. In order then to underline that this was a theoretical and not a personal objection he publicly rebuked the Bishop of Ross who suggested the very same addition 'as settled by law' to the Act that Sharp himself had suggested to Lauderdale.[17]

This attempt at subtlety was a waste of effort. Sharp's 'long set speech' was quite simply ignored.[18] He had still not given up, however, and some days later he approached Tweeddale with a new project.[19] A paper had been drawn up and circulated among the bishops which expressed their fears of the possible implications of the king's erastian control of the church. Sharp wished this to be presented to Lauderdale, presumably as a demonstration of episcopal disaffection. Lauderdale's reaction was so unfavourable that Sharp was content to take the paper back and promise that it should be forgotten:

When I [Tweeddale] gave him [Sharp] an account of my Lord Commissioner's thoughts of it, he was content to take it back, and assure it should never be more seen, but that he would behave himself with all resignation and confidence of the king.

Thus the act was able to pass in Parliament without overt and public opposition from Sharp.

Sharp's opposition to the Indulgence had been comprehensively destroyed. The cost, however, had been enormous, not only in terms of time and trouble, but in terms of the side-effects of such a colossal assault on episcopal independence. Tweeddale wrote confirming his original warnings of the damage it would do, and the necessity for an antidote:

> it will heighten jealousies and fears and raise vain hopes higher than ever, and alarm all sorts and persuasions of people if more be not done to terminate them for this time, and it will be warm living and ruling the roast here till the next session of Parliament. [20]

Sharp's opposition to the Indulgence had had the ultimate effect of threatening the government's ecclesiastical policy. The opposition of the Archbishop of Glasgow was to prove equally far-reaching. Alexander Burnet's consistent reaction to unwelcome developments in the church since his translation to Glasgow had been to express his opinion publicly. His letters to Sheldon had long since earned him Lauderdale's enmity. His reluctance to play the politician had brought him in conflict with Sharp. Since the episode of the attempted petitioning of the king in 1667, relations between Sharp and Burnet had grown progressively cooler. In October 1668 a further attempt by Burnet to petition the king directly, without reference to the Privy Council, had been quashed by Sharp. [21]

Burnet's opposition to the Indulgence was no secret. Very likely it was regarded as further useful ammunition in the continuing campaign against him. What had not apparently been anticipated, despite Burnet's previous record, was that he would attempt to draw up yet another petition. The public clamour that this paper was to arouse, and the resulting dismissal of the archbishop, were to prove far more troublesome than his original opposition to the Indulgence.

As early as the end of July it was known that Burnet, in consultation with other bishops, was planning to send a representative to the king to complain of the Indulgence. Only Sharp had dissuaded him from this course of action. [22]

The fear was that open petitioning would demonstrate publicly the weakness and insecurity of the episcopal settlement, and thus give rise to even more confidence and boldness among dissenters. As Tweeddale said:

> treuth is the Arch Bishop of glascow and his clergy ther grumblings and open professing ther groundles fears and aprehensions doe rais thes peopel mor then all is doun. [23]

Furthermore, there was the constant apprehension in the circle of policy makers that the king might choose to believe Burnet's account of events, rather than their own, and thus endanger their political security. It was therefore absolutely necessary that the policy of dividing the dissenters by means of the Indulgence should be a success 'least anything should com to the King's ears by any of the Bishops'. [24]

In August Tweeddale had been in favour of bringing Burnet into line by threatening him with an extraordinary visitation of the west if he failed to comply with government policy towards dissenters, not only in the matter of the Indulgence, but also in purging of episcopal ministers in his province. That scheme had been vetoed by Lauderdale. The threat, however, had certainly seemed to have the desired effect on Burnet, who promised to amend.[25]

In September, when no visitation had taken place, Burnet recovered sufficiently to oppose the admission of a further batch of outed ministers under the terms of the Indulgence.[26] This provoked some anxiety and again induced Lauderdale to think how the danger might be removed:

> What does concern L.F. [Long Face, that is, Burnet] must have an answer, and he some way of mortification . . . for otherwise it seems he is soon again apt to misken himself.[27]

These apprehensions were soon to prove all too well-founded.

At the Synod of Glasgow held in mid-September, a paper, immediately christened the New Remonstrance, was drawn up by Ramsay the Dean, with the help of two other ministers.[28]

The document[29] began with a self-justification of the episcopal clergy. It alleged that charges of wickedness had been maliciously levelled against them by conventicle keepers, and that while the orthodox clergy were thus reviled, conventicles attended 'by persons of neither good principles nor practices either towards God or the King' were tacitly condoned despite the laws against them.

Secondly the Remonstrance stated the Synod's resentment against the Indulgence, and fears of the *de facto* schism that it would create. Lastly, the document regretted the lack of progress towards 'an Uniformity in the Church both for worship and discipline, whereby wee might have had the splendor of a setled Church'.

It seems possible that the whole idea of the paper came from Ramsay and not from Burnet, but Burnet was present at the Synod and tacitly condoned it. No sooner was this done than Tweeddale was informed from at least four independent sources of the paper's existence. About ten days afterwards Tweeddale was in possession of a copy. When Burnet realised that the paper was public knowledge, he went to Tweeddale and justified it as a draft of a paper to be offered to the bishops at their next meeting together. To Tweeddale, however, it seemed seditious: 'somewhat like the presbyters [in] '48, and not unlike the beginning of the troubles'.[30] Burnet was therefore summoned before the Privy Council.

Even at this stage Tweeddale was conscious of the danger to the ecclesiastical policy that the whole affair threatened. He therefore suggested privately to Burnet that if the petition were suppressed and removed from the records, nothing more should be said:

> and all to avoid the raising too much dust about the bishops' ears wherewith we fear to raise the fanatics too high.[31]

Burnet was not to be bought off, and asserted that he could give no such undertaking without consulting with the Synod. It was therefore necessary for him to appear before the Council.

In the meantime the whole matter had been relayed to the king by Robert Moray. Charles' reaction was as violent as that of Tweeddale. He too saw opposition to royal policies as sedition, indistinguishable from that of the presbyterian rebels. This opinion was similarly echoed by Lauderdale who arrived in Edinburgh for the Parliament to find this situation.[32]

Ever since 1667 Lauderdale had been looking for a pretext to get rid of Burnet. This seemed a golden opportunity. Sharp was certainly not prepared to stand up for Burnet.[33] Lauderdale therefore proceeded on a course intended to depict Burnet as the promoter of sedition. Not even this part of the proceedings went smoothly. The Dean of Glasgow and his colleagues bore out Burnet's original assertion that the initiative for the Remonstrance had come from them. That, however, was not enough to save him from a 'mortification' long planned. Towards the end of November Lauderdale suggested Burnet's dismissal to the king, who duly signed the warrants requiring resignation.[34] The form of the warrant provided for Burnet to be summoned before the courts for his mismanagement if he should attempt to resist his dismissal. Burnet knew that he was beaten and, albeit with some show of reluctance,[35] tendered his resignation on 24 December.[36]

Thus Burnet's resistance to the Indulgence, like that of Sharp, had been destroyed, although not without much trouble. The Remonstrance had certainly come to public attention, and the subsequent dismissal of the Archbishop, particularly when the Act of Supremacy was also considered, constituted a massive assault on the public prestige of the episcopate. The necessity of crushing the opposition of the two archbishops to the Indulgence had thus threatened the whole basis of government ecclesiastical policy.

Opposition to the policy had, however, been encountered not only within the ranks of the orthodox clergy, but also among the dissenters. One matter for concern was whether a sufficient number of ministers would accept the Indulgence. The basic intention of the Indulgence was to divide the dissenters. The success of this policy clearly depended on the acceptance of the Indulgence by as many as possible of the outed ministers. From the very beginning Lauderdale was doubtful whether the scheme would work:

> They [the dissenters] are unsatisfiable. What they would have begged before, they will reject when offered. Oh, they are a terrible insolent generation.[37]

Immediately after the first ministers were licensed to preach by the Council, notice came to Tweeddale of attempts made among the dissenters to dissuade the parishioners from listening to the indulged ministers. Both he and Lauderdale began to wonder whether the scheme would work at all.[38] Hard on the heels of this report came reports that English and Irish dissenters were trying to persuade their Scottish brethren not to accept the Indulgence.[39] It was to be expected that there would be controversy among the dissenters — that was what the Indulgence had been intended to provoke — but if the anti-Indulgers were too successful the policy would fail.

To this anxiety was added a second, concerning the conduct of the indulged ministers themselves. When the first twelve had been licensed, George Hutcheson had made a little speech promising their future good behaviour. [40] Almost immediately, however, reports came to Tweeddale that the licensed ministers not only regarded their admission as the first step towards the admission of all outed ministers and triumph over the orthodox ministers, but had reverted to the presbyterian habit of 'lecturing' before the church service. [41] This habit was particularly suspect because lecturing had in the past been the opportunity for making political comment while ostensibly expounding scripture.

A third danger emerged. The Indulgence had been used specifically to deal with the situation in the west. Concessions had been extended to ministers there, but not in other parts. The result was dissatisfaction among the outed ministers in parts of the country previously peaceable:

> Another difficulty I [Kincardine] find in it [the Indulgence] is, a great grumbling in these parts of the contrie which have continued quiet, that they, because they have been so, must be denied the benefit which the westerne parts have procured to themselves by their being turbulent. [42]

The earl of Home reported to Tweeddale that the orthodox minister of the parish of Hilton in the presbytery of Kelso had been usurped from his own pulpit by the former minister, now outed. The usurper declared to the parishioners, who supported him, that he saw no reason why he too should not benefit from the Indulgence:

> he preached and before sermon told that since the Council had given licence to several nonconformists to preach, he saw no reason the same indulgence should not be granted to him, being of the same principles and guilty of no other crime, and so thought he had undoubted right to that Church. [43]

Thus the schism against which Sharp and Burnet had so often warned seemed to be already in the making.

Considering the assaults on the policy of Indulgence from both within and without the church, it is not surprising that when an alternative policy began to emerge it should have been taken up and explored. The policy in question was the comprehension of moderate presbyterians within the church in exchange for concessions to be made by the bishops. It was, that is to say, the very same policy first tentatively advanced by Leighton in the summer of 1667.

The first sign that these ideas had any general support among the orthodox clergy came at the time of the Glasgow Remonstrance in September. The diocese of Glasgow was split into two synods for ease of administration. When the half that met at Glasgow drew up the Remonstrance, the other half, due to meet at Peebles a few weeks later, drew up a counter-petition which they intended to present to Alexander Burnet at that time. [44] An outline of this document was sent to Tweeddale before that time, signed by more than thirty of the ministers. It seems that the petition voiced two desires: one that the church should be purged of unworthy ministers; the other to consider what share it might be appropriate for ministers to have in the episcopal jurisdiction.

Tweeddale was uncertain what to do because of the political danger of making such a document public. He gave permission, however, for it to be presented to Burnet at the Synod, and promised to consider the matter further. In the event Burnet did not attend the Synod and thus the petition was not presented. [45] Nevertheless the germ of a policy had been born, and during the next few weeks Tweeddale made tentative further moves.

Early in November he proposed to Robert Douglas, now among the indulged, [46] that if presbyterians would co-operate in keeping the peace, the nature of the bishops' authority might be modified:

> if the presbyterians would sober their pretensions, and have regard to the peace and quiet of the church, probably somewhat might be obtained to soften episcopacy to them. [47]

Tweeddale went on to remind Douglas that episcopacy had not always been so repugnant to Scots as it was now: 'their presbyterian predecessors did not so boggle at bishops as they did now.' Douglas was bound to agree, but pointed out to Tweeddale that circumstances had changed since 1637:

> He acknowledged it was so, but that there had not only engagements against them intervened, but [that also] these last bishops had so violented the government, that they had rendered most of that [presbyterian] persuasion irreconcilable to it.

Douglas then proceeded to speak very plainly. He told Tweeddale that there was no hope of getting presbyterian ministers to acknowledge episcopacy, and that the policy of Indulgence counterbalanced by the suppression of conventicles should be pursued:

> Purge the church of unworthy persons and bring in more of the soberest of that persuasion whom the disaffected people to the present government will hear, and then proceed with all severity against conventicles 'which' said he, 'I was ever and am still against, as much as any bishop is.'

When Tweeddale then went on to point out the dangers of schism inherent in this situation, Douglas made little of them, and expressed the hope that in time animosities between the two groups would die down.

This was not a hopeful sign for a policy of Accommodation. Moreover, when the scheme had been retailed to Robert Moray he had expressed displeasure and suggested that the whole idea should be abandoned. Tweeddale was bound to agree that it had not been a very encouraging encounter:

> So we [Lauderdale and Tweeddale] have fully complied with you as to the laying aside further prosecution of that almost desperate design of uniting the divided parties in the church. [48]

The only recourse left, therefore, was to make the Indulgence policy work as well as possible and at the same time remove as many as possible of the unacceptable orthodox ministers, as both Douglas and his colleagues and the authors of the anti-Remonstrance had urged. The guiding hand for this policy, it was decided, should be Leighton who in November had already been selected as Alexander Burnet's successor. [49] Tweeddale had high hopes that he would prove an agent of reconciliation and a means of inducing the indulged ministers to attend presbyteries:

> the change of single bishops short F[ace, Leighton] for L[ong Face, Burnet] will signify more than all expedients and engines whatever, and supply a visitation . . . and like enough bring those men to presbyteries, who nothing else could, as he has done in his own diocese. [50]

This proposal won the king's support, and arrangements were therefore made for him to succeed Burnet, as soon as he should tender his resignation. [51]

There was only one major objection to this scheme: Leighton did not want to be archbishop of Glasgow. Early in January 1670 Tweeddale first broached the subject. Leighton's immediate reaction was to refuse, and even when assaulted by the arguments of Lauderdale and the Earl of Lothian 'with that fury as well nigh made him cry', he could not be persuaded. [52] So insistent were they, however, that Leighton framed an account of the reasons for his refusal:

> The foolish strifes that are raised about religion I have as much as I could always avoided; . . . the secular advantages of that place I do disgust as much as the trouble of it. [53]

At a second meeting a few days later, Leighton was subjected to a further barrage of arguments why he should accept the see, with such violence this time 'as wrung tears from his eyes', but with the same result. Meantime, however, events provided Tweeddale with a more effective lever than simple vehemence.

Over the months since the Indulgence was passed Gilbert Burnet had continued to send reports to Tweeddale of the situation in the west. [54] In December 1669 he had been promoted from his parish of Saltoun to Professor of Divinity at the University of Glasgow. [55] He was thus from that time ideally situated for sending bulletins on church affairs. These reports had been anything but encouraging about the working of the Indulgence policy, and confirmed earlier reports that the indulged ministers left their parishes, attracted congregations away from orthodox ministers and generally failed to observe the terms on which they had been licensed. [56] As a result of such reports Lauderdale had passed in Council an order forbidding lecturing and proposed legislation forbidding indulged ministers to officiate in parishes where violence had been used on the orthodox minister. [57] In addition, as a reaction to the continuing reports of conventicles, orders were renewed to the forces requiring them to seize the ministers and important men there and send them to the Council. [58] This was the first renewal of legislation against dissenters since the Indulgence.

The implication was that the period of restraint imposed by the Indulgence was coming to an end. It was this project that Tweeddale now used to bend Leighton:

> After Council I went to the Bishop of Dunblane's lodging and gave him an account [of] what was done, and of the necessity there would be of laying aside Indulgence and lenity with those people if he continued obstinate in his resolution.[59]

Tweeddale had no instant success, but felt that at least some progress had been made:

> I thought him more mollified so that I am not so hopeless, but I will never promise for him till he accepts.[60]

Leighton, however, refused so steadfastly that eventually Lauderdale decided to require his obedience by a direct command from the king. Accordingly on 22 March a letter was dispatched to Leighton to this effect.[61] Even this did not immediately have the desired result and Tweeddale again attempted to bring him round.[62] Leighton as before refused and begged that he might be excused Tweeddale's importunity:

> My advice therefore, and humble desire, is that your lordship would lose no more thoughts nor pains on that which is so exceedingly unworthy of the smallest part of those you have bestowed on it already, for I shall not be able to prevail with myself to engage in that employment upon what terms soever.[63]

At the same time he replied to Lauderdale's command in the negative.[64] In May, therefore, as a last resort he was summoned to London to have the king require his obedience in person,[65] and in June he eventually capitulated[66] and returned to Edinburgh before the end of the month.[67]

Thus by his long and vehement delays Leighton had rendered Tweeddale's policy ineffective. Tweeddale had intended that the policy of Indulgence should be strengthened and the goodwill of the government towards the dissenters should be demonstrated by the swift replacement of a hardliner by a moderate. Instead the serious disorders in the west had been compounded and encouraged by the absence of any archbishop.[68] Numerous reports of conventicles[69] made it impossible to wait until Leighton should take up his appointment and win over the dissenters by persuasion. More immediate methods had to be found. A further proclamation was therefore issued on 3 February instructing sheriffs and others in authority to arrest conventicle keepers and send them to the Council.[70] Plainly this was no more likely to be effective than other such proclamations. At the continuing prospect of disorder Tweeddale was ready to give up:

> Oh, but I be weary of taming the shrew, and now I despair of all my labour under the sun.[71]

Further reports from Gilbert Burnet[72] of the neglect of church-going and abuses committed on orthodox ministers led in April to a more vigorous approach. A committee of the Council, appointed to consider how orthodox ministers might best be protected, recommended the appointment of a Commission of the Privy Council to put the acts against dissenters into effect in the worst-affected shires. [73] The Commission seems to have had some success in establishing a degree of order, at least temporarily. Reports indicated that the indulged ministers were held to the terms of their licensing and dissenters were punished. [74] At the same time the Provost of Edinburgh made determined efforts to enforce attendance at church and put an end to conventicles. [75] These measures were, however, only a repetition of policies that had been tried before and found to fail.

In June and July, when the Commission had finished its work, it was reported from all hands that outrages against orthodox ministers and conventicling had increased again. [76] Rumours of a further Indulgence demonstrated the increasing confidence of dissenters. [77] Meanwhile Tweeddale's hope of purging the western clergy had proved impossible to put into action without Leighton, although complaints of their inadequacy continued. [78] Sharp's resistance to the Indulgence continued as implacably as before, and with some justification his comment on a worsening situation was 'I told you so.' [79]

By the summer of 1670, therefore, the policy of Indulgence was beginning to look extremely sickly. Sharp was still opposed to it. Burnet's place had remained empty. The indulged ministers had not kept their part of the bargain. The project of splitting the dissenters had succeeded only in vastly increasing their numbers. Despite repeated entreaties, no purging of orthodox ministers had taken place. It was plain that if the situation were not to run completely out of control, the Parliament due to meet in August and the new archbishop would have to find some new way of dealing with the problem.

8
In Search of a Policy, 1670-1672

THE legislation passed in the Parliament of 1670 seemed to be truly Draconian.[1] Failure to inform against conventicles or to condone them in any way was now made a crime punishable by fining and imprisonment or by banishment.[2] Assaults on orthodox ministers were now punishable by death and confiscation of goods.[3] The holders of indoor conventicles were required to find surety of 5,000 merks that they would not do the same thereafter or remove themselves from Scotland. Attendance at indoor conventicles was to be punished by fines amounting to a quarter of the offender's annual income with extra heavy fines for those who allowed the conventicle to take place. The holding of outdoor conventicles, 'the Rendezvous of Rebellion', was punishable by death and confiscation of goods. Attendance at field conventicles was punishable by fines double those for house conventicles.[4] This act against conventicles was the notorious Clanking Act. In addition irregular baptism was subject to fines,[5] as was failure to attend church. Persistent absentees from church were to sign a bond that they would not rise in arms. Failure to sign was again punishable.[6]

Generally these measures have been taken to demonstrate that Lauderdale had totally abandoned any sort of leniency or moderation and thereafter proposed to obliterate dissent as quickly as possible.[7] There are a number of reasons, however, for supposing that this legislation was not quite what it seemed. Partly the measures were intended to demonstrate to dissenters the government's implacable opposition to active dissent.

In the Parliament of 1669 a measure had been planned which should convey the government's determination to crush active nonconformity. The idea had been abandoned, presumably until it should become clear how the Indulgence was working. The Indulgence had been a very limited success and so the legislation was introduced in the next session of Parliament.

During 1670 a number of rumours had together suggested to dissenters that the policy of rigour was over, and this despite overt action to the opposite effect. The Commission to the West, it was reported by William Sharp to Tweeddale and Lauderdale in London, had given the impression that it was not serious in its action against dissent:

> I am told quietly, and I say it thus truly to your lordship only, that the dissatisfied in the west spare not to say that they very well knew this Commission was not designed for any hurt to them.[8]

Kincardine, the only member of the Lauderdale party on the Commission,[9] had objected against the failure of the members to return to Glasgow and consolidate its work there:

> It was against my will that we did not adjourn to Glasgow [at] the end of this month, that the very fear of our return might have kept the people in awe.[10]

The implication for dissenters was that conventicling was being deliberately allowed to continue. Rumours were started that a further Indulgence was intended for the Parliament of 1670.[11] Although these were immediately scotched by Tweeddale,[12] the combined effect could not be but to encourage the dissenters. What was needed, therefore, was a massive dose of disillusionment — a programme of legislation *ad terrorem*. This course of action had already been suggested.

In January Gilbert Burnet, who was certainly thought by Tweeddale to be a reliable judge of the situation, had written emphasising the value of uttering threats:

> A little terror will quell the boisterous insolence of the rabble. The more roundly you threaten and shake the whip, there will be less need of laying [it] on.[13]

Part of the intention of the acts passed in 1670 was therefore to crack the whip.[14] It was most improbable that penalties could or would be exacted as was laid down.

The point was very soon to be illustrated. At the end of June a particularly large conventicle had taken place in Fife at Hill of Beath.[15] It seemed especially disturbing to the government because it took place in an area of the country that had previously been quiet. People were reported to have gathered from places as far apart as Glasgow and east Fife, some of them armed. More than a thousand were reported to have been there, perhaps as many as two thousand, and it was a source of anxiety that so many people could travel so far, apparently immune from enquiry by the forces of law and order. So sinister did such an assembly seem that there were fears it was a preliminary to another rising, and the forces were therefore alerted. It was thought that there was some connection between conventicles held in London and that at Beath.

When therefore in September the two ministers who had held the conventicle were arrested, exemplary punishment might have been expected. Even though the Clanking Act was not retrospective, one might have anticipated severe treatment. On Lauderdale's express instructions, however, and with the concurrence of the king and the advice of other Scots in London, moderation was counselled:

> They advised that if those ministers would sign the bond themselves with caution as you [Tweeddale] propose, that it be accepted, and they indemnified for the future. Then I [Lauderdale] asked the king's commands in it, and he was very clear that caution should be accepted as you propose. This is also my opinion, for I desire we may be quit of their conventicling and that their bygones be bygones.[16]

If the Clanking Act had indeed been passed in a repressive and savage spirit, the two ministers would have known the difference.

A second and related purpose of the legislation was most likely the subduing of Hamilton. He was the dominant member of the Commission to the West whose activities had been so equivocal. At the end of June he wrote to Lauderdale complaining that it was impossible to subdue conventicles with the militia, and implying that a standing army should once more be raised.[17] That was a suggestion from which he stood to gain. There was also a report sent to Lauderdale suggesting that the frequency of conventicles and the numbers at them had been deliberately exaggerated.[18] Similarly there was a report of the corruption among the officers of the few standing forces, as Kincardine reported:

> I have reason enough to think that they are rather obstructors of anything may lend to the public service, than that they either can or will do anything themselves.[19]

The possible benefit to him and others of continuing disorder had not escaped Kincardine's notice. He commented that there were

> too many discontents amongst us that would be glad of a mischief, and are at present well satisfied with the disorderliness of that people.[20]

If the legislation convinced him that his furtive condoning of dissent was hopeless, then it would have been useful. It cannot be coincidence that during the same Parliament Hamilton was granted indemnity from a debt owed to Earl Forth by his father-in-law, the first Duke.[21] Settlement of his finances had been deliberately delayed by Lauderdale as a lever to use with Hamilton. Clearly he had now decided that it would be more useful as a bribe. Government policy towards dissent was laid out, plain for all to see, and Hamilton was offered inducement to follow it.

A third purpose of the legislation was the placating of the English bishops. Lauderdale and his allies had felt some anxiety in late 1669 about the possible reaction from Sheldon and the English bishops to the dismissal of Alexander Burnet.[22] There was a fear that Burnet would manage to create a party of sympathisers among the English bishops.[23] In the event Burnet's realisation of his utter powerlessness destroyed any fear that he would be a focus for any protest,[24] but the danger existed. In 1670, however, the ascendancy of the high-flying English bishops in the church and of the Anglican party in the Commons was demonstrated by the acts against conventicles.[25] If Lauderdale wished to protect himself politically in England, he would do well to appear to follow a less lenient policy. The placating of the Parliament may well have been the reason why Charles, whose natural sympathy was for toleration, was prepared to condone overtly repressive measures. The draft instructions for the legislation laid down that its most important function was the maintaining of order and security in Scotland: 'and generally and above all, for securing the peace of that our Kingdom.'[26] Charles was having difficulty enough with England; there could be no relaxation of the need for security in Scotland.

Lastly, this programme of legislation would serve to content Sharp. The primate was too valuable a man to be altogether ignored or discarded. He had proved himself useful in compelling his fellow-bishops to agree to the Act of

Supremacy. Who could tell when he might again prove invaluable? This set of laws would go some way to restoring his confidence in Lauderdale's intentions for the church.

There thus seem to be adequate grounds for thinking that Lauderdale's measures were designed to serve certain specific political ends, rather than that they were an expression of rage or malice. It is also most probable that they were of his own devising. When this legislation has been considered, it has sometimes been supposed that Lauderdale's association and then marriage with the countess of Dysart was to blame. His second wife is made responsible for egging him on to severity and repression.[27] In fact a letter from her to Tweeddale in March 1670 points out in the most moderate terms that no imminent solution but containment could be hoped for:

> Where remedies are chiefly applied to quiet the party to keep danger from breaking out, it is the work of time must effect the settlement.[28]

The duchess went on to point out that no legitimate grievance among the dissenters should be ignored, and that only 'the good works, the diligence and the example of those in higher orders' would finally reconcile the dissenters to the established church. This hardly bears out the story of an insatiable desire for revenge on presbyterians.

There is, however, a further series of reasons for supposing that Lauderdale's legislation had more to it than meets the eye. The first is a number of minor provisions in the legislation and the instructions concerning it. The Clanking Act was to have effect for three years only.[29] The implication behind this limitation was that it was extraordinary legislation for an emergency, and that correspondingly when the crisis was over the penalties would lapse. It was, that is to say, an example of carrot and stick psychology, which held out hopes of reward for good behaviour. Such a provision could have no part in purely punitive and repressive measures.

Again the draft instructions contain a section which stresses that all the king requires is outward and public conformity. The legislation is not intended to perform the function of an inquisition, but simply to keep the peace:

> our pleasure is that no minister be preiudiced or molested for his privat opinions concerning Church Government, providing he is in with the Church meetings and submit to the present Government, and . . . do behave himself peaceably and orderly as becomes a minister of the gospell.[30]

It was most unlikely that the dissenters would accept any such distinction between a public and a private judgment. The idea, however, does seem to show a disposition to tolerate passive dissent. Nonconformists were being severely dealt with as a matter of political expediency, not from any desire to extirpate their views.

Much more substantial support, however, is given to the idea that the Clanking Act and supporting legislation should not be taken at face value, by the support of Lauderdale and his allies for Leighton's policies of moderation.

Leighton's acceptance of the archbishopric in June 1670 had been conditional. He would take on the job provided that he was allowed to put his Accommodation scheme and related policies into practice,[31] and provided that he need not accept the title or office of archbishop of Glasgow, but only the functions of the position. Twice before in 1667 and late in 1669 some attempt had been made to re-unite the church on these terms, and there are suggestions of other less formal initiatives to the same end during this period.[32] None of those gestures had met with the slightest success. It cannot therefore have been with any great hope of success that Lauderdale and his allies viewed the king's concession to Leighton on this issue. Furthermore they could be certain from the tone of Sharp's recent letters that he was in no mood to make concessions to presbyterian scruples. The prospects for Leighton's scheme winning support from the primate therefore seemed remote.

It was undeniable, though, that the Indulgence was not having the success hoped for it. Any alternative to simple force with all its attendant risks to security was therefore attractive. Since 1667 the rival merits of comprehension (or Accommodation) and toleration (or Indulgence) had been under discussion in England.[33] It had been suggested that comprehension was appropriate for presbyterians and toleration for other sectaries. This seems to have been a policy for which Charles himself had some enthusiasm. A bill for comprehension, however, had been heavily defeated in April 1668 in England. It therefore seems likely that Charles was enthusiastic about the possibility of trying out such a scheme in Scotland.[34]

In addition to the scheme of Accommodation Leighton managed to gain government support for measures designed to answer some of the complaints levelled at the established church. At his first synod held at Glasgow in June, a committee was appointed to investigate complaints against scandalous ministers. To this committee were joined six local gentlemen by order of the Privy Council.[35] No doubt the intention was to reinforce the doubtful authority of orthodox ministers with that of local figures. It certainly suggested that Lauderdale was prepared to back measures designed to purge the established clergy.

When the committee came to do its work, Leighton reported that the worst offenders had already fled and that only the mediocre were left to be dealt with:

> such of our own as are neither good enough, nor bad enough; not so bad as to be legally removeable, nor so good as to be able to overcome the prejudices of a distempered people.[36]

Tweeddale was certainly pleased with the progress made, and he regretted to Robert Moray the dislocation that the insufficiency of ministers had caused:

> Judge you how this country hath been lost with planting of such fellows, and the severities used to make them hear such pitiful creatures.[37]

In addition, in the winter of 1670-71, Leighton conducted a further purge of
the orthodox clergy.[38] At about the same time six orthodox ministers
sympathetic to Leighton's ideas were sent to preach in the west.[39] One of the
most persistent complaints from the dissenters had been the continuing
number of vacant parishes, and their consequent deprivation of sermons.
'Leighton's Evangelists', Gilbert Burnet, James Nairn, Lawrence Charteris,
Patrick Cook, James Aird and Walter Paterson, were therefore sent to fill the
gap, and travelled round for about three months. During their stay they
seemed to have had some success and it was hoped that they would make the
acceptance of the Accommodation proposals easier.[40] Reports came of huge
congregations turning out to hear Leighton himself and his six helpers.[41] These
ministers had been temporarily transferred from their own parishes, with
government consent.

All these measures, however, were temporary palliatives. The solution to the
problem of dissent was felt to be contained in the Accommodation proposals.
In August 1670, therefore, when Lauderdale was present in Edinburgh for the
Parliament, a series of meetings with the leading dissenters began. Leighton,
Lauderdale and some of the Privy Council met with six of them, including
Hutcheson, Wedderburn and Bairdie: all indulged ministers. On these
occasions Leighton proposed his scheme which, as before, consisted of a
reduction of the bishop's role to that of permanent president, in exchange for
the recognition of this moderate episcopacy by the presbyterians. No
agreement was reached at the meeting, but ministers agreed to discuss the
matter with their brethren.[42]

Lauderdale's attitude to these meetings was moderately sanguine: 'It may
doe good, but certainly it shall doe noe hurt.'[43] Moray from London
confirmed the impression that it was hoped that it might be a successful way of
dealing with the problem:

> It were a mighty happy thing if these dissenters could by any means [be] gained to conform.
> Sure, nothing will be left unattempted that looks like hopeful to compass it.[44]

Tweeddale shared in this restrained optimism and reported early in September:

> My intelligence is that there is a great disposition to obedience, and I hope to a compliance
> with the proposition for Accommodation.[45]

Towards the end of September Tweeddale met with Leighton and three of
the ministers to enquire what their judgment was on the proposals.[46] They
replied that in the time so far elapsed the meetings they had held with other
ministers had not been able to come to a conclusion, and consequently they
desired further time. Tweeddale was assured that they would give their answer
about mid-October. Clearly this delay boded no good. Leighton was prepared
to allow more time without hesitation, and he urged Tweeddale not to ruin the
plan by being over-hasty:

> I must again recommend [the scheme for Accommodation] to your lordship, and earnestly
> entreat the preventing of its miscarriage; and that if no better can be, it be rather delayed than
> precipitated into that posture that cannot in haste be rectified again.[47]

Tweeddale on the other hand was keen to apply a little pressure. He took Hutcheson aside after the meeting and impressed upon him that this was the last chance for him and his brethren. Failure to come to terms would have dire results:

> I talkid with Mr George apart of uhat I thought not proper to be said in publike; first that upon his returne did all the hops of accomadatione depend, the regulatione of episcopacy to a primitive model, and the allowance of presbetry; that if this condescendenc failed of settling and composing differencis, uhich was lik to prove the ultimus conatus, the consequencis uold be troubelsom to them.[48]

He further urged on Hutcheson that it was a waste of time to consult with the outed ministers as a whole since some were not committed to presbytery. At Hamilton, Tweeddale met Lady Margaret Kennedy, a close friend of the duchess of Hamilton, who was known for her sympathies to presbyterians. Since 1660 she had corresponded with Lauderdale constantly, urging him to grant concessions and favours to dissenters.[49] Tweeddale asked her and the duchess[50] to use their influence to get the Accommodation accepted by those dissenters who were former Resolutioners. At the same time he put about the threat that if the Accommodation were not accepted, the indulged ministers would not be paid their stipends.[51] The necessity to take such underhand measures was, however, proof enough that it would be no simple matter to come to a satisfactory conclusion.

These events had made Tweeddale revise his former optimistic forecasts. The report of them had the same effect on Lauderdale, who displayed great irritation with the delay in an answer:

> The carriage of the dissenters pleases me as little. Sure they think themselves mighty considerable from Fife to the West, their papering and disputations and their delay. With them I shall modestly differ also. I shall delay turn about, and shall find them in a modester sense before I shall be disputed into a consent to make further offer of the king's intended favour.[52]

In October the meeting at Irvine of which Tweeddale had been told duly took place. It too was inconclusive because no reply to the proposals had been received from the ministers in Fife and Lothian. A further extension of the time allowed was therefore asked.[53] In November nothing had yet been agreed, but letters to Tweeddale began to indicate which way the wind was blowing. There was a body of support for the Accommodation, but it would coalesce only if Leighton's proposals were enacted into law:

> There are divers among the dissenting brethren who are much inclined to peace and union. I [Leslie Charteris] have spoken with some of them, but I fear none of them will be moved to yield to what is desired until the government of the church be modelled and settled by law according to the proposals made to them.[54]

It is likely that Leighton had originally intended that his programme should be made law.[55] The temper of the government, however, made it most unlikely that that would happen without some preliminary demonstration of good will from the dissenters. They, on the other hand, had very little reason to trust to the word of the government that the concessions would be extended. In this atmosphere of mutual distrust Leighton made a last attempt to rescue the ruins of his proposals. A meeting was arranged between him and about thirty dissenters in Paisley in mid-December.[56]

Leighton's report on what had passed was not wholly pessimistic:

> it is likely the most rational of them returned, if not fully convinced, yet with something of doubt and suspicion that their model is not so singly and clearly the cause of God and the kingdom of Christ as they have been used to trumpet it.[57]

He noted that although progress was slow, the dissenters had been unwilling to bring the series of meetings to an end. He recommended that more time should be allowed to them, although it might only be that they wished to avoid the charge of being responsible for breaking off discussions. Finally he urged most strongly that the proclamation incorporating the proposals, unknown to any but him, should be made public:

> the sooner they [the proposals] be now made known, I believe they will the better serve those good ends for which they were designed.[58]

As far as the government was concerned, however, the moment for concessions had passed months before. In Tweeddale's view the dissenters had missed their opportunity by their slowness and reluctance to compromise:

> The bishop of Dunblane is called a new meeting of the west country ministers at Paisley on Wednesday last, but I doubt he troubles himself in vain, and I wish he had forborn it. They are sought too much, and grow insolent upon it.[59]

The application from the meeting at Paisley to Tweeddale for yet further time to consult therefore met with a cool reception:

> I told him I had been commanded to require their answer before I went last to London [in November 1670] and I had stayed so long as I might have reasonably expected it before I went, but none coming I had no commands about that affair, nor would I take upon me to give them any new day.[60]

It was plain that the whole project was moving rapidly to an unsuccessful conclusion, whose only effects, as Tweeddale prophesied, would be a worsening of the situation:

> the effects are like to be embittering of their spirits to greater opposition and so the further discouraging of the Bishop who he [Gilbert Burnet] says will retire and leave them.[61]

In January the ministers formally presented their reply,[62] which as Tweeddale commented was 'not worth the having'.[63] Their refusal to accept the proposals as he reported to Moray could only mean a return to severity.[64] Lauderdale was long since totally disillusioned and only wrote to say 'I told you so':

nor am I surprised with the little success of the conferences that have been kept with the dissenters. I know them to be a peevish, wilful, and an unsatisfiable generation, and although I acknowledge it was rational to try those ways first, yet I never expected good of it, because I think that party desires no peace. I wish sober men's eyes may be opened to see at last what those people drive at when they refuse so reasonable offers, and that some solid course may be laid down to prevent the mischief that certainly they would do if they could.[65]

It is probably not true that Lauderdale had 'never expected good' of the Accommodation proposals. Much suggests that at the time of the Parliament of 1670 he had been reasonably sanguine of Leighton's programme. It is certain, however, that in the months that followed he had begun to despair of reconciling the dissenters and to take a more and more unfavourable view of their failure to accept wholeheartedly the government concessions. This trend towards severity was to be hastened over the next few years, but for almost two years it was tempered by a decline in conventicling and a continuation of moderate policies.

After the Parliament of 1670 the conventicling in Scotland had for the time died down.[66] The reasons for this are obscure. Possibly it was the effect of the Clanking Act, or the reduced activity of fellow-dissenters in England following the 1670 legislation against them. When the Council had dealt with those involved in the spate of incidents culminating in the Hill of Beath conventicle, no further dissenters came before them that year. When the negotiations over the Accommodation proposals came to such an inauspicious conclusion in January 1671, there was therefore no immediate need for a new policy to be found at once.

For some time Tweeddale, Kincardine and Leighton continued to hope that the dissenters might be induced to come round, and were for that reason eager to continue their moderate policies. The kingpin among the clergy continued to be Leighton. The first concern of Tweeddale was therefore to ensure that he would continue at Glasgow, despite his own oft repeated reluctance. Leighton gave a qualified undertaking to continue:

he was brought to say he would continue therein as long as in any public station whatever, and as long as he had any hopes to do good.[67]

In an attempt to make that assurance more sure, Lauderdale urged that Leighton should be pressed to permit himself to be installed as archbishop of Glasgow, rather than simply hold the office as Commendator.[68] Lauderdale's intention thereby was undoubtedly to augment the authority of the bishop and thus give more effectual backing to the idea of moderate episcopacy. At this date therefore it seems clear that he had not yet abandoned hopes of a moderate settlement. Kincardine, Lauderdale and Tweeddale all urged Leighton to accept, and finally in October, when Lauderdale had threatened that if he did not accept it would be necessary to return to severity,[69] he capitulated with characteristic reservations:

In [the] end he condescended that if the king's majesty will be pleased to understand his acceptance not to be an engagement to continue longer in that station than he thinks his service can be useful, he would submit.[70]

Lauderdale expressed his pleasure at this conclusion of the matter,[71] and accordingly, with Sharp's reluctant concurrence, he was translated to the archbishopric, although without the formal ceremony.[72]

Throughout 1671 efforts were made to salvage something from the wrecks of former projects. In an attempt to induce conformity, the indulged ministers were by new proclamations required to keep to the terms of the original agreement under which they had been licensed. Leighton, Tweeddale and Kincardine together decided on the necessity of an act confining indulged ministers to their parishes on failure to attend presbyteries.[73] This was duly passed in Council on 26 January.[74]

Lauderdale approved of this measure on the grounds that since leniency had not induced them to conform, possibly a little severity would:

> Fair offers gains nothing on them. It is time that they be put to the conditions on which they were first indulged to preach.[75]

In July lecturing by indulged ministers was again forbidden, and they were required to observe the anniversaries of the king's birth and restoration.[76]

Strangely enough this method seemed to prove effective. Kincardine reported that the refusal of the Accommodation had dissatisfied many of the outed ministers who wanted churches.[77] There was thus pressure on the indulged ministers from both sides to conform. In May Gilbert Burnet was involved in a scheme whereby indulged ministers in the presbytery of Hamilton should join with their fellow ministers in presbytery meetings, provided that they were not for the moment pressed also to go to synods. Robert Moray and Tweeddale were in favour of the experiment,[78] and Gilbert Burnet himself held out the highest hopes for it as *de facto* Accommodation:

> I believe not without reason that their example would be quickly followed by their brethren. And thus, by the blessing of God that design of Accommodation which was hitherto looked on as desperate is in a pretty forwardness.[79]

By October, however, Burnet reported that Leighton no longer had any hopes for Accommodation: 'He sees any truce with our peevish neighbours to be despaired of.'[80] Burnet himself was of a more robust frame of mind, and accordingly when he went to London soon thereafter he made certain proposals which were to form the basis of the second Indulgence of September 1672.[81]

The basis of Burnet's proposals was the recognition that it had proved impossible to fill the vacant churches in the west. It was not for want of trying that parishes remained empty.

After the failure of Accommodation, attempts were made to fill vacant parishes. In January 1671 Leighton calculated that there were twenty-five vacancies in the west. With the concurrence of Tweeddale and Kincardine he proposed the filling of a third with experienced ministers, a third with young men from college, and leaving the most unruly and disorderly parishes vacant 'till the people come to a better sense'.[82] This scheme met with Lauderdale's approval.[83] In March Sharp was called upon to be willing to release ministers in his province for this work.[84] This order, which had been foreshadowed in Lauderdale's instructions the previous year,[85] was a recognition of Sharp's lack of sympathy for such a course of action, but also a demonstration of the government's support for it. In July further government support was shown by an order requiring heritors to present to vacant parishes on pain of their rights of election lapsing in favour of the bishop.[86] Most probably heritors with presbyterian sympathies had been keeping out orthodox ministers by refusing to elect. From London Moray urged the planting of vacancies.[87]

This procedure, however, was not without its troubles. When a minister, approved by Leighton,[88] was presented to the vacant kirk of Shotts in September, he was threatened not to preach,[89] and a riot took place which effectively persuaded him not to try again.[90] Thereafter Leighton began to despair, since all efforts to fill vacancies had by October proved vain:

> But for our vacant parish kirks in the west, I wish it were taken into consideration and well resolved on what way of supplying them will be fittest in order to the public peace.[91]

The bankruptcy of government initiatives was made painfully clear by Leighton's plaintive request for help from Gilbert Burnet in London:

> I waited on the Lords of Council this week, but they have given me neither any clear command nor advice in these particulars, which till I receive from some that have power to give it, I must forbear to attempt anything and rather let things rest as they be than by endeavouring to better them, run the hazard to make them worse.

It was in fact clear that for the moment the worst parishes must be left vacant.[92]

Accordingly, when Burnet made his proposals to Lauderdale he began with the assumption that it would not be possible to fill vacancies with orthodox ministers. He suggested therefore a general indulgence of all outed ministers and their allocation in pairs to vacancies, there to share the stipend between them, but to be confined to their respective parishes.[93] In March 1672 this scheme was submitted to the Privy Council for its consideration.[94] In the same month a Declaration of Indulgence had been declared in England;[95] correspondingly the Scottish proposals have the appearance of an equivalent concession. Moray, Tweeddale and Leighton all supported the proposals.[96] In September, therefore, while Lauderdale was in Edinburgh for the Parliament, the act was passed in the Privy Council.[97]

Thus it seemed that while earlier schemes had failed, this second Indulgence would after all prove the means either of achieving peace, or of dividing the dissenters in a way that the first Indulgence had failed to do. Nevertheless, during the period from January 1671 to September 1672 which had been employed by some in promoting principles of moderation in the church, other developments had seemed likely to ensure that the Indulgence would be no more successful than other schemes.

From the Parliament of 1670 to January 1671 there had been no conventicling and no disturbances brought before the Council. Thereafter there was a gradual resumption of activity. In January Tweeddale noted that a conventicle had been held near Glasgow.[98] In February there was news that ministers who had temporarily gone into exile had returned again to the west 'from Ireland and other lurking places'.[99]

In March it was felt necessary to appoint a committee to consider how conventicles were to be prevented,[100] since Rothes and Lauderdale anticipated that, with warm weather and the return of spring, conventicling would resume.[101] Shortly thereafter the justices were ordered to put into force the acts against dissenters passed the previous session of Parliament.[102] Although there was some reluctance among the justices themselves, Kincardine and others felt that it was a necessary warning to dissenters at that time: 'the generality of the Council judged it a very good expedient to let that people see we are in earnest.'[103] Similarly the sheriffs of Lanark, Ayr and Renfrew were ordered to exercise their authority and punish dissent.[104] In July even Leighton was reported by Kincardine to have complained of conventicles, but not as freely as Sharp:

> He [Leighton] complains a little of their conventicling, but says it is not considerable, but St Andrews says that conventicles are frequent and numerous in that country.[105]

Disorderly baptisms and failure to baptise children were prevalent enough by the end of June for the Council to urge the bishops to take notice of such cases and report them.[106]

In September the Kirk of Shotts riot took place, and again in January 1672 the minister of Auchinleck in Ayrshire was attacked.[107] In February conventicling was sufficiently overt in Glasgow to warrant an order to the magistrates to enforce the laws.[108]

By the time that the Parliament met on 12 June 1672, therefore, there was some reason to suppose that continued moderation had not put a decisive end to dissenting activity.[109] The Indulgence was therefore tempered by a series of acts designed to punish active nonconformity. By now it was clear that dissent had grown beyond the scope caused by the original outing of the ministers. It had acquired a momentum of its own. In order to prevent a second generation of nonconformists emerging, ordinations outwith the orthodox church were made punishable by confiscation of goods and banishment.[110] Evasion of the baptism of children by the orthodox clergy by simply refraining from having them baptised at all was noticed by the Parliament — the acts of Council not apparently being thought sufficient — and made punishable by fines.[111] 29 May was again ordained to be kept by ministers and people.[112] The acts against conventicles and absence from church services passed in the Parliament of 1670 were renewed for a further three years and enlarged.[113]

The initiative for these acts was almost certainly Lauderdale's. In his instructions for the Parliament he was given virtual *carte blanche* to do whatever he thought fit for settling the church:

you shall take such ways as you shall upon the place judge most conducible for quieting the minds of peaceable people and curbing seditious conventicles.[114]

The actual incidence of conventicles was not, however, the only or the sufficient cause for the legislation then enacted. There were other pressures acting upon Lauderdale.

During the years 1671 and 1672 Lauderdale had gradually discarded the two principal moderate voices among his advisers: Moray and Tweeddale. In the case of Moray the actual reason for the break is hard to determine. Burnet asserted that Lady Dysart was jealous of Moray and deliberately fostered mistrust between him and Lauderdale.[115] Certainly from 1668 there had been a cooling in their friendship, and by early 1671 there had occurred the first serious breach.[116]

The quarrel with Tweeddale, Burnet also ascribes to Lady Dysart's influence.[117] No doubt this is partly true, but Tweeddale was also most anxious to be free of the cares of government and to be able to concern himself with his neglected family and domestic affairs.[118] In addition, disagreement had grown up between them over the fate of Lauderdale's first wife's jewels. These had been intended for her daughter, Tweeddale's son's wife, but Lady Dysart wanted them, and secured them for herself.[119] After October 1671 Tweeddale no longer wrote to Lauderdale, nor did he receive letters from him, and after November 1673 he no longer attended the Privy Council.[120]

These two men had been replaced in Lauderdale's confidence by Kincardine and his own brother Charles Maitland, Lord Hatton. Kincardine had been one of the triumvirate of moderates who had been advanced after Rullion Green. He had always been the weakest of the three, and it seems probable that when isolated in the Council he lacked the strength of purpose or vigour to propose moderate initiatives. Hatton was a man whose career had been advanced only very recently. It is possible that Lady Dysart had deliberately advanced him — although she knew him to be worthless — as a counter-balance to Tweeddale.[121] As his later corrupt behaviour in his capacity as Treasurer-Depute was to show, he was more than usually self-interested and rapacious among the Scottish nobility.

During the period when the influence of Moray and Tweeddale was waning, to be replaced by that of lesser men, Lauderdale himself was gradually moving towards the conviction that severity was the only appropriate way to deal with dissent. It is true that the negotiations towards the second Indulgence could not have taken place without his support. On the other hand, his mode of referring to dissenters grew gradually more extreme. They were 'a peevish, wilful, and an unsatisfiable generation';[122] 'they can neither be quiet nor let others be quiet beside them';[123] they were 'incorrigible rogues who wait but for opportunity to rebel';[124] and 'seditious and disaffected persons'.[125]

Moreover, at a time when moderate councillors were losing favour, and Lauderdale's own sympathy for dissent was rapidly waning, a number of factors made it politically desirable for him once more to demonstrate his intention to suppress active nonconformity with rigour.

The first of these was renewed war with Holland. The Parliament of 1672 had been called to provide men and money for the third Anglo-Dutch war. It did not require a very long memory to recall that the Pentland Rising had taken place in the first of such wars, and accordingly the king's letter to the Parliament required members to 'provyde fitting remedies against all accidents that may befall throw this occasion [of the war]'.[126] The Clanking Act had seemed more effective than any leniency in producing calm; it was probably with this in mind, therefore, that additional penal laws were passed.

There were also developments in Scottish political alliances that made an expression of rigour again seem desirable. Hamilton was gradually moving towards an identification with the cause of dissent, or at least of moderation. Since he was by far the most considerable political rival in Scotland, Lauderdale was in consequence pushed further towards an identification with orthodox episcopacy.

During 1671 the fencing between the two continued by correspondence.[127] Hamilton, however, became less and less willing 'to be a good bairne in tyme comeing'.[128] He was reluctant to complete investigations into the Kirk of Shotts riot.[129] In October he confided to Gilbert Burnet, who conveyed this to Lauderdale, that he could not put the acts against conventicling into force because they were too severe:

> He complains much that the authority of the Council is exposed to such contempt by the frequent making of acts, and the slipping from them without more ado, so that he protests he knows not what to do.[130]

In January 1672 he refused to be a member of the commission to investigate the Auchinleck riot.[131] This dereliction of duty was not by any means allowed to escape Lauderdale's notice, but was reported by Kincardine:

> Tis a hard matter that men for their private grudges will neglect (to say no worse) the king's service, and hazard their country's quiet.[132]

In March Hamilton was required to consult with other members of the Council on the matter of an Indulgence for Scotland.[133] This request he refused:

> since you will take the concurrance and advise of those that much better knowes and understands matters of so great concernement my absence wull be of no prejudice to the bussines.[134]

Clearly Hamilton was creating for himself the role of political opposition, an opposition moreover in which obstruction of Lauderdale's ecclesiastical policies would play an important part. Hamilton was identified through his wife with presbyterian sympathisers. Any identification with them or moderates on his part, however, was almost certainly the fruit of expediency rather than conviction.

Finally Lauderdale was faced with the real possibility of a serious breach in the church. If the Indulgence were to be put into force without any indication to Sharp and his allies that dissent was to continue to be noticed, he was likely to be faced with schism. Sharp had been no better pleased with the Accommodation proposals than he had been with the first Indulgence. When the negotiations came to an end he did not scruple to make his satisfaction known,[135] or his displeasure at continued attempts to effect it. In 1671, therefore, he used the opportunity of a number of vacancies among the bishoprics[136] and senior positions within the church to try and promote his candidates rather than those of Leighton and his allies. This policy was quite evident to Moray, who conveyed his thoughts to Lauderdale:

> he [St Andrews] considers nothing but setting up of faction according to his old presbyterian principles.[137]

Sharp proposed his own candidates in opposition to those of Leighton and his allies for the Professorship of Divinity in the New College at St Andrews, and the bishoprics of Dunblane, the Isles, Edinburgh and Galloway.[138] It seems, moreover, that not one of the four bishoprics was filled with Sharp's candidates, although compromises were made. If Sharp was to be kept loyal to Lauderdale, some recognition of his point of view was necessary. More than that, Sharp had renewed his old alliance with Rothes, as informants were again eager to convey to Lauderdale.[139] It was possibly a safety precaution that in November Rothes was removed from the Presidency of the Privy Council,[140] but such a move alone could not dissolve that new confederation. Furthermore, if it were a question of choice, Lauderdale could not now afford to abandon Sharp. His moderate allies no longer existed; he could not possibly ally with Hamilton; the only course that remained to him was to hang on to Sharp. If the price was further legislation against dissent, it would have to be paid.

Thus, despite the relatively successful record of moderate policies in 1671 and 1672, political pressures were working on Lauderdale in such a way that the Indulgence of 1672 marked, not the successful conclusion of years of progress towards toleration, but the beginning of a return to more repressive policies.

H

9

The Slide to Severity, 1672-1675

DURING the period from the second Indulgence of September 1672 until 1675 Lauderdale found himself under increasing political pressure. The high point of his reign as Secretary of State for Scotland had passed, and he was assailed by political rivals, who by 1674 were strong enough to threaten him with impeachment. Throughout the period from 1660 it seems most likely that Lauderdale's consistent preference had been for the moderate low-key treatment of dissent. This had not only accorded with his natural sympathy for his former Covenanting and presbyterian allies, but with his judgment of what would most effectively secure his major political purpose: the maintenance of peace and security in Scotland. During the period from 1667, however, he had witnessed the consistent failure of conciliation to put an end to active nonconformity. Correspondingly, Lauderdale's sympathy for 'lenity' had been eroded. Furthermore, by 1672 he found himself facing the growing, confident opposition of 'the party', the phrase used by contemporaries, of Hamilton and his allies, while at the same time bound to rely on Sharp for political support. The result was the reinforcement of his growing tendency to severity with dissent.

Throughout the period 1672-75 Hamilton made plain both his hostility to Lauderdale and his alliance with the moderate party in the church. In the same period a major dislocation in the church brought into the open the hostilities that had been developing from 1667. In this dual crisis Lauderdale was forced to rely on Sharp to restore order within the church and to support him politically. The price of that alliance was an effective end to any further attempts at conciliation and an increasingly unsympathetic attitude, on the part of the government, to nonconformity.

The first and most immediate factor to diminish further Lauderdale's sympathy for dissenters was the failure of the second Indulgence to create peace and order. In 1669 the Indulgence seems only to have been extended to those who were known to be prepared to accept it. In 1672, however, a list of outed ministers was drawn up, apparently without consulting them, and they were assigned to parishes selected for them.[1] About eighty ministers were thus disposed of. The psychology behind this move was probably to make the dissenters seem responsible for any failure in the Indulgence. Even before the Indulgence was granted, however, the rumour of erastian conditions prompted protest meetings in Edinburgh in August.[2] In September, after the conditions were made public, further meetings were held among the dissenters, and resulted in drawing up a paper of 'Grievances as to the Indulgence'.[3] The net result was that many of those named to parishes did not take up their posts.[4] From March 1673 repeated orders were issued requiring ministers to take up the positions to which they had been assigned, but more than twenty never seem to have complied.[5] So far had the dissenters grown in confidence that they were now prepared to reveal the government's weakness, and thus by definition Lauderdale's ineptitude in managing them.

Hard upon the heels of the failure of this last attempt at compromise followed the development of a close association between Hamilton and the moderates among the orthodox clergy. This was an alliance fraught with danger for Lauderdale, and its effect was to alienate him from the party among the clergy associated with Leighton.

After the passing of the second Indulgence Hamilton's attitude with regard to the church continued to be less than satisfactory. Conventicling activity had been reported by Hamilton to Lauderdale in November 1672. The tone of the letter raises the suspicion that Hamilton was pleased with the failure of the Indulgence and anxious to make it public. In May 1673, in view of the continuing conventicles and unrest, a Commission was appointed of Hamilton and four others to keep quiet the Diocese of Glasgow.[6] Previously Hamilton had declined to involve himself in church affairs, and it is most likely that this Commission was intended to silence his complaints about ecclesiastical matters by forcing him to take responsibility for them. Hamilton was fully capable of evading such a challenge, however, and declined the Commission as a quite impossible task for so few men:

> for if you will consider this commission for five of us to putt in execution that which has been the greatest worke of the councill this ten year past and yet I fear will be a harder taske now then when they begunne . . . how then it can be expected to be undertaken by so few a number, or upon what reason so great a bussines and of so great consequence ought to be imposed upon us, and how more can be expected from such a commission than from the Councill, pases my understanding, or currage to undertake.[7]

In June 1673 he gave notice to the Privy Council that he had fined certain conventicle keepers, but again remarked on the widespread abuse of the Indulgence.[8] Such tactics seemed to demonstrate a strategy of seeming to do his duty while in fact making public the bankruptcy of ecclesiastical policy. The response from Lauderdale followed its former pattern. A Commission was granted to the duke and others for putting the law into execution concerning church matters in the Diocese of Glasgow.[9] Again Hamilton raised difficulties and refused to undertake it.[10]

By the time of the Parliament of 1673, therefore, it seemed clear that Hamilton was set on a course of opposition to Lauderdale's ecclesiastical policy, whatever that might be. The Parliament, however, contrary to its usual custom, did not tackle ecclesiastical matters first. Instead Hamilton set himself in opposition to Lauderdale and before the Parliament was well begun forced the discussion of three grievances concerning the importation of salt, tobacco and brandy.[11] The vigour and unexpectedness of this attack obliged Lauderdale to resort to the device of adjournment.[12] In early December he announced to the Parliament an adjournment until 28 January 1674, and gave notice of his intention in the meantime to begin the consideration of ecclesiastical affairs:

> I am by the King's authority to make a short recess and in the interim it shall be my constant care, with his Majestys settled judicatories, to take effectual course for securing religion and the peace of this kingdom. [13]

In fact the Parliament did not meet again. No ecclesiastical legislation was therefore proposed, and no opportunity presented itself for Hamilton to stage a full-scale public opposition to Lauderdale's ecclesiastical policy. In late December Hamilton went to court and continued his campaign against Lauderdale, with Tweeddale and others as his allies. [14] In London they associated with Lauderdale's political enemies with whom they had apparently been in correspondence for some time. In January Lauderdale was attacked in the Commons. There were rumours that he had created an army in Scotland to march against England and would be tried for treason, and insinuations that he had asserted the king's right to arbitrary power. The king, however, was much too shrewd to surrender to these attacks on Lauderdale. His Secretary had served him extremely well and he would not be abandoned. The English Parliament was prorogued on 24 February and the Scottish Parliament was thereupon adjourned by Lauderdale. The party were sent packing from court without obtaining much satisfaction. In Scotland Hamilton and his allies continued their opposition in the Privy Council. [15] When therefore in May an opportunity offered in Council for an assault on ecclesiastical policy, they were not slow to take it.

After the second Indulgence much anxiety had been provoked among orthodox clergy by the increase in dissenting activity. The failure of the Indulgence has already been described. In addition, between September 1672 and June 1674 there were renewed assaults and protests against orthodox ministers. [16] In Edinburgh a riot concerning the election of a new provost seemed at bottom to be caused by the preference of dissenters for his predecessor's leniency in noticing nonconformity. [17] It was found necessary in March 1673 once more to expel outed ministers from Edinburgh. [18] Conventicles reappeared. [19] The Declaration against the Covenants was found not to have been required from office-bearers in some burghs. [20] The 29th of May was widely ignored in 1673. [21]

In December 1673 the diocesan Synod of Glasgow had sent a petition to the Privy Council and Lauderdale, then in Scotland for the Parliament, complaining of disorders in the church. This petition had been ignored. [22] During the following months the ecclesiastical laws had been increasingly flouted. In the spring of 1674, therefore, a feeling of discontent had grown among the orthodox clergy in several dioceses in Scotland. This discontent crystallised in the Diocese of Glasgow in the form of a desire for a National Synod. The moving spirit behind this development was Gilbert Burnet himself, despite what he says. [23] He, with Leighton's approbation, analysed the dilemma of the church in succinct terms and proposed either that episcopacy be abandoned or that, if it were to be maintained, disorder be repressed. Secondly he proposed that a National Synod be called to settle orthodox clergy and give an opportunity for dissenters to be heard. Thirdly, he suggested that since the laws against dissent were too severe to be put into practice, they should be revised. [24]

These views were sufficiently current in the Diocese of Glasgow by April 1674 to prompt them to renew their address to the Privy Council when it was discovered in the Synod held that month that the petition from their former meeting had been ignored. [25] The question of a National Synod was not included in this petition nor discussed at the meeting, [26] perhaps because of the absence of Gilbert Burnet. He meanwhile was in Edinburgh where, on the same day as the Synod of Glasgow, the Synod of Edinburgh was to meet. On the night before the meeting Burnet met with a number of ministers who asked his opinion about what could be done for the church. He urged them to petition for a National Synod. [27] He also told one of them that a petition to the same effect would be offered from the Synod of Glasgow. [28] Perhaps emboldened by that prospect, three of the ministers of the Diocese of Edinburgh, Cant, Turner and Robertson, petitioned the bishop to intercede with the primate and the rest of the bishops to persuade the king to call a National Synod to deal with evils in the church. [29]

The bishop was taken aback by this sudden proposal. His immediate reaction was that it was a matter of far greater importance than it was appropriate for the Synod to initiate without reflection. The petition was therefore laid aside, [30] and instead an address was made to the Privy Council representing the disorders in the church and begging the Council

> that in their great prudence they may apply such remedies to these evils as they shall judge to be most suitable. [31]

During the days that immediately followed the drawing up of these two petitions it became evident that Hamilton and his allies were fully aware of these developments, had perhaps been involved in setting them afoot, and intended to make use of them as part of a general attack on the state of affairs in the church. They had arranged to pack the Council with their supporters when it considered the petitions, and to press that conventicles and disorders were of such danger to the peace of the country that the king must be immediately informed. [32] The danger to Lauderdale of such a public intimation of disorders in the church was evident, and accordingly his supporters in Scotland were rallied. On 6 May the Council considered the petitions at an unusually well-attended meeting of twenty-one members. [33] Hamilton moved

> that the Council should do their part here, and now send the papers given in from the Synods to my Lord Commissioner [Lauderdale] and acquaint his Majesty with all.

Rothes replied that the moment was not right and that first it should be decided whether the Council as a whole or a committee should make further investigation. The Lauderdale party were against a committee:

The danger of the Committee was the naming of persons who might have prepared work enough from the present occasion, and in wording of the representation words and clauses might have been insert which all the teeth of some would not have got pulled out.

In the vote which followed, the motion for investigation and report by the whole Council was carried. Hamilton then pressed that preliminary notification of the petitions should be given to the king. Again this was defeated by a vote, and the whole matter deferred by a request to the Synod of Edinburgh to amplify the details of their complaints. [34]

Thus the immediate threat to Lauderdale had been averted, but that was by no means the end of the story. After the meeting of the Synod of Edinburgh, James Ramsay, Bishop of Dunblane had, according to the Dean of Edinburgh, 'expostulated' with the Bishop of Edinburgh for laying aside the motion for a National Synod. He had then written to the presbytery of Auchterarder and 'did prevail with them to petition for a National Synod'. Similarly he encouraged the presbytery of Edinburgh to do the same. Meanwhile Leighton had made known his regret that the Bishop of Edinburgh had suppressed the original motion and had condoned further 'such petitions from some presbyteries in the south part of his diocese'. The intention was that these petitions should be presented to the bishops and, if they would not co-operate, directly to the king. [35] Turner, the minister who had originally been approached by Gilbert Burnet before the Synod of Edinburgh, then compounded his errors by canvassing members of the Privy Council. Robertson had canvassed support in Fife. [36]

Despite the extremely chilly reception by the Bishop of Edinburgh of the petition from members of the presbytery of Edinburgh and his forwarding of the document with unfavourable comments to Lauderdale, [37] Turner and his allies were unabashed. They sent a letter to Lauderdale protesting the innocence of their motives and begging Lauderdale to further their desire for a National Synod. [38] At a meeting of the bishops at St Andrews in July concerning conventicles, Ramsay attempted once more to raise the issue of a National Synod, but he was unsuccessful. [39]

It is not impossible that Lauderdale might have been willing to consider a National Synod had circumstances been different. In a letter to Leighton in June he had been prepared to acknowledge the value of Synods at least in principle. [40] Furthermore his desire for Leighton to continue as archbishop of Glasgow even after he had condoned the campaign for the National Synod certainly suggests continued preference for moderate episcopacy. In the situation in mid-1674, however, it was idle to hope that he would support such a motion.

It was made quite clear to him by numerous reports that the main activists behind the campaign were Gilbert Burnet and James Ramsay, Bishop of Dunblane. There could be no doubt in either case of the very strong connection of these men with the Duke of Hamilton's interest. Burnet had first been introduced to the Hamiltons in 1668 but had got to know them well through his research for his lives of the first two dukes. The papers were in the hands of the duchess, and consequently he had had occasion to spend considerable periods of time at Hamilton Palace.[41] At one time Burnet had been so intimate with both Lauderdale and Hamilton that he had been able to effect temporary reconciliations between them in 1671 and 1672, but at about the time of the Parliament of 1673 Lauderdale broke with Burnet, possibly out of jealousy of the favour he had won at court. During the tempestuous Parliament of 1673 Lauderdale laid on Burnet the blame for egging on Hamilton.[42]

The report of Burnet's alliance with Hamilton caused him to fall from favour at court.[43] From that time relations between Burnet and Lauderdale were bad. When in the summer of 1674 the names of both Burnet and Hamilton were linked with the National Synod campaign, that circumstance was a further inducement for Lauderdale to oppose it.

Ramsay was as closely associated with Hamilton. From 1664 he had been minister at Hamilton by virtue of his appointment as Dean of Glasgow until his consecration to Dunblane in 1673.[44] In that position he had certainly had occasion to know the Hamiltons. Their intimacy with him was later revealed by their close interest in his case.

Secondly, if Lauderdale were to consider supporting the move for a National Synod, the only two bishops he could rely on were Ramsay and Leighton. Ramsay had blotted his copy-book irretrievably, and Leighton was again bent on retirement. Leighton had written to Lauderdale in the months following the Indulgence with a typically melancholy report, conveying his despair of any real improvement in the situation, and hoping only for the containment of dissent:

> And truely I beleev that the utmost that is to bee expected from the best counsels relating to this affair is the preventing of mischeif and keeping things from running to extream confusion. But for church order and cordiall agreement I confesse I have given over to look for it in these parts for our time.[45]

In April, therefore, he decided to resign his see, and made his way to London to do so.[46] This prospect was so disturbing to Ramsay, who no doubt saw himself in future lonely isolation among the bishops, that he wrote to the duchess of Lauderdale urging her to use her influence to prevent it.[47] Apparently this request was successful, and Leighton was required by the king to spend a further year in his diocese from August.[48] Although he had thus been 'remanded back to this station for a little time',[49] Leighton from that time concentrated on his future retirement. In June Kincardine reported that he could hardly be induced to discuss business during his visit to London, 'he being so full of his demission'.[50] In November he reminded Lauderdale that he had only returned to his post conditionally.[51] During the winter of 1673 the increasing disorder in the church and the consequent failure of a proposal by Leighton to extend the second Indulgence to a further twenty-five parishes drove him deeper into despair:

what shall be the date of our recovery He alone knowes who rwles times and seasons and all men's hearts and all thinges.[52]

In May he was asked to make a journey to London to give his views on church matters. He declined on the basis that the situation was so bad that to give advice was a pointless waste of time:

> the truth is they [public concernments] are of late run to that incredible height of confusion
> . . . that I should think him a very confident man that would of himself undertake so long a
> journey to offer advice in that matter, and would not rather studiously decline it unless he
> were expressly called and commanded to it.[53]

In June he had given some support to the movement for a National Synod, but even this he seemed to think would be useless in restoring order.[54] At the end of that month he made his way to London apparently to resign from August as the king had agreed.[55]

By the time the National Synod campaign was well under way, therefore, Lauderdale was aware that its obvious senior member had to be counted out. It is perhaps an indication of how Lauderdale would have liked *mutatis mutandis* to have given that campaign his support that Leighton's renewed desire to resign caused him great irritation. Because of his anger, Leighton was induced to continue until the end of 1674.[56]

While a combination of forces was alienating Lauderdale ever more completely from the moderates within the church, other pressures were driving him just as inexorably towards an alliance with Sharp. The attack on Lauderdale in the Commons in January 1674 had not succeeded, as had been intended, in removing him from office. It had, however, left him politically isolated except for his alliance with the English High Church party.[57] Now their ally in Scotland was still Sharp, and contact between Sharp and Sheldon was still sufficiently close for Sharp to write to Sheldon at the time of the National Synod campaign with complaints of 'fire in our own bedstraw' and a loud cry for help.[58] The way for Lauderdale to retain his remaining allies in England was therefore to befriend their ally in Scotland. There is little sign that this procedure was grateful to Lauderdale; relations with Sharp had never returned to their original cordiality after 1666. Yet although Lauderdale had consistently favoured moderation, he had as consistently preferred his own political survival over any other cause whatsoever. Moreover, not only did Sharp enjoy an alliance with the English High Church party; he was virtually the only major political figure left in Scotland with whom Lauderdale could ally. Hamilton was his rival, Tweeddale had joined his party, Moray was dead, Rothes was as ever weak and untrustworthy. Moreover, in the summer of 1674 Lauderdale broke with Kincardine.[59] It was essential for the Secretary of State to have allies in Scotland, and Sharp was the only possibility.

The price of that alliance was to accept Sharp's interpretation of troubles within the church, and his solutions for them. Thus the supplicants for a

National Synod were severely punished with the support of Lauderdale.[60] John Paterson, Dean of Edinburgh, and Alexander Young, Bishop of Edinburgh, had already shown by their letters to Lauderdale that they were firm supporters of Sharp. In mid-June Paterson had suggested on what grounds action could be taken against Turner, Cant and Robertson.[61] The bishop of Edinburgh attempted to deal with them, but the ministers refused to co-operate and appealed to the Council.[62] On 2 July, therefore, a committee of the Privy Council including Sharp had been appointed to consider the case.[63] When they came before the Council the ministers were sufficiently overawed to promise to obey the bishop and undergo their sentence of a month's suspension.[64] It was not, however, likely that the matter would stop there when the ministers had behaved so obstructively. The details conveyed to Lauderdale and the king resulted in their suspension from Edinburgh together with the removal of a fourth minister, Hamilton, until the king's further pleasure.[65] At the same time Ramsay, Bishop of Dunblane, was removed to act as bishop of the Isles.[66] Burnet had been wise enough to take himself to London, but he found that retribution awaited him there, where Lauderdale had ensured that he was met with no favour from the king.[67]

Ramsay first petitioned the Council against his sentence, but the Council had now been reconstituted so that Hamilton's allies were no longer members. Hamilton himself was apparently unable to help Ramsay although he was present, and consequently the petition was simply forwarded to Lauderdale.[68] Ramsay was unwise enough to seek the duke of Hamilton's further help, and with backing from him set off in March 1675 to present his case at court.[69] It was unfortunate for him that Sharp was at that time in London. A letter to the primate in June from Ramsay, threatening him with public revelations of the primate's wickedness, received an extremely sharp reply and damaged his own cause.[70] Turner, Cant and Hamilton petitioned Lauderdale in June 1675, but equally without success.[71] Not until April 1676 were the sentences on both Ramsay and the ministers lifted, although their cases were reviewed in September 1675, and two of the four ministers were informally restored.[72]

Just as the treatment of the movers for a National Synod reflected Sharp's growing power with Lauderdale, so too did the treatment of dissent. At the time of the Parliament of 1673 Lauderdale had seemed to Gilbert Burnet to be willing to turn a blind eye to dissent.[73] Certainly he had ignored the report of the Synod of Glasgow in December 1673. In March 1674 a proclamation made public when Lauderdale was still in Scotland remitted all unpaid fines, releasing dissenters from all their debts,[74] and thereby hoped to reclaim them to loyalty and obedience. In the spring of 1674 he was certainly considering an extension to the second Indulgence and a conference with dissenters.[75] That he should even think of doing so at such a late date indicates the strength of his preference for Leighton, whose scheme it probably was, over Sharp, and methods of moderation over severity. After mid-1674, however, there is less and less sign of these preferences and much evidence of the influence of Sharp and his allies.[76]

Sharp's view of dissent had been unremittingly severe since before the Pentland Rising. His attitude to the programme of conciliation in operation since 1667 had been unwaveringly hostile. In 1674, however, he had more than usual reason for those sentiments. The dissenting activity had caused unrest not only in the Synods of Edinburgh and Glasgow, but also in his own Synod of Fife. Although the complaints of ministers had been managed more discreetly there, yet still Sharp had found himself faced with the job of presenting a paper embodying their complaints to the Privy Council. In the circumstances of the Council meetings of May 1674 he had seen fit not to present the paper, but as he expressed it in a letter with which he forwarded it to Lauderdale, orthodox ministers had ample reason for complaint and were entitled to some redress:

> Those regular ministers being sensible that the case is very grievous, and more exposed to injustice and oppressions than any other order of men in the nation, as if they were destitute of protection and countenance from the laws and authority, are necessitated to apply to the civil authority, with all becoming humility and modesty, for a speedy and effectual help and relief from these evils.[77]

The National Synod movement was a threat to Sharp's control of the church; his attitude to Leighton and his supporters therefore was hostile. The petitions were a threat to law and order, to royal authority and to the unity of the orthodox clergy:

> divisive, and of a tendency destructive to the establishment of the church and highly injurious to his Majesty's authority.[78]

Thus he was willing to take severe measures to quench the 'fire in our own bedstraw'.

On the other hand Sharp was far too astute not to recognise that the generally disturbed nature of the Scottish church was the result of continuing active dissent. If the episcopal establishment was to survive, then some way had to be found to put an end to such dissent. He pointed out to Lauderdale that as leniency had not worked in the past there was no reason to suppose that an extension of the Indulgence would prove any more satisfactory now:

> I am still confident that any further Indulgence will be far from a tendency to the cure of our schism or quieting of that party who will not be satisfied though the heads of all the bishops were given them in a charger, and presbytery set up next month.[79]

The only solution to the problem in his view was the decisive end to dissent, of whatever nature, if law and order were to be preserved:

> unless this kingdom find there is a king over it whose authority must be so regarded as it be not permitted to any person or party to assume to do good in their own eyes in matters relating either to church or state it is impossible it can be well with us.[80]

If any further impetus was needed to persuade Sharp of the necessity of stern measures, it was given by a scuffle in the streets of Edinburgh during which he was threatened.[81] The implications of this event were not lost upon Lauderdale. Lady Dysart wrote to Sharp conveying their understanding of its importance:

> I assure your Grace wee have with faithfull hairts given God thanks for his marcy to us in your Graces safty. Wee are sensible of our great interest therein, and shall ever consider all your concernes as our owne.[82]

By June 1674 Lauderdale was persuaded of the necessity to accept Sharp's view of dissent as well as that of the National Synod.[83] In a reconstituted Privy Council from which many of Hamilton's supporters had been omitted, although Hamilton was left in, presumably because Lauderdale was not yet strong enough to exclude him,[84] action was taken against conventicles. It was acknowledged that the remission of fines had failed to reclaim dissenters to loyalty and good behaviour, and that conventicles and other disorders had continued. The Council was therefore exhorted to apprehend the ringleaders with the use of both standing forces and militia should that be necessary. A Commission was then given to Sharp and others authorising them to put this policy into force.[85] Shortly thereafter an act was passed whereby landlords were obliged to procure from all their tenants, and masters of households from their servants, an undertaking not to attend conventicles. Disobedience was punishable by expulsion from service or tenancy. Furthermore, magistrates of royal burghs were made responsible for conventicles within the burgh.[86] Accordingly during June and July very brisk action was taken against conventicles.[87]

In August Sharp went to London,[88] where he stayed with Lauderdale until the following spring, 1675, while Lauderdale continued to wrestle with his English political adversary. In the autumn of 1674 Lauderdale's reliance on Sharp was underlined by the reappointment of Alexander Burnet to the archbishopric of Glasgow. He was apparently persuaded to this course of action by Sharp and the English High Church party.[89] Only three years before, in February 1671, Lauderdale had gone out of his way to express his aversion to Burnet and his firm resolve never to reappoint him:

> As for the late Archbishop Burnet, I wonder how you can so much as let it enter your mind that ever I will so much as think of readmitting him. That would quite ruin all. No, I shall never, never so much as consent to it.[90]

Yet by September 1674 Alexander Burnet was back in Glasgow[91] and by October had resumed correspondence with Lauderdale in his old style:

> I wish I could tell you that all were well here, but I must not conceal my fears from your Grace. There are, in all probability, combinations among us, not yet discovered, and designs to drive all our differences and debates to the greatest extremity, and dispose the giddy multitude to a rebellion . . . But I hope by the prudence and vigilancy of his Majesty's ministers, it may yet be prevented and hot spirits reduced to a better temper.[92]

In December he was readmitted to the Privy Council.[93] Furthermore Paterson, the Dean of Edinburgh, who had given Sharp such wholehearted support over the National Synod, was made bishop of Galloway.[94]

By the end of 1674, therefore, policies had been decided which put the church back on a course of severity and repression. This new direction was confirmed by Lauderdale's political fortunes in early 1675. The attack on Lauderdale and other royal officers in 1674 had been followed by the prorogation of the English Parliament. When it reassembled in April 1675 it immediately returned to Lauderdale's case. Gilbert Burnet, whose new-found enmity to Lauderdale was well known, was used by Lauderdale's enemies in the hope of getting him to implicate Lauderdale in treason. His depositions encouraged a further attack.[95] As before, the king brushed it aside,[96] but there were two further addresses made against Lauderdale in May and June, and a noticeable decline in support for him.[97] Sharp, and now Alexander Burnet,[98] were correspondingly all the more essential to Lauderdale, and he more and more fixed to their policies.

10

The Bishops Call the Tune, 1675-1679

FROM 1675 Lauderdale embarked on policies that were intended simultaneously to preserve his alliance with Sharp, Burnet and the English High Church Party, to subdue dissent in Scotland and to destroy Hamilton and the party. The keynote of these policies was an increasing readiness to use force, and that in turn was to prove Lauderdale's undoing. His actions from 1675 lent themselves only too well to their interpretation by Hamilton as arbitrary misuse of power. The support for the party both in England and Scotland obliged the king to rescind Lauderdale's policies in 1678 and thereafter. The murder of Sharp and the Bothwell Brig rising demonstrated his incapacity to fulfil the basic requirement of maintaining peace and security, and in September 1680 he was obliged to resign as Secretary of State.

While Sharp was still in London in 1675, Alexander Burnet continued action against dissent in the spirit of the legislation of 1674. Apparently under Burnet's influence,[1] and at the instigation of letters from court,[2] the Privy Council ordered the garrisoning of a large part of the countryside for the prevention of conventicles.[3] In addition those persons ordered to appear before the Council since the indemnity of March 1674, and who had not done so, were now to be intercommuned. Furthermore, the acts of Parliament of 1670 against conventicles and absence from church, valid initially for three years and renewed in 1672, were recommended for renewal once more.[4] Thus legislation which had not been put into effect was now to be renewed in circumstances which suggested that now it might well take effect. Royal permission for its renewal was given in August.[5] The use of a standing army to garrison the countryside was an extension of the former system of quartering soldiers on disaffected towns or areas. It too betokened a new spirit in the government.

It seems improbable that the explanation for these edicts is to be found in the incidence of conventicles or the influence of Burnet, contributory factors though these doubtless were. Conventicling still continued but, so far as can be seen, at no greater rate than at any time over the previous eighteen months. Burnet would have been prepared to advocate the use of troops at any time in his career and indeed had frequently urged it. The crucial difference is to be found in the realignment of parties in England in early 1675. Sheldon had been no more in favour of the policy of leniency towards dissent, sporadically urged by the king in England since 1667, than Sharp had been in favour of its equivalent in Scotland. By February 1675, however, Charles had recognised that his desires could not be implemented. His recognition of that fact returned Sheldon and his party to their role of allies of the crown.[6]

Correspondingly the king was now prepared to condone measures of severity in Scotland. Furthermore, Lauderdale, still dependent for his political survival on Sheldon and his allies, was the more ready to propose policies to extend the new-found English zeal for conformity across the border.

Accordingly, after Sharp's return to Scotland in autumn 1675, the policies already initiated were continued and extended. Delays in establishing and equipping the projected garrisons were condemned in September.[7] In December the Commission for the suppression of conventicles was renewed. It had a quorum of only three and widespread powers to take action against dissent.[8] At the same time the Declaration was again required from all holding public office.[9]

In January 1676 action was taken against James Mitchell, the man who had attempted to assassinate Sharp in 1668. Mitchell had been arrested in February 1674[10] and, while Lauderdale was still in Scotland, interrogated in March by a committee of the Privy Council. Perhaps because Lauderdale was still at the time endeavouring to promote moderate policies, Mitchell was promised his life, by authority of Lauderdale and the Privy Council, provided that he made a full confession.[11] Mitchell had then been left in prison and allowed to consult lawyers and friends,[12] until in December 1675 he was unwise enough to attempt to escape.[13] This apparently brought him to the attention of the Privy Council once more in January 1676, in circumstances very different from those of March 1674. Mitchell was asked to renew his confession, but without any renewal of the promise of life. Such a confession would of course have permitted his immediate condemnation to death by the Justiciary Court, and it is probable that it was intended as a brisk example to fellow-dissenters who were particularly active at the time. Mitchell naturally refused to co-operate and was therefore put to torture.[14] This method was no more effective in extracting a confession, and accordingly Mitchell was re-imprisoned, this time on the Bass Rock.[15]

This rigour continued in the spring of 1676, with increasing numbers of cases being brought before the Privy Council. In March a royal proclamation announced further measures to be taken for the suppression of conventicles, and required indulged ministers to keep to the terms of the Indulgence.[16] In addition the universities were ordered to be purged by the application of the Oaths of Allegiance and Supremacy.[17] Commissions were then appointed to put the acts into force locally.[18] In April the act of 1669, making heritors responsible for conventicles held on their property on pain of fining, was extended from the western shires to the whole of Scotland[19] - an act that was in itself a demonstration of the spread and increase of conventicles. In the same month a Commission was appointed to suppress conventicles in the south-western shires.[20]

In quelling dissent the policy of severity was a failure. As far as can be gauged from the cases before the Council and the nature of the legislation itself, conventicling was increasing rapidly. The principal reason for this is probably to be found in the increasing sophistication of the organisation of dissenters. Until about 1672 there is very little evidence of any attempt by the dissenters to form regular methods of communication and consultation. These had doubtless been slowly evolving for some time, but the consultations over the second Indulgence seem to be the first major occasion on which dissenters were able to meet for negotiation on their own initiative. No doubt repeated government requests for dissenting opinion on Accommodation had developed a system of communication. After 1672 their organisation expanded greatly, until by 1674 it was possible for them to hold an assembly in Edinburgh, attended by delegates from alternative presbyteries all over Scotland, at which resolutions were taken as to agreed procedures in their alternative congregations.[21] In August 1676 Burnet complained that these arrangements were so complete that dissenting congregations existed in virtually every parish with impunity:

> most parishes in this country have ministers assigned to them who preach, baptise, publish banns (at their field meetings) and marry; and those ministers have their respective elders who advise and assist them in the exercise of discipline, and . . . advertise the people of the times and places appointed for their meetings.[22]

On the other hand these policies were successful in at least one respect. They cemented Sharp and Burnet to Lauderdale's interest, and they were induced thereby to do what they could to extend his political support in Scotland, although without much success.[23] Sharp had for some time been on good terms with Rothes. From autumn 1675 he did what he could to effect a reconciliation between him and Lauderdale.[24] Similarly Sharp attempted to ensure that Lauderdale and his brother Lord Hatton remained on good terms; Hatton's son had offended Lauderdale, which had caused a breach in relations.[25] In November 1675 he went so far as to attempt a reconciliation between Lauderdale and Hamilton.[26]

In fact, although Sharp and Burnet remained staunch allies, they did not succeed in extending Lauderdale's support, while Hamilton refused to abandon his opposition. Instead, from the autumn of 1676 Hamilton began to use the severity of ecclesiastical policy as a pretext for yet another major assault on Lauderdale. In October Gilbert Burnet, now thoroughly confirmed in his antagonism to Lauderdale, suggested to Hamilton the drawing up of a comprehensive list of charges against Lauderdale to be presented to the king. The duke of York had expressed his willingness to back such an indictment, and Burnet indicated that there would be widespread support for it in England.[27] It was some time before this project came to fruition, but in the meantime Hamilton was not idle.

In the early months of 1676 Hamilton was in London and apparently suggested that a further Indulgence was the best means of settling the church.[28] This suggestion caused Alexander Burnet grave alarm and caused him and other bishops to protest fiercely against such a scheme.[29] Sharp conveyed to Lauderdale his conviction of the alliance between Hamilton and the presbyterians implied by this suggestion, and of its political importance:

It is now apparent that the party have taken off their mask, and whence the fanatics have taken their encouragement and for what end they have been and are connived at and upholden, though their practices and way are no less absurd than their principles are known to be pernicious and destructive to order and humane society. All discerning men [?] see that neither religion nor tenderness of conscience are in the case.[30]

This protest caused Hamilton some embarrassment,[31] and for the moment he was advised by his allies to lie low.[32] In March Sharp was hopeful that this reverse, combined with the renewed measures against nonconformity, would put an end to the party, although his hopes, justifiably as it turned out, were tempered with some doubt:

I wish I could say that the heart and hopes of that party were quite broken, but [I] do not despond that if the way now taken for making the fanatics here, and their supporters, find they must live under the king and his laws, the faction and their evil designs will soon melt away and come to signify nothing.[33]

In July, however, Hamilton seriously overstepped the mark in a further attack on Lauderdale's ecclesiastical policies, and thereby gave Lauderdale the opportunity to deal him a significant blow.

James Kirkton had been minister of Mertoun in the presbytery of Earlston until he was outed in 1662.[34] In 1672 he was licensed to preach at Carstairs under the terms of the second Indulgence.[35] In March 1673 Kirkton had not yet taken up residence in his parish and was among those warned by the Privy Council to do so by 1 June.[36] By November he had still not appeared and was reported to be in England.[37] In June 1674 he was accused of having taken part in a conventicle at Cramond[38] and of having failed to appear before the Council. In July he was declared a rebel and an outlaw.[39] Kirkton was therefore the sort of dissenter the Privy Council was most interested in bringing to justice: a minister who had deliberately flaunted his contempt for the royal concessions to dissenters; a man known to move about the countryside and therefore likely to be involved in intrigue with dissenters in England as well as throughout Scotland; in short a wanted man.

In 1676 Kirkton was in Edinburgh when he was recognised by Captain William Carstares. Carstares was a notorious thug who in May 1675, while a lieutenant, had used the troops under his command to kidnap five men, apparently for his personal profit. Although he was brought before the Council and punished,[40] yet in July 1675 he was restored by royal command to his place in the same company.[41]

When Carstares recognised Kirkton, his duty was to arrest him and deliver him to the Council. Possibly Carstares tried and failed to get a warrant to do so from the Council and so instead took Kirkton to his own home and there tried to blackmail him. Kirkton's shouts eventually brought help and he escaped, leaving Carstares unhurt.[42] Kirkton had no legal redress since he was in any case an outlaw, but Carstares, probably in fear of complaint against him to the Council, reported those who had helped Kirkton escape. These men were then fined and required to produce Kirkton before the Council themselves, since he had immediately again been reported as preaching at conventicles.[43]

This case was exactly the opportunity that Hamilton and his allies had been looking for, where they could allege that in taking action against dissent Lauderdale was exercising arbitrary power and depriving nonconformists of their ordinary civil rights. When Baillie of Jerviswood appeared before the Council, Hamilton, Kincardine, Cochrane and Dumfries alleged that the charges against him were not relevant on the grounds that the arrest was illegal. To this a warrant was produced which had apparently been ante-dated by members of the Council.[44]

It was obvious that Hamilton had hit on a case which was potentially very dangerous for Lauderdale's allies. This was exactly the sort of misuse of authority to which Charles was sensitive, as Turner's disgrace over the Pentland Rising had demonstrated. Lauderdale's nephew, Hatton's son, Sharp and the committee of the Council first involved in the case all wrote to Lauderdale to represent Hamilton and his friends as wilful opposers of the royal commands concerning dissenters.[45] Lauderdale recognised his opportunity, and in a reconstitution of the Privy Council, Hamilton, Dumfries, Kincardine and Cochrane were all omitted, a development which gave Sharp much satisfaction:[46]

It is sufficiently apparent that the disloyal and fanatic party have taken boldness and encouragement to affront the king's authority and the laws by the connivance they have met with from those who by their offices are obliged to suppress them, and by the janglings and clamorous debates kept up by some discontented at the Council board . . . And now that by the late Commision the Council is thus purged, it is hoped the proceedings of that board shall be carried with more smoothness and unanimity, and that the king's authority shall be more vigorously owned and have a greater awe with the people.[47]

This blow to Hamilton was followed early in 1677 by an order relieving him of his commissions in the militia,[48] and from September 1677 all officers of state were declared to hold office during his Majesty's pleasure, rather than as previously for life.[49] Thus the necessity for any further reconstitutions of the Council was avoided, and Lauderdale was in effect given control of its membership.

Although Hamilton had thus been defeated at least temporarily over his opposition to Lauderdale's ecclesiastical policy, the implications for that policy were much wider reaching. The treatment of Mitchell was itself disquieting in that it demonstrated a positive desire to make examples of dissenters on the part of Lauderdale's allies; the Kirkton-Carstares case continued and amplified a tendency towards severity by any means. It is not certain whether Lauderdale was given an alternative version of Carstares's action, but in condoning his allies' interpretation[50] he was giving the seal of approval to what amounted to the public perversion of justice. Clearly Sharp and the rest had placed him in a very awkward position by their inept handling of the case. Whether or not he was informed of the other version of events,[51] he could not afford to abandon his allies in the face of Hamilton's attack. Yet by supporting them he was committing himself to an interpretation of ecclesiastical policy that could only offer further opportunities for opposition to Hamilton and the party. Furthermore, now that they had been excluded from the running of the country, their opportunities for opposition were that much greater in that they were no longer identified with the policies of the regime.

When to these considerations is added the continued failure of ecclesiastical policy to perform the major function required of it, to restrain dissent, it seems clear that Lauderdale's alliance with Sharp and Burnet had led him into ever deeper waters. Lauderdale's reaction to this situation in 1677 was to come to Scotland to deal with the problem himself, and there to attempt to moderate the policies now in force against dissenters. Such a course of action, if successful, would have a number of desirable effects. Hamilton's reputation with the dissenters would be diminished and his opposition to Lauderdale thereby rendered more difficult; Lauderdale himself would be released from the stranglehold that had been imposed by his alliance with Sharp; the increasing problem of active nonconformity would be moderated, or at the very least the long-awaited split in the solidarity of the dissenters, which had begun to emerge after 1672, would be enlarged and continued.

Lauderdale arrived in Scotland in July 1677 and very soon set about negotiations with the dissenters. A number of the outed ministers from the west petitioned Lauderdale for some favour to dissenters in anticipation of a favourable reply.[52] Certainly by the end of August Hamilton had heard rumours of 'underhand treaties betuixt the phanatiks and those in pouer'.[53] By early September he had heard that a further Indulgence was intended, and he assumed that it would be passed with Sharp's approbation.[54] By 20 September, however, it was plain to Hamilton that Lauderdale was acting on his own initiative without the support of the bishops or his other allies:

> for I find many of those of his partie begins to be disgusted; and for the affair off the Indulgence, he keeps them all strangers to itt, and they dare not ask questions. I believe the archbishops ar ill pleased with him, iff they knew how to helpe itt.[55]

Understandably these developments caused disruption among Lauderdale's supporters, as Hamilton noted early in October. By 12 October the negotiations had obviously broken down, since Lauderdale made a declaration in the Council that no such thing as an Indulgence had ever been intended.[56]

The knowledge of the failure of this project now placed Lauderdale in a worse position than if it had never been attempted. It was no doubt for this very reason that he had tried to conduct the negotiations in secret so that a *fait accompli* could simply be announced. Instead of strengthening his position, Lauderdale had weakened it by alienating himself from his Scottish allies.[57] Furthermore, he evidently feared he had also alienated his English High Church allies, for his chaplain Dr George Hickes wrote to his friends first of all denying Lauderdale's intention of granting an Indulgence[58] and then asking them to convey to their colleagues Lauderdale's continuing loyalty to the church:

> If this story of the Indulgence be bruited about London, I hope you'll both contribute to confute it, especially among our brethren of the clergy, who ought to look upon my Lord as the most sincere and zealous patron they have in the world.[59]

Hickes was politically naive. His letters are therefore a good index of what Lauderdale wanted to be believed about his activities. But not only had Lauderdale sown doubts among his allies by this procedure: he had encouraged the opposition party. Hamilton noted to his allies with delight that Lauderdale's party was in disarray, and took the opportunity to organise meetings of his own party to discuss tactics.[60] Hamilton's advantage was improved by the effects of the rest of Lauderdale's ecclesiastical policies.

From 1667 Lauderdale had always hoped that it would be possible to divide the dissenters by lenient policies. He had anticipated that Indulgence or Accommodation would appeal to a moderate majority and that once they had been reconciled to the government the remaining irreconcilables could simply be obliterated forcibly. This policy had never worked because those prepared to fall in with the government's offers had never been in the majority. Always the numbers of those still alienated had been too great for it to be politically possible for the government to destroy them. In 1672, however, divisions had undoubtedly appeared among dissenters. Denunciation of those who accepted the Indulgences grew stronger. By 1677 these divisions were evident to the government, and Lauderdale had certainly hoped to exploit them. As he wrote to Danby, 'all rational courses are taken to divide them and to quiet them'. The details of the proposed Indulgence are unknown. Certainly Lauderdale's terms were unacceptable. While these negotiations were going on, however, Lauderdale was at his old trick of applying pressure through harsh legislation against those who failed to accept the government's bounty.

Accordingly on 2 August former legislation requiring heritors to be responsible for their tenants' attendance at church and obedience to ecclesiastical law was renewed, requiring the swearing of an oath to attend church by each tenant at the instance of the heritor.[61] On 7 August commissions were granted for the suppression of conventicles in the various shires.[62] The days when these acts might have been effective had long since passed. As Hamilton laconically remarked:

> that itt will be possible to reclame the people from conventickls or gett them to take this bond I much doubt of itt.[63]

In fact in October it proved so difficult to secure obedience to the swearing of the bond that a committee of the Council suggested that it be waived.[64] Instead of damaging Hamilton's reputation with dissenters, therefore, the utter ineffectiveness of Lauderdale's policies could not but improve it.

Once again, therefore, Lauderdale was faced in the autumn of 1677 with the old intractable threefold problem of dealing with the dissenters, the party and his allies at the same time. In October he hit upon what later became known as the Highland Host. An army would be sent to quarter upon the western shires. The use that was made of this campaign by Hamilton, its transmission to posterity by Wodrow, and its description by a pro-dissenting historian in the twentieth century[65] have conspired together to obscure what logic this course of action might possess. It can well be understood that in October 1677 it offered certain distinct advantages to Lauderdale.

In the first place the army could be instructed to deal with the dissenters once and for all, and this could be represented to the bishops as a favour done to them and a demonstration of Lauderdale's fidelity to the church. Secondly, the army could be used not only to quarter upon the lands of Hamilton and his allies in the west and thus impoverish their tenants, but also to alienate the dissenters from the party, who would be shown to be utterly ineffectual in protecting them.

Initially it seems possible that Lauderdale had intended only to frighten dissenters with talk of an army. In October he explained to the king via Danby that only preliminary action had been taken in case of rebellion:

> And yet we have only made preparations, but will not raise any forces, only make them ready in case they [the dissenters] shall rise. For we would not alarm this kingdom nor the king's other dominions till there be cause for it.[66]

However, it is more likely that' this was intended merely as a plausible preliminary notice of his intentions. Similarly, talk of rebellion seems very likely to have been mere rhetoric to make more plausible his intended action. To do this was to follow the example of others before him in Scotland and exaggerate the danger of rebellion to serve one's own end. Certainly there seems to have been increased conventicling activity at this time, but it was Hamilton's opinion that the notion of a rebellion had been deliberately raised to justify action against the west,[67] and that the Highland Host was intended to provoke resistance which could then be mercilessly repressed.[68] In all likelihood there was some truth in this assertion, since it was repeated in January by Hickes:

> I wish they would try as they did in 1666 whether God would work miracles for them or no.[69]

The Highland Host was the other half of the policy of extending Indulgence. If the dissenters would not accept it, they had no one to blame but themselves for their subsequent repression. A rumour circulated by Tweeddale years later[70] accused Lady Dysart of offering the dissenters an Indulgence in 1677 in return for £10,000. When they refused to pay, the Highland Host was unleashed in revenge. It is hard to credit that the money could seriously have been expected, but the implication that the Highland Host was the reply to the failure of the plan for an Indulgence may very well have some truth in it. This reasoning was certainly not fit for public consumption. The notion of rebellion and the accompanying alerting of forces in England and Ireland[71] provided an admirable screen for less exalted intentions.

The details of the instructions for the campaign reveal that the dissenters were to be as far as possible permanently extinguished, as Lauderdale himself vowed:

> this game is not to be played by halfes, we must . . . crush them, so as they may not trouble us any more in hast.[72]

It is arguable, however, that the action to be taken against the dissenters represented only one aspect of the functions of the Highland Host, and that not necessarily the most important. It was certainly intended also to destroy the party, 'done out of desygn to catch Duke Hamilton in one snare or another,' as one observer remarked.[73] The various acts which had tried to make heritors responsible for the actions of their tenants, culminating in that of summer 1677, had been attempts to force the nobility, greater and lesser, to take their share of maintaining government authority. The disaffection of such men from ecclesiastical policy had been the root cause of the ineffectiveness of ecclesiastical legislation throughout the reign. By launching a campaign against those men who most overtly supported dissent, Lauderdale was attempting to demonstrate that such culpable disaffection would not be allowed to continue.

On a number of occasions Hamilton had failed to accept Commissions to deal with dissenters in his own area of influence. He was of course no longer on the Privy Council. In order to demonstrate the equal lack of co-operation from his friends, Lauderdale wrote in October to the earl of Dundonald and others requiring them to suppress disturbances in Ayr and Renfrew.[74] Early in November the Council received a reply protesting that it was impossible for them to do so and allegedly suggesting an Indulgence instead.[75] No doubt by now it was true that suppression was impossible, but to make such a blunt reply was to play into Lauderdale's hands. Their refusal was relayed to Danby in terms that justified an attack on the noblemen and officials of the west:

> And lately I gave notice what orders we had given for calling together the gentlemen of those two most disaffected shires, not that we expected much from them, but to try their puls and render them inexcusable.[76]

When it was represented to the king that there was danger of rebellion from dissenters, and that that rebellion was encouraged by the nobility, it was virtually certain that Lauderdale would be given *carte blanche* to do as he would. Accordingly a royal letter was sent to the Privy Council in December approving of measures taken to make ready highland forces and the militia, and to proceed to the west, there to quarter upon and punish all dissenters.[77] Hamilton was not convinced by Lauderdale's tactics and agreed with Queensberry that there was more to the campaign than met the eye:

> I am apt to be of your judgment that the calling of these forces together to Glasgow is more for perticular prejudices to sume of us, or upon sume designes we understand not, then for what is pretended.[78]

A third purpose of the campaign was to convince the bishops, both English and Scottish, that Lauderdale was indeed a friend to the church and an enemy to dissent. This view of the Highland Host was diligently peddled to High Church circles in London by Hickes:

> The methods to be taken for reducing and suppressing them [the dissenters] will much credit the wisdom, and manifest the honesty of my lord and his unfeigned love both to the king and church.[79]

This interpretation of Lauderdale's activities was also conveyed to the English episcopate in an account of Scottish affairs written by the Bishop of Galloway and sent to the Bishop of Rochester.[80] Such representations had the desired effect in London at least. The Bishop of London was moved to write a fulsome letter thanking Lauderdale for his protection of the Scottish church in the name of all the English clergy with whom he had been in contact.

In Scotland, where the bishops were closer to events, the proposals were not met with such enthusiasm. In December Hickes reported disaffection among some of the bishops he had met, whose doubts of Lauderdale's good faith he attempted to quell:

> And yet the lords of the party had so far insinuated themselves into the clergy as to make some of them suspect his [Lauderdale's] sincerity to the church. This I found everywhere in the late tours I made about the country, and I think I was more capable than any other single man to cure their jealousies, wherewith some bishops were but too much possessed.[81]

In late December a list of suggestions for the conduct of the campaign was drawn up by the bishops.[82] On the whole it repeated the terms of the king's letter to the Council in December, but it also took the trouble to insist that the troops should confine themselves to quartering on dissenters:

> and thus ye innocent and orderlie people will find themselves eased and encouraged to continue in their orderliness and obedience.

They further urged that the fines should be paid into a central fund. It is possibly significant that the instructions of 18 January 1678 did not include these *caveats* and were not signed by the two archbishops although they were present.[83] These stipulations perhaps may be thought to betray a fear that the soldiery would simply indulge in indiscriminate quartering and plundering. In February, when the grotesque excesses of the campaign had become apparent, Sharp made his disapproval of events very plain to Sir William Bruce, who had taken him to task.[84]

Even though Lauderdale's policy had perhaps failed to win over the Scottish bishops to wholehearted endorsement, their complaints and hesitations were negligible compared with the truly colossal rage of Hamilton. From the time when the project became public knowledge, he made up his mind not to be associated with it in any way. He intended at first to retire to England[85] until that was made impossible by a decree of the Privy Council on 3 January.[86]

When he was ordered to attend a committee of the Council with reference to the coming campaign,[87] he pleaded sciatica and did not attend.[88] By this means he no doubt meant to keep his own hands clean, the better to accuse others. As early as 3 January Hickes was anticipating that Hamilton would ally himself with the English Parliament and complain of arbitrary government in Scotland.[89] The conduct of the campaign gave him ample extra ammunition, for as might have been expected the soldiery ran wild and plundered and destroyed indiscriminately from their mobilisation late in January until the end of April.[90] Possibly for this reason the Council ordered the Highlanders to be sent home at the end of February,[91] and their duties were taken over by militia regiments.

To compound all these errors, the fact that English and Irish troops had been alerted before the campaign was begun created grave suspicion of what Lauderdale might do with the very considerable number of troops thus amassed, and gave the perfect excuse for his English political allies once more to attack him. It is extremely difficult to know whether Lauderdale had carried on this campaign with half an eye to Charles's interests in England. Gilbert Burnet certainly thought that the whole venture was to justify keeping up an army,[92] and Wodrow thought so too.[93] Sir John Dalrymple of Stair, a presbyterian sympathiser, who had been at some trouble not to get involved with the campaign, thought it was part of a larger plot to raise an army by the duke of York.[94] All of these men had good reason to draw such an interpretation, and there seems to be no more objective evidence. It is certain, however, that this was how Lauderdale's political enemies found it convenient to interpret his actions.

The deeper waters into which Lauderdale was thus plunging were made ever deeper by a further manifestation of the policy of severity against dissenters: the trial and execution of James Mitchell. The act of 4 September 1677 appointing officers of state to hold office only during royal pleasure had probably been the means of replacing Nisbet as Lord Advocate with Sir George Mackenzie. There are a number of reasons given for this change. Perhaps the most convincing is that given by Hickes in which he asserts that Nisbet was a sympathiser with presbyterians; 'being a fanatic' is Hickes's phrase.[95] Mackenzie was instructed in October to bring Mitchell to trial.[96] The trial eventually took place in January and was badly mismanaged. The excerpt from the Privy Council Registers was read out in court, showing that Mitchell had been granted indemnity in 1674, and although it was declared inadmissible evidence, Lauderdale, Sharp, Hatton and Rothes, who had sworn in court that no promise had been made, were publicly shown to have committed perjury.[97] It seems that Lauderdale had forgotten that the promise had been made, or so it was explained by Gilbert Burnet,[98] who had no interest in exonerating him. Possibly a more likely explanation was that he had never considered it possible that the excerpt could be read. Indeed, it was only made possible by the defection from Lauderdale's party of Sir Archibald Primrose who obtained the extract,[99] and it was he who was Burnet's informant. Here again, whatever the truth of the matter, it was certain what interpretation would be put upon the episode by Lauderdale's political enemies.

As early as February reports were reaching Charles of the excesses of the Highland Host. At a meeting in late March Hamilton's son Arran heard the king justify Lauderdale's conduct against complaints made of it. [100] When the party ventured to London to state their case themselves, [101] the danger was much greater. Hickes exhorted his London friends to stand by Lauderdale for, in his opinion, the whole future of the church and monarchy lay in the balance:

> If his Majesty be persuaded to hearken to them [the party], and so much as check the Council, and stop their proceedings, farewell the Church, and the royal authority for ever in this land. [102]

In fear of their political life, Lauderdale and the Privy Council sent representatives to London to justify their behaviour, [103] and these were accompanied by Alexander Burnet to support Lauderdale and present the bishops' approval of what had been done. [104] In addition Hickes, with Lauderdale's approval, [105] had printed at London his account of Mitchell's trial in a pamphlet entitled *Ravillac Redivivus,* [106] and an account of the Council's proceedings was ordered to be published in Edinburgh. [107]

For two months, from early April to early June 1678, the war between the two Scottish parties was carried on in London. [108] Lauderdale's allies attempted to influence the king by emphasising the danger of rebellion and the necessity for severity at a time of crisis. Such an appeal was well calculated at the outset of the political manoeuvres later to be known as the Exclusion Crisis. [109] It was not, however, a strong enough line to prevent Charles enquiring into the truth of allegations about the Highland Host, and being prepared to listen to the Hamilton party's version of events. Moreover, during their time in London the party made it their business to confer with members of the House of Commons and to provide them with further ammunition for a renewed attack on Lauderdale in May. In addition the king ordered the disbanding of all troops but the Life Guard and an end to imposing fines, [110] although an indemnity was offered to those involved in the expedition. [111] The king also forbade the Privy Council to proceed against those members of the party who had gone to London in defiance of the proclamation of 3 January. [112]

Nevertheless the contest was by no means a clear victory for the party. The attack on Lauderdale in the Commons failed because of the king's continued support for his Secretary. The English bishops stood firm by him also. The king granted Lauderdale permission to hold a Convention in Scotland with himself as Commissioner, [113] and not a Parliament as the party had wished, thus denying them the occasion for a full-scale ventilation of their grievances like that attempted in the Parliament of 1673. Furthermore, this Convention was summoned for the express purpose of levying money for the support of troops to repress dissent. [114] The next step for Hamilton, therefore, was to use the Convention to attack Lauderdale [115] despite the fact that such assemblies were intended only for granting supply. This challenge was repulsed with the help of the bishops and Lauderdale, for the moment in control, returned to court.[116]

Lauderdale's temporary escape from political disaster had been effected to a considerable extent by his ecclesiastical allies. He could not hope that Hamilton would now cease to challenge him, and consequently he was, as before, still dependent on Sharp and Alexander Burnet in Scotland. Their letters made it crystal clear in the remaining months of 1678 that their tactics and sentiments with regard to the dissenters remained unchanged, and that they expected Lauderdale to continue the policies implied in the Highland Host expedition. In July Burnet wrote to Archbishop Sancroft, Sheldon's successor at Canterbury, expressing dissatisfaction with the defeat of the party and hoping for a return to severity against dissent:

> I shall only say, that there is now a foundation laid for suppressing the insolencies of our seditious conventiclers; and if our forces be well commanded, and the laws duely putt in execution, we may hope yet to see a serene calme.[117]

Similar expressions of rigour were contained in letters from the Bishop of Galloway in September[118] and from Sharp in November.[119] Moreover, in November a gathering of eight of the bishops decided to dispatch one of their number to urge the king to action

> upon reasons which appear to us to be of great importance for the quiet and interest of this church.[120]

The nature of the advice to be so offered could hardly be in doubt. In January 1679 the Committee for Public Affairs, of which Sharp and the Bishop of Galloway were members, made recommendations to the king for the continued repression of dissent by means of the lately raised forces.[121]

These policies, however, must indubitably drive Lauderdale yet further into danger from Hamilton who, in the late summer of 1678, after the Convention, had again complained of Lauderdale to the king, and although not triumphant had at least been heard,[122] and according to report had gone so far as to tell the king that it was impossible to establish episcopacy in Scotland. The potential danger of this situation progressively increased from the summer of 1678 over the Exclusion Crisis. The revelations of the Popish Plot had been used by the opposition to the king in the English Parliament to destroy Danby, the king's most skilful supporter. It was extremely doubtful whether Charles would be able to rescue his Secretary from yet another onslaught.

In 1679 that onslaught came.[123] The English 'Cavalier' Parliament had been dissolved in January of 1679 after the Commons under Shaftesbury's guidance had proved capable of exploiting the revelations of the Popish Plot. The First Exclusion Parliament which replaced it was considerably less well disposed to the court interest. Consequently, when Lauderdale was attacked first of all on 25 March by Shaftesbury in the Lords and then on 8 May in the Commons,[124] he could not expect the same degree of support. Shaftesbury's speech had specifically criticised the Highland Host expedition, and it seemed clear that he was being prompted by Hamilton. Events in Scotland proceeded to make Lauderdale's position even less secure. Growing unrest, exemplified by the conflict between a conventicle and troops at Lesmahagow,[125] culminated on 3 May 1679 in the murder of Sharp,[126] and was followed in early June by a defeat for the government forces at Loudoun Hill.[127] These events were represented by Shaftesbury in a meeting of the English Privy Council as further evidence of Lauderdale's misgovernment. Although Charles stood by Lauderdale, he met Hamilton and a number of supporters in July[128] and allowed them to make their complaints at a conference at which both sides were represented.[129]

There were three published attacks on Lauderdale made in 1679. All of them seem to have been made on the basis of information supplied by Hamilton and his allies, and each included a specific condemnation of ecclesiastical policy. The first such paper, *An Account of Scotland's grievances under Duke Lauderdale tendered to the King,* was probably the substance of Hamilton's argument at the meeting at Windsor in July. The second paper, *Particular Matters of Fact relating to the Administration of affairs in Scotland under the Duke of Lauderdale,* was circulated in Scotland, where Lauderdale made efforts to suppress it.[130] The third paper was *Some farther matter of Fact relating to the Administration of affairs in Scotland, under the Duke of Lauderdale.* It is interesting that despite these attacks Lauderdale apparently made no attempt to get his own back with attacks on Hamilton. Furthermore, because the Scottish Privy Council had written to Lauderdale that the Scottish troops would be unable to control the rising,[131] English troops under Monmouth were sent north[132] and defeated the rebels at Bothwell Brig on 22 June.

Thus not only had Lauderdale been attacked by the Parliamentary opposition to the crown at a time when it was progressively more difficult for Charles to defend him; his ecclesiastical policy had proved inadequate to perform its most essential function of maintaining peace in Scotland. Events had provided Charles's enemies with exactly the opportunity of using Scotland as a lever against him, which it had been Lauderdale's function to prevent. The solution, therefore, seemed to be to silence the opposition, both English and Scottish, by putting into practice policies of leniency which Hamilton had so long espoused.

It is just possible that Lauderdale was behind the instructions to Monmouth[133] and the Declaration of Indulgence which was proclaimed with an indemnity for the rebels on 4 July,[134] and the invitation sent to Leighton on 16 July asking him to go to Scotland and there help to put into force policies of 'clemency'.[135] Lauderdale may have thought that the death of Sharp would release him from his dependence upon the bishops and their policies, and that he could triumph over Hamilton by appropriating his ideas. As had previously been demonstrated on numerous occasions, Lauderdale was by no means implacably set against Indulgence and may have hoped that this time it would succeed where previously it had failed. If indeed this was Lauderdale's judgment, it was a truly colossal gamble that he could recoup his fortunes by an about face. Furthermore he was almost certainly not behind one manifestation of the new policy of leniency. William Veitch, a conventicle preacher, was arrested in England and sent to Edinburgh for trial. He was able to inform Shaftesbury of his case. Shaftesbury then took the opportunity to represent the case as an unwarrantable assault on the rights of an English subject. Under such pressure the king ordered the Privy Council to release the prisoner. This instruction was a direct affront to Lauderdale's authority. [136]

A more likely explanation of this reversal of policy, and one that accords with the king's decision to confer with Hamilton, is that Charles was prepared to sacrifice Lauderdale in the interests of the crown's political fortunes in England. On August 13 a special meeting of the Privy Council was called and as many members as possible required to be present to hear a royal statement of policy on the course of action to be pursued in the wake of the rising. [137] On that day a letter was read from the king indicating that, despite previous declarations of support for Lauderdale as recently as 17 July, [138] the king had been greatly influenced by the party's representations, and publishing an indemnity extending the king's pardon to virtually all past offenders against ecclesiastical law. [139] By October the decision had been taken that the duke of York should go to Scotland. The effect of this move was to bring an end to Lauderdale's control of ecclesiastical policies and to permit new initiatives.

11
Epilogue: The Wheel Turns

IN the period 1660-1679 it has been possible to trace how Lauderdale was gradually pressured, by considerations primarily political, into abandoning the presbyterian sympathies of his youth and acquiescing in the imposition of an erastian episcopacy. Furthermore it has been possible to see that the difficulty of this task had by degrees induced him to acquiesce in methods of enforcement ever less acceptable to the political nation.

When Monmouth declared indemnity and indulgence in 1679, it seemed possible that the entail of Lauderdale's political inheritance might be broken and that an opportunity for a fresh perspective on the ecclesiastical situation might be taken. Such hopes were possible throughout the duke of York's first visit to Scotland but did not survive the summer of 1680. By 1681 it was clear that ecclesiastical policy would continue on the same melancholy path. Moreover it was also clear that the continued repression of dissent was the result of the political self-interest of the parties concerned, and not of any objective analysis of dissenting activity.

In August 1679 Charles had suddenly been taken ill and it seemed as though he might die. James his brother was at this time discreetly in exile in Brussels and was hastily summoned to England. When Charles recovered, James's place of exile was commuted to Edinburgh. This move did not meet with Lauderdale's favour. When the duke was required to take the Oath of Allegiance on becoming an active member of the Council, he refused as a Catholic. The Council applied to Lauderdale for advice[1] and he advised that James must take the oath.[2] It seems possible that by this means he hoped to make it impossible for James to supplant him. The move failed, and James took his place in the Council without swearing the oath, with the king's allowance.[3] James was active in the Council in Scotland from December 1679 to February 1680 and again from October 1680 until 1682. Although he was a known papist and therefore hardly the man to appeal to the dissenters, yet it seems that the initial effect of his presence was to calm the raging animosities of Scottish politics[4] and commend policies of moderation. According to Gilbert Burnet, he was recommended for the position by Tweeddale, who was anxious to keep Lauderdale out and thought that James would avoid party politics.[5] The first stay was too brief for much to be gleaned from it, but three factors point to a more reasonable temper of affairs. Firstly the bishops were by no means satisfied by the turn of events. They protested in July to Lauderdale against 'the prevalence of schism and libertism',[6] by which Monmouth's concessions were clearly meant. In September and again in December Alexander Burnet, now archbishop of St Andrews, complained of the Indulgence and the plight of the church.[7] He did not dare complain of James and indeed in January 1680 admitted in a letter to Sancroft that James had treated the bishops well:

> His Royal Highnesse hath been very faire and friendly to us since he came into this country, and gives us all the encouragement that in justice and reason we can expect.[8]

It was clear from their complaints, however, that the days when the bishops dictated policy to Lauderdale were over, and that James was bound by no such ties.

A second more hopeful feature of James's first brief visit was the return of members of the opposition to the Privy Council. Queensberry, who had begun to assume the leadership of the party from Hamilton, had been admitted to the Council in July 1679[9] and began to attend regularly from September. Dundonald, who had been absent for much of 1679, returned to regular attendance in December. Atholl and Perth, who had both deserted Lauderdale after the Highland Host, both began to attend the Council regularly in December. If the Council could once again comprehend a variety of opinions instead of representing simply a claque of Lauderdale's supporters, there was hope that ecclesiastical policy might be redeemed from the nadir to which it had lately sunk.

Lastly, James associated himself with a desire for moderation. Before he left Scotland in 1680, he addressed a homily to the Privy Council in which he exhorted them to reasonable courses:

> he recommended to them to continue in promoving his Majesties service and the peace and quiet of the kingdome, and therein to use such moderation as may most conduce to these ends and purposes.[10]

There is little doubt that James spoke in this vein from political motives. Monmouth's initiatives after Bothwell Brig in ecclesiastical affairs had been a great success and had given him much political support among Scots. James needed to transfer that support to himself and hoped to do so by taking a middle line. On at least one occasion, in 1675,[11] he had been prepared to support the Hamilton party in London, so although his natural affinity was for the very party and policies that Lauderdale had espoused, there was some opportunity for him to draw support from a wider base and to commend less extreme measures. He voiced these sentiments in a letter to England in December:

> I live here as cautiously as I can, and am very carfull to give offence to none, and to have no partialitys and preach to them laying a side all privat animositys and securing the King his owne way . . . and tho some of either party here might have hoped I should have shewd my partiality for them . . . yett I am convinced it was not fitt for me to do it . . . I find the generality of best men much troubled at the indulgence . . . and say it will encourage them to another rebellion. I am of that opinion, tho I do not think it proper to take it from them till they forfitt it againe.[12]

The implication of the letter was that, when convenient, the middle way of moderation would be abandoned - and so it very soon proved.

In the period from March till James's return to Scotland in October 1680, this hopeful interlude was brought to an end. The fundamental reason for this change seems to have been that the bishops, fearing their loss of power under the terms of the third Indulgence, sent a representative to London who by intrigue with Lauderdale, Sancroft and James procured an end to it, and a return to policies of repression. The initiative for this development came from the English bishops, as Alexander Burnet confided to Lauderdale in February 1680:

> We had the honour to receive a very kind letter from his Grace of Canterbury and some others of my lords of the English clergy, by which we are encouraged (if not invited) to send up one of our member . . . to represent to them the true state and condition of our affairs.[13]

In a further letter Burnet went on to indicate just what the description of their 'affairs' would amount to, and to solicit Lauderdale's help:

> We judged it necessary to send up my lord of Edinburgh to attend you and the bishops of England, and to represent by your joint advice and assistance some things which are very grievous and uneasy to the orderly clergy here.[14]

The object of the English bishops in extending this invitation was to find an additional rod to beat Monmouth. It was a project in which the Scottish bishops were happy to concur, as Burnet revealed:

> Your Grace knows how and by whom that Indulgence was obtained, and how furiously it was driven on, and in what a business which was so much precipitated it is no wonder that many things may deserve a second and serious consideration.[15]

It was also, however, a project congenial to James, as his letter from Scotland had shown. In the early months of 1680, after his return from Scotland, James had much influence at court and was eager to score against an ever more obstreperous Monmouth.[16] Thus a policy was devised which effectively put an end to Monmouth's concessions.[17] In June orders were given to proceed against those attending conventicles, or those who had not yet accepted the indemnity, and to return to the policy of garrisoning the west.[18] This was followed by instructions for 'regulating' the Indulgence[19] which placed many more restrictions upon the terms on which it could be conferred. Not surprisingly, this development gave the bishops much satisfaction and induced them to pay their thanks to Sancroft and the English bishops:

> We have been exceedingly refreshed . . . with the success of our brother's negotiation, by which . . . we are much relieved from our fears of the irreparable prejudice the Church and the monarchie must needs have sustained by the late unhappy indulgence granted to the bitter and irreconcilable enemies of both; had it not been brought within due limits by this just and necessary regulation.[20]

A number of conclusions can be drawn from these events. First it is clear that the reversal of Monmouth's policy was not primarily the result of dissenting activity. Presbyterian writers[21] and the Privy Council records testify to the absence of conventicling at this time. The long-awaited major split among the dissenters had finally become public and unmanageable over Bothwell Brig.[22] As a result the concessions offered by Monmouth had met with a much better reception than previous similar concessions. In the months following the battle the majority of the dissenters had shown themselves willing to comply with the Indulgence. The only significant opposition had been from an irreconcilable minority. Their doings were known to James but were dismissed by him as of no great importance.[23] Not until March 1680 did the Privy Council find it necessary to reconstitute the Committee for Public Affairs to deal with conventicles,[24] whereas the Bishop of Edinburgh had left for London in February. The Council's action then and their suggestions for further measures to be taken, in April and May,[25] were doubtless taken into account in framing the new legislation, but it seems fairly clear that the nature of the measures had already been decided.[26]

Secondly this redirection of policy indicated the return of the bishops to their role as makers and arbiters of policy. The implications for ecclesiastical peace were not hopeful.

Lastly the brief opportunity to settle the Scottish church had been allowed to disappear. The members of the party, once returned to participation in the Council, had apparently abandoned their concern for the dissenters. It is probably not too harsh to say that their opposition to Lauderdale's ecclesiastical policy lasted only so long as they were barred from policy-making themselves.

From the summer of 1680, therefore, ecclesiastical policy reverted to the policies of severity that Lauderdale had latterly been unwillingly brought to espouse. The details of those policies and their day-to-day evolution are beyond the scope of this book. Suffice it only to say that the excesses of the Cameronians in the summer of 1680[27] lent colour to the claim that dissenters were a continuing danger, and allowed the continued maintenance of military forces. The resignation of Lauderdale as Secretary of State was followed by the appointment of the Earl of Moray, a nominee of Lauderdale,[28] and totally acceptable to the Scottish bishops who claimed him as

> the most affectionate and constant friend, that we have met with; and . . . as much concerned for this poore Church as any of our owne number.[29]

Finally, the duke of York returned to Scotland in November 1680, no longer desperate for support but entrusted with a Commission to settle the kingdom. His interpretation of that instruction confirmed in 1681 the direction which ecclesiastical policy had already resumed:

> His [James's] administration in Scotland against non-conformists . . . was a continuation of the rigours of Lauderdale, who, by the fury of his temper, had brought a great part of his countrymen to such a state of mind, that it was become impossible to govern them, either by mercy or severity.[30]

During the next five years provocative policies kept the issue of dissent alive. The extirpation of the Cameronians, the most radical of the presbyterian nonconformists, was carried out at the same time as much more moderate men were inflamed by the legislation requiring subscription of the Act of Succession and the Test Act of 1681, which implied that the Catholic James would succeed to the throne. Ministers who refused the Test were deprived of their livings and thus enlarged further the number of outed ministers. Continued conventicling was meanwhile punished by quartering and fining and the Test used as a universal gauge of loyalty, and nonconformity was punished by imprisonment, transportation and even execution. Such was the fury of persecution between 1684 and 1687 that the period has become known as the 'Killing Times'.

This terror was brought to an end in 1687 by Indulgences designed to benefit James VII's Catholic subjects, but in the process offering considerable relief to presbyterians. The Revolution marked the end of the story, with the eventual triumph of toleration and the removal of religion from the sphere of politics. [31]

Abbreviations

APS	Acts of the Parliaments of Scotland
BM	British Museum
CSPD	Calendar of State Papers Domestic Series
GUL	Glasgow University Library
HMC	Historical Manuscripts Commission
LP	Lauderdale Papers
NLS	National Library of Scotland
RPC	Registers of the Privy Council
RSCHS	Records of the Scottish Church History Society
SHR	Scottish Historical Review
SHS	Scottish History Society
SRO	Scottish Record Office

K

Notes

Chapter 2

1. For a general outline of the progress of negotiations to that end see G. Davies, *The Restoration of Charles II* (London, 1955).

2. The early stages of this breach are described in David Stevenson, *Revolution and Counter-Revolution in Scotland, 1644-1651* (London, 1977). F. D. Dow, *Cromwellian Scotland* (Edinburgh, 1979) details much of the later development of the factions.

3. *Records of the Commissions of the General Assembly,* 3 vols., ed. A. F. Mitchell and James Christie (Edinburgh, 1892, 1896, 1909), III, 3.

4. For a comprehensive outline of the negotiations culminating in Charles's arrival in Scotland see *Charles II and Scotland in 1650,* ed. S. R. Gardiner (Edinburgh, 1894).

5. For Cromwell's justification of his actions see 'A Declaration of the Army of England upon their march into Scotland', *The Writings and Speeches of Oliver Cromwell,* 4 vols., ed. W. C. Abbott (Cambridge, Mass., 1937-47), II, 283-8.

6. For the deteriorating military situation see John Nicoll, *A Diary of Public Transactions and Other Occurences, chiefly in Scotland, from January 1650 to June 1667* (Edinburgh, 1836), 18-32.

7. *Records of Commissions* III, 10-12, 15-17, 26, 28-9, 33-40, 41-2, 49-58, 63-5.

8. *Ibid.,* III, 557-62, 94-106.

9. The text of the Engagement is most conveniently to be seen, with an accompanying explanatory note, in *A Source Book of Scottish History,* vol. III, ed. W. C. Dickinson and G. Donaldson, 2nd ed. (Edinburgh, 1961), 134-9.

10. This was an old argument, dating from the Act of Classes, for which see *Acts of the Parliaments of Scotland* [hereafter APS] VI, part ii, 143-7.

11. *Records of Commissions* III, 561.

12. *Ibid.,* III, 53, 57. As the Resolutioners later pointed out, *ibid.,* III, 395-6, to select from those declaring themselves repentant only those thought to be sincere, was an exercise hard to justify.

13. *Ibid.,* III, 129-30.

14. *Ibid.,* III, 130-2, 132-3.

15. *Ibid.,* III, 131, 132-3.

16. The existence of what was virtually a private army in the west of the country had been a matter of concern for some time. See for example *Records of Commissions* III, 62-3. Wariston in his diary speaks of it in terms of a partisan force, *The Diary of Sir Archibald Johnston of Wariston,* vol. II, ed. D. H. Fleming (Edinburgh, 1919), 28-30 and note. See also Nicoll, *Diary,* 30, 35-6. The role of Gillespie and Guthrie, *Records of Commissions* III, 124, 128-9, was clearly also of concern to the Committee of Estates and the Commission.

17. *Records of Commissions* III, 132, and *sederunts.*

18. The best sources of information on this period are David Stevenson, *Revolution and Counter-Revolution in Scotland, 1644-1651* (London, 1977) and Walter Makey, *The Church of the Covenant, 1637-1651* (Edinburgh, 1979).

19. See the *sederunts* for 28 November and thereafter: *Records of Commissions* III, 130ff.

20. This process had been going on since mid-September, but numbers increased enormously after the split, *ibid.,* III, 135ff.

21. *Ibid.,* III, 164-5, 193-5, 216-28, 236-40.

22. The names 'Protester' and 'Remonstrant' seem to have been used with equal freedom, but for the sake of consistency the word 'Protester' will here be used to apply to the party of ministers within the church.

23. From the following presbyteries, *Records of Commissions* III: Stirling (173-82); Glasgow (196-9); Aberdeen (243-51); Paisley (255); Deer (274-6); Irvine (276-9); Dunfermline (293); Ayr (298); Hamilton (362-3) and from the Synod of Dumfries (460-2).

24.   From the following, *ibid.,* III: Province of Fife (379-81); Synod of Angus (386-7); University of St Andrews (412-4); Synod of Moray (418-9); Presbytery of Chanrie in Ross (429-31); Presbytery of Glasgow (464-6); University of Glasgow (466-8); Presbytery of Dumbarton (487-9); Province of Perth (490-2).

25.   For arrangements for such meetings, often abortive, to July 1651, *Records of Commissions* III, 233-4, 252, 260, 273, 293, 294, 311, 392-3, 397-400, 403, 411-2, 420, 421, 428-9, 444-5, 460.

26.   J. D. Ogilvie, 'A Bibliography of the Resolutioner-Protester Controversy, 1650-1659' *(Edinburgh Bibliographical Society Publications* XIV, 1928-30), 59-74.

27.   *Acts of the General Assembly of the Church of Scotland, 1638-1842* (Edinburgh, 1843), 220; *Scotland and the Commonwealth,* ed. C. H. Firth (Edinburgh, 1895), 19.

28.   *Records of Commissions* III, 525, 532-4, 539-40, 540-3, 550-1, 552-6; Wariston, *Diary* II, 93-4, 98, 135 and note, 150 and note, 164, 169, 180-1.

29.   *Register of the Consultations of the Ministers of Edinburgh and some other Brethren of the Ministry,* 2 vols, ed. Wm. Stephen (Edinburgh, 1921, 1930), I, 2.

30.   *Scotland and the Commonwealth,* 47-8, 133, 260; *Scotland and the Protectorate,* ed. C. H. Firth (Edinburgh, 1899), 32-3; *A Collection of the State Papers of John Thurloe,* 7 vols., ed. Thomas Birch (London, 1742), I, 664.

31.   Thurloe, *Papers* I, 159; *Calendar of State Papers (Domestic Series) Interregnum* [hereafter CSPD], 1651, 400.

32.   See for example the fulminations on these issues in Wariston, *Diary* II, *passim,* on the Protesting side; for the Resolutioner view see *Consultations of the Ministers of Edinburgh* I, 80-7, and also Robert Baillie, *Letters and Journals* [hereafter Baillie] 3 vols., ed. D. Laing (Edinburgh, 1822), III, 166, 174, 316.

33.   *Scotland and the Commonwealth,* 6-7, 192, 265, 369-70; Thurloe, *Papers* I, 478.

34.   Baillie III, 207-8 and note, 244, 245, 248.

35.   *Ibid,* II, 249; H. R. Trevor-Roper, 'Scotland and the Puritan Revolution', in *Historical Essays 1600-1750, presented to David Ogg* (London, 1963), 78-130.

36.   See for example their reaction to 'Gillespie's Charter', which was one of the Cromwellian programmes for concessions to the Protester party: *Register of Consultations* I, 57-69.

37.   See Wariston's repeated agonising on this point: *Diary* II, *passim.*

38.   *Scotland and the Commonwealth,* 122-3, 241, 271; *Scotland and the Protectorate,* 62, 80.

39.   *Scotland and the Commonwealth,* 122-3, 127, 242, 262, 271; Thurloe, *Papers* II, 18; *Scotland and the Protectorate,* 41, 57, 65.

40.   Wariston, *Diary* II, 214-5 and note.

41.   *Consultations of the Ministers of Edinburgh* I, 70.

42.   Wariston, *Diary* II, 250, 258.

43.   Thurloe, *Papers,* II, 221, 261.

44.   For an account of these see Baillie III, 276, 279, 296-7.

45.   Thurloe, *Papers* IV, 56-8, 127-8, 223, 250, 282, 479, 557-9, 646, 741; V, 301, 323. J.M.Buckroyd, 'Lord Broghill and the Scottish Church, 1655-1656' *(Journal of Ecclesiastical History,* XXVII, 1976), 359-68.

46.   Baillie III, 352, 357, 361.

47.   GUL Ms Gen 210, 18, 21, 23, 54, 64.

48.   There is no even moderately satisfactory biography of Sharp. The only full-length work ever attempted is Thomas Stephen, *The Life and Times of Archbishop Sharp of St Andrews* (London, 1839). Unfortunately it is a violently partisan work.

49.   An attempt is made in the *Annals of Banff,* ed. W. Cramond, 2 vols. (Aberdeen, 1891-3), *passim,* to sort out some of the details of Sharp's early life.

50.   S. J. Spalding, *History of the Troubles and Memorable Transactions in Scotland 1624-1645* (Aberdeen, 1830) and J. Gordon, *History of Scots Affairs,* 3 vols. (Aberdeen, 1841).

51.   There are two contemporary or near contemporary biographies of Sharp, neither of them very reliable. The first, *The Life of Mr James Sharp,* was published while Sharp was still alive in 1678. The second, *A True and Impartial Account of the Most Reverend Father in God Dr James*

Sharp, was not published until 1723, although it is said to have been written some years earlier. This particular detail about his performance at the grammar school comes from *True and Impartial Account,* and is reluctantly seconded by *Life of Mr James Sharp.*

52.　*Roll of Alumni in Arts of the University and King's College,* ed. P. J. Anderson (Aberdeen, 1900), 12.

53.　*Officers and Graduates of the University and King's College of Aberdeen, 1485-1860,* ed. P. J. Anderson (Aberdeen, 1893), 187.

54.　*True and Impartial Account,* 28.

55.　W. G. S. Snow, *The Times, Life and Thought of Patrick Forbes, Bishop of Aberdeen 1618-1635* (London, 1952), 154-5.

56.　*Ibid.,* 83; G. D. Henderson, *The Burning Bush* (Edinburgh, 1957), 75-6.

57.　Snow, *Patrick Forbes,* 82-3.

58.　I am indebted to Professor E. G. Rupp and Dr I. B. Cowan for helpful discussions on this issue.

59.　Snow, *Patrick Forbes,* 83; Henderson, *Burning Bush,* 75-6.

60.　J. Gordon, *History* I, 50-1, 82-3, 87-94.

61.　For a bibliography, J. D. Ogilvie, 'The Aberdeen Doctors and The National Covenant' *(Edinburgh Bibliographical Society Publications* XI, 1912-20), 73-86.

62.　J. Gordon, *History* II, 226.

63.　*True and Impartial Account,* 29; *Life of Mr James Sharp,* 13.

64.　The assertion in the *True and Impartial Account,* 29, that Sharp associated with Taylor, Hammond and Sanderson is almost certainly wrong.

65.　This has been established by Mr Smart, archivist of St Andrews University, to whom I am indebted. The document is: St Andrews University Muniments SL705/1, 147.

66.　*Life of Mr James Sharp,* 13-15. There seems no good reason to doubt this, especially as the author goes to such lengths to excuse Henderson's error of judgment.

67.　For the negotiations and examinations from 3 Nov. 1647 to 27 Jan. 1648 leading up to his admission as minister of Crail see *Selections from the Minutes of the Presbyteries of St Andrews and Cupar,* ed. G. R. Kinloch (Edinburgh, 1837), 37-8.

68.　*Life of Mr James Sharp.* 18-25.

69.　I am indebted to the minister of Crail and his Kirk Session for permission to study the transcript of the Kirk Session records for the seventeenth century.

70.　*The Diary of Mr John Lamont of Newton,* ed. G. R. Kinloch (Edinburgh, 1830), 3-4.

71.　*Ibid.,* 11; *Records of Commissions* II, 310.

72.　The Edinburgh end of the correspondence in 1650 survives in first draft form in NLS Wodrow Folio LXV f.274, 276, 277, 278.

73.　*Minutes of the Presbyteries of St Andrews and Cupar, passim.*

74.　*Selections from the Minutes of the Synod of Fife 1611-1687,* ed. C. Baxter (Edinburgh, 1837), 155, 166, 177.

75.　*Record of Commissions* III, *passim.*

76.　Lamont, *Diary,* 34; Nicoll, *Diary,* 56-7.

77.　He was released from the Tower on 10 April 1652: CSPD 1651-2, 213, and on 1 July reported to the governor of Edinburgh Castle: *ibid.,* 312.

78.　*Records of Commissions* III, 535, 556. He was moderator of the provincial assembly of Fife held at Kirkcaldy in 1654, and was present at its meeting in 1655 which was dissolved by Cromwellian troops despite protest from Sharp. Lamont, *Diary,* 79, 86.

79.　*Register of Consultations* I, 201.

80.　*Ibid.,* I, 204ff.

81.　*Ibid.,* I, 204; II, 130.

82.　*Ibid.,* II, 130.

83.　*Ibid.*

84.　*Ibid.,* II, 148; Lamont, *Diary,* 113.

85.　*Register of Consultations* II, 191-2.

86.　*Ibid.,* II, 192.

87. *Register of Consultations* II, 192-3.
88. GUL Ms Gen 210, 3; R. Wodrow, *The History of the Sufferings of the Church of Scotland from the Restoration to the Revolution* [hereafter Wodrow], 4 vols., ed. R. Burns (Glasgow, 1828), 5n.
89. Davies, *Restoration,* 297-8.
90. Baillie III, 302, 326, 340.
91. GUL Ms Gen 210, 10.
92. *Ibid.,* 17, 27.
93. *Ibid.,* 11, 17, 20.
94. *Ibid.,* 11, 19.
95. *Ibid.,* 22. For a full-length statement of their desires in both civil and ecclesiastical government see *ibid.,* 66-74, reprinted in Wodrow I, 13-16n.
96. *Ibid.,* 17, 19, 57, 66, 75, 85.
97. *Ibid.,* 22, 23, 24, 42, 44, 47-8, 49, 52, 54, 58, 59-60.
98. *Ibid.,* 82, 85.
99. *Ibid.,* 86-7.
100. *Ibid.,* 18, 19, 21, 35, 37, 51-2, 55, 57, 64.
101. *Ibid.,* 20, 22, 24, 39, 50, 52, 53-4, 58, 59, 61, 63, 65, 75, 77-9, 83-4, 85-6, 87.
102. *Ibid.,* 3, 5, 11, 34, 36, 39, 50, 51, 56, 61, 64-5.
103. *Ibid.,* 85, 86.
104. *Ibid.,* 87.
105. *Ibid.,* 88-9, 93-6.
106. *Ibid.,* 96.
107. *Ibid.,* 96-7; Wodrow I, 23n, paras 1, 2, 3.
108. GUL Ms Gen 210, 97-8; Wodrow I, 24n.
109. Lauderdale's career is yet another aching void in seventeenth century Scottish historical writing. The biography of W. C. Mackenzie, *The Life and Times of John Maitland, Duke of Lauderale 1616-1682* (London, 1923) is outdated, but not so far replaced by a more modern work. Colin Beattie, 'The Early Career of John Maitland, Duke of Lauderdale, 1637-1651' M.A., McGill, 1977, was completed too late to be used for this book.
110. Maurice Lee's biography, *John Maitland of Thirlestane* (Princeton, N. J., 1959) gives an idea of their stature.
111. The following details of the first earl's political career are taken from Stevenson, 'Covenanters', 195, 307, 331, 378-9, 401.
112. Stevenson, 'Covenanters', 307, 309, an instance when father and son voted differently on the same issue.
113. I am indebted for this information to Mr R. Smart, Keeper of the Muniments at the University of St Andrews.
114. For this period at St Andrews see R. G. Cant, *The University of St Andrews,* new edition (Edinburgh, 1970), 45-66.
115. Gilbert Burnet, *The History of My Own Time,* 2 vols, ed. O. Airy, (Oxford, 1897, 1900) I, 184; *Lauderdale Papers,* [hereafter *LP*] 3 vols., ed. O. Airy (London, 1884-5) I, 157.
116. I am indebted to the present earl of Lauderdale for a copy of the catalogue.
117. For Lauderdale's career to 1647 see Baillie I, 379, 389; II, *passim;* Stevenson, 'Covenanters', 342, 365, 535.
118. Stevenson, 'Covenanters', 536.
119. *Ibid.,* 542, 544.
120. *Ibid.,* 545.
121. *Ibid.,* 552-3.
122. *Ibid.,* 556.
123. *Ibid.,* 557.
124. *Ibid.,* 563.
125. *Ibid.,* 559-61; Baillie III, 33-4.
126. Stevenson, 'Covenanters', 588, 602; Baillie III, 64.

127. Stevenson, 'Covenanters', 588-9; Baillie III, 52.

128. Stevenson, 'Covenanters', 602.

129. *Ibid.,* 669.

130. APS VI ii, 143-8.

131. Stevenson, 'Covenanters', 621-2.

132. *Ibid.,* 641-5; Baillie III, 73.

133. Stevenson, 'Covenanters', 684.

134. *Ibid.,* 722, 732, 736-7.

135. Baillie III, 230, 265, 401.

136. *Register of Consultations* II, 35, 36-8, 89, 98, 151; Thurloe, *Papers* VI, 238-9.

137. GUL Ms Gen 210, 7, 11, 14, 16.

138. *Ibid.,* 18, 20, 28, 51, 56, 62, 65, 66, 80, 81.

139. *Ibid.,* 24, 29-33, 38, 55, 63-4.

140. *Ibid.,* 20, 22, 39, 50, 53, 54, 58.

141. G. H. Jones, *Charles Middleton* (London, 1967). Chapter I gives a biography of John Middleton.

142. *Records of Commissions,* III, 90, 156, 172-3; James Kirkton, *The Secret and True History of the Church of Scotland from the Restoration to the Year 1678,* ed. C. K. Sharpe (Edinburgh, 1817), 109; Burnet, *Own Time* I, 227.

143. James Turner, *Memoirs of his Own Life and Times* (Edinburgh, 1829), 100-131.

144. *Calendar of the Clarendon State Papers,* 5 vols., ed. W. D. Macray and F. J. Routledge *et. al.* (Oxford 1872-1970) IV, 59, 62, 439, 509.

Chapter 3

1. For this expedition see *LP* I, 23, 24-8; GUL Ms Gen 210, 92-3, 100-1, 108-10, 113-4, 116-20; *Cal. of Clarendon Papers* IV, 603, 647; V, 5, 6; Burnet, *Own Time* I, 165.

2. GUL Ms 210, 29-33.

3. *Ibid.,* 77.

4. *Ibid.,* 104-5. For more on this issue see J. M. Buckroyd, 'The Resolutioners and the Scottish Nobility in the early months of 1660' *(Studies in Church History* XII, 1975), 245-52.

5. Edward Hyde, Earl of Clarendon, *The Continuation of the Life of Edward Earl of Clarendon* (Oxford, 1761), 51-2. For this work the Mss page numbers are cited throughout.

6. Burnet, *Own Time* I, 195-6.

7. *Cal. of Clarendon Papers* IV, 624.

8. *LP* I, 28-30; Alexander Robertson, *Sir Robert Moray* (London, 1922), 105-8.

9. Burnet, *Own Time* I, 196-7.

10. GUL Ms Gen 210, 130, 133-4, 136.

11. GUL Ms Gen 210, 137.

12. *Ibid.,* 138-91.

13. Text in Wodrow I, 80-1.

14. Wodrow I, 80-2; Kirkton, *History,* 74-5.

15. Burnet, *Own Time,* 197-9; G. Davies and P. Hardacre, 'The Restoration of the Scottish Episcopacy' *(Journal of British Studies* I ii, 1960), 37.

16. *The Life of Robert Blair . . . containing his autobiography from 1593 to 1636 with supplement . . . to 1680 by his son in law Mr Wm Row,* ed. Thomas M'Crie (Edinburgh, 1848), 361-3; NLS Ms 2512 f. 3.

17. NLS Ms 597 f. 50; Baillie III, 441; Nicoll, *Diary,* 272, 279.

18. *Extracts from the Records of the Convention of the Royal Burghs of Scotland, 1615-1676,* ed. J. D. Marwick (Edinburgh, 1878), 499-503.

19. GUL Ms Gen 210, 136; Kirkton, *History,* 65-6; Nicoll, *Diary,* 295.

20. GUL Ms Gen 210, 122, 130; Row, *Life of Blair,* 353-4.

21. *LP* I, 32-3.

22. Davies & Hardacre, 'Restoration', 36.

23. CSPD 1660, 205, sec.73; Sir George MacKenzie of Rosehaugh, *Memoirs of the Affairs of Scotland,* ed. T. Thomson (Edinburgh, 1821), 10-12; Nicoll, *Diary,* 297.

24. See Wodrow I, 68-75 for documents relating to this incident. The minutes of the Committee are still extant in SRO Parliamentary Papers. Other accounts are found in Baillie III, 446ff; Row, *Life of Blair,* 356ff; Kirkton *History,* 72ff; Nicoll, *Diary,* 298; Burnet, *Own Time* I, 204; Mackenzie, *Memoirs,* 16.

25. BM Add Ms 23114 f. 42; Row, *Life of Blair,* 359.

26. Daniel Defoe, *Memoirs of the Church of Scotland* (London, 1717), 140.

27. *LP* II, App. B, lxx-iv. See also the letter from Douglas and Hutcheson to Lauderdale: *ibid.,* I, 35.

28. *LP* I, 39. The instructions are dated 17 Dec.

29. The only source for this meeting is Clarendon, *Continuation,* 54-7.

30. Davies & Hardacre, 'Restoration', 40.

31. GUL Ms Gen 210, 132; Baillie III, 406.

32. *Cal. of Clarendon Papers* V, 176; for further description of this document see Davies & Hardacre, 'Restoration', 39-40.

33. Row, *Life of Blair,* 353; Kirkton, *History,* 59.

34. Kirkton, *History,* 66-7.

35. *LP* I, 291.

36. *Mercurius Caledonius* 31 Dec. 1660-8, Jan. 1661; Nicoll, *Diary,* 310-1, 315-6; Kirkton, *History,* 87.

37. APS VII, 6-7.

38. For this incident see Cassillis' letters, *Camden Miscellany* VIII (London, 1883), 'Letters to the Earl of Lauderdale', 2-7; Mackenzie, *Memoirs,* 23; *LP* I, 62, 63; Row, *Life of Blair,* 372-3; Baillie III, 461; Kirkton, *History,* 91.

39. *LP* I, 291, 62.

40. *Ibid.,* 293.

41. APS VII, 12, 13.

42. Kirkton, *History,* 91-2.

43. APS VII, 16.

44. *Ibid.,* VII, 18.

45. *LP* I, 66.

46. *Ibid.,* I, 70, 72.

47. Text in Wodrow I, 110.

48. *LP* I, 70-71.

49. *Ibid.,* I, 71; Baillie III, 454.

50. *LP* I, 71, 72-3; for additional details on this issue see J. M. Buckroyd, *'Mercurius Caledonius'* (*SHR* LIV, 1975), 11-21.

51. APS VI, pt. 2, 287; *LP* I, 72.

52. *LP* I, 72.

53. *Ibid.,* 74, 75; text in Wodrow I, 111.

54. *LP* I, 77, 91.

55. *Ibid.,* I, 77.

56. *Ibid.,* I, 85.

57. *Ibid.,* I, 81-2.

58. Row, *Life of Blair,* 343, 356-7.

59. Mackenzie, *Memoirs,* 16.

60. Baillie III, 404. See HMC Laing I, 311-5 for a particularly vivid account of the Resolutioner attitude to the return of the king.

61. Baillie III, 448.

62. *Ibid.,* III, 415, 417.

63. *LP* I, 36-7.

64. *Ibid.,* I, 41, 84.

65. Kirkton, *History,* 70-1, 98, 109.

66. APS VII, 26.
67. *Ibid.,* VII, 12.
68. Row, *Life of Blair,* 376-7; Kirkton, *History,* 70.
69. Row, *Life of Blair,* 364, 376; *LP* I, 59; Nicoll, *Diary,* 321-3; Kirkton, *History,* 77, 117.
70. *LP* I, 61, 65, 68; *Mercurius Caledonius* 8-16 Jan., 16-25 Jan., 1-8 Feb., 1-8 Mar., 22-28 Mar; Row, *Life of Blair,* 374, 375, 377.
71. *Cal. of Clarendon Papers* V, 75.
72. Baillie III, 448; Row, *Life of Blair,* 370, 381; *LP* I, 91.
73. *LP* I, 69, 72.
74. Kirkton, *History,* 69, 78.
75. *Camden Miscellany* VIII, 'Letters to Lauderdale', 1-7; HMC Laing I, 319.
76. Row, *Life of Blair,* 373; Mackenzie, *Memoirs,* 23.
77. APS VII, 162; BM Add Ms 23116 f.1; Row, *Life of Blair,* 383.
78. *LP* I, 63.
79. *Cal. of Clarendon Papers* IV, 647.
80. Nicoll, *Diary,* 308; Row, *Life of Blair,* 360, 368.
81. *LP* I, 77. Burnet, *Own Time* I, 214 has 'Primrose proposed, but half in jest . . .'.
82. Row, *Life of Blair,* 378. Sir James Lockhart of Lee is a possible candidate for the fourth place. Sir John Gilmour was involved with Lauderdale's legal affairs and so attached to his interest: HMC Laing I, 316-7.
83. Davies & Hardacre, 'Restoration', 41.
84. *Ibid;* Kirkton, *History,* 88.
85. *Cal. of Clarendon Papers* V, 85-6.
86. *Ibid.,* V, 88, 90; Davies & Hardacre, 'Restoration', 44-5.
87. Davies & Hardacre, 'Restoration', 45; R. S. Bosher, *The Making of the Restoration Settlement* (London, 1951), 211.
88. *Cal. of Clarendon Papers* V, 88.
89. APS VII, 86-8.
90. For more on this, see Davies & Hardacre, 'Restoration', 45-6; Mackenzie, *Memoirs,* 27-9.
91. Burnet, *Own Time* I, 214-5.
92. Burnet, *Own Time* I, 216; Row, *Life of Blair,* 382.
93. NLS Ms 2512 f.6.
94. Burnet, *Own Time* I, 215; Row, *Life of Blair,* 381-2. Hamilton's dissent was on political grounds: HMC Hamilton (Supp.), 80-1.
95. Baillie III, 458-60.
96. *Ibid.,* III, 461.
97. Mackenzie, *Memoirs,* 28.
98. Kirkton, *History,* 117-8.
99. Wodrow I, 112-30.
100. BM Add Ms 23116 f.21.
101. Burnet, *Own Time* I, 216.
102. Mackenzie, *Memoirs,* 7, 8-9.
103. *Ibid.,* 6.
104. BM Add Ms 23115 f.71, 84.
105. *Ibid.,* f.29, 82; Add Ms 23116 f.27.
106. *LP* I, 92; Baillie III, 459.
107. BM Add Ms 23116 f.39.
108. APS VII, 193.
109. *LP* I, 45-94 *passim.*
110. Baillie III, 484-5.
111. APS VII, 193.
112. Baillie III, 460, 461.
113. NLS Ms 2512 f.8; Row, *Life of Blair,* 384.
114. NLS Ms 2512 f.6.

115. Baillie III, 468.
116. *LP* I, 96-7; NLS Ms 2512 f.8.
117. *LP* I, 89.
118. Row, *Life of Blair,* 362.
119. This document was known in Scotland: *ibid.,* 368.
120. Bosher, *Restoration Settlement,* 186-9. I am indebted to Dr H. Roseveare of the Institute of Historical Research for discussion on this point.
121. NLS Ms 2512 f.8.
122. Bosher, *Restoration Settlement,* 212-7.
123. Davies & Hardacre, 'Restoration', 48.
124. *LP* II, App. lxxviii.
125. That is the meaning I take from the sentence: 'And by what he [Clarendon] did ask of me and communicat to me of the King's purpose in reference to this Church and our Church, I found that which your Grace [Middleton] was pleased often to tell me was not without ground.'
126. *Cal. of Clarendon Papers* V, 73.
127. *LP* I, 88; Mackenzie, *Memoirs,* 24.
128. Burnet, *Own Time* I, 237.
129. *Ibid.,* I, 234. This is, I think, the likely interpretation of Burnet's comments on Sharp's behaviour at this time. Burnet was not, of course, present. See also NLS Ms 2512 f.6.
130. *LP* II, App. lxxviii.
131. *Ibid.,* Introduction.
132. Text in Wodrow I, 151-2n.
133. *LP* II, App. lxxxi.
134. NLS Ms 3136 f.143.
135. Row, *Life of Blair,* 399-400.
136. BM Add Ms 23116 f.76.
137. Kirkton, *History,* 128; Mackenzie, *Memoirs,* 52. For the atmosphere in London at this time and its effect on presbyterians see *The Diary of Alexander Brodie of Brodie* (Aberdeen, 1863), 197-236.
138. Mackenzie, *Memoirs,* 52-6; Burnet, *Own Time* I, 233-6; Kirkton, *History,* 129; Row, *Life of Blair,* 387, 390.
139. Text in Mackenzie, *Memoirs,* 57-9.
140. Mackenzie, *Memoirs,* 24-5; Row, *Life of Blair,* 381; Burnet, *Own Time* I, 194.
141. BM Add Ms 23116 f.86. They did not leave until the bishops were brought into Parliament: Row, *Life of Blair,* 407.
142. Mackenzie, *Memoirs,* 19, 52; Burnet, *Own Time* I, 230, 234.
143. Davies & Hardacre, 'Restoration', 50.

Chapter 4
1. Row, *Life of Blair,* 390-1; Burnet, *Own Time* I, 236-7.
2. Kirkton, *History,* 134.
3. See for instance Rothes' expressions of respect: *LP* I, 17.
4. NLS Ms 3922 f.17. This is the letter that Davies & Hardacre could not find: 'Restoration', 50n.
5. NLS Ms 2512 f.10; Row, *Life of Blair,* 395.
6. Kirkton, *History,* 135; NLS Wodrow Ms Quarto LXIII.
7. NLS Ms 2512 f.10.
8. Row, *Life of Blair,* 396.
9. Hew Scott, *Fasti Ecclesiae Scoticanae,* new ed. (Edinburgh, 1920), III, 240.
10. Appointed only to the Commission of the General Assembly of August 1652: *Register of Commissions* III, 519.
11. Baillie III, 468.
12. Burnet, *Own Time* I, 238; RPC I, 353.

13. *Mercurius Caledonius,* 8-15 March 1660.

14. Baillie III, 19, 34.

15. Robert Keith, *An Historical Catalogue of the Scottish Bishops,* new ed. (Edinburgh, 1824), 265.

16. Row, *Life of Blair,* 377n.

17. *Mercurius Caledonius,* 1-8 March 1661; Row, *Life of Blair,* 377.

18. For Leighton's early life see E. A. Knox, *Robert Leighton, Archbishop of Glasgow* (London, 1930), chapters V-XI; D. Butler, *The Life and Letters of Robert Leighton* (London, 1903), chapters V-X.

19. Burnet, *Own Time* I, 242-3.

20. *Ibid.,* I, 242.

21. Thurloe, *Papers* II, 513.

22. Butler, *Leighton,* 335, 338.

23. Row, *Life of Blair,* 399; Kirkton, *History,* 137; Burnet, *Own Time* I, 247-8.

24. Butler, *Leighton,* 305-7.

25. Baillie III, 487.

26. Kirkton, *History,* 120.

27. Keith, *Scottish Bishops,* 281.

28. Row, *Life of Blair,* 398. I am indebted to Professor G. Donaldson for bringing this fact to my notice.

29. Keith, *Scottish Bishops,* 62-3, 133.

30. *Ibid.,* 203-4, 218.

31. *The Humble Address of the Synod of Aberdeen* [Edinburgh, 1661], not signed by Patrick Forbes.

32. John Paterson, *Tandem Bona Causa Triumphat* (Edinburgh, 1661).

33. Scott, *Fasti* VI, 117.

34. *Ibid.,* IV, 230.

35. Row, *Life of Blair,* 375.

36. *Mercurius Caledonius,* 16-25 January 1661.

37. Scott, *Fasti* III, 77.

38. Baillie III, 134, 236, 279, 393, 420, 561; *Register of Commissions* III, 529.

39. Kirkton, *History,* 136.

40. *Register of Commissions* III, 500, 519.

41. Keith, *Scottish Bishops,* 152.

42. BM Add Ms 23117 f.17, 33, 34, 44, 46.

43. *Registers of the Privy Council of Scotland,* third series [hereafter RPC] I, 174.

44. *Register of Commissions* III, 499, 519.

45. Scott, *Fasti* V, 461.

46. *Ibid.,* II, 188.

47. Row, *Life of Blair,* 377n.

48. *Ibid.,* 415.

49. Kirkton, *History,* 131-2.

50. RPC I, 119, 130.

51. BM Add Ms 23117 f.11.

52. APS VII, 372, 376.

53. *Ibid.,* VII, 376.

54. Kirkton, *History,* 106-8; Row, *Life of Blair,* 386.

55. Mackenzie, *Memoirs,* 64-5; *LP* I, 147.

56. APS VII, 405-6.

57. Burnet, *Own Time* I, 258n.

58. Row, *Life of Blair,* 440-3. See Burnet, *Own Time* I, 230-2 for an earlier demonstration of Middleton's hostility to Crawford.

59. Mackenzie, *Memoirs,* 77-8; Burnet, *Own Time* I, 269; Kirkton, *History,* 149-50. The number of those initially outed is very uncertain, but it is almost certainly not as high as the three hundred which Kirkton claims, and which is the likely total to about 1666.

60. BM Add Ms 23115 f.84; Add Ms 23116 f.21.
61. Burnet, *Own Time* I, 187.
62. Mackenzie, *Memoirs*, 60-1.
63. RPC I, 36-7, 41-2, 53-4, 57-8, 61, 206; *LP* I, 99-103; BM Add Ms 23117 f.57; Burnet, *Own Time* I, 228, 230-1.
64. *LP* I, 103-5.
65. APS VII, 420.
66. Kirkton, *History*, 146; Row, *Life of Blair*, 417.
67. Mackenzie, *Memoirs*, 62-3; Row, *Life of Blair*, 403.
68. Nicoll, *Diary*, 365-6; Lamont, *Diary*, 146-7; Row, *Life of Blair*, 406-7.
69. Burnet, *Own Time* I, 252; W. R. Foster, *Bishop and Presbytery* (London, 1958), 38.
70. Row, *Life of Blair*, 399; Kirkton, *History*, 137; Burnet, *Own Time* I, 247-8.
71. NLS Ms 597 f.75; Row, *Life of Blair*, 405.
72. NLS Ms 2512 f.11. These indications of moderation are borne out by the continuation of existing forms of worship: G. D. Henderson, *Religious Life in Seventeenth Century Scotland* (Cambridge, 1937), chapter VII.
73. Row, *Life of Blair*, 425-6.
74. Kirkton, *History*, 150, 152; Burnet, *Own Time* I, 268-9.
75. *LP* I, 120; RPC I, 273-4.
76. RPC I, 312-5; Kirkton, *History*, 154.
77. Row, *Life of Blair*, 426.
78. Kirkton, *History*, 149.
79. Burnet, *Own Time* I, 251, 253.
80. *Ibid.*, I, 256; Row, *Life of Blair*, 409.
81. Mackenzie, *Memoirs*, 66-70, 73-7; Row, *Life of Blair*, 427-8; Kirkton, *History*, 146-7.
82. *LP* I, 118; Burnet, *Own Time* I, 191-2.
83. See *LP* I, 114 for a sample list.
84. This was Mackenzie's reading, but it would argue that Clarendon had not been involved earlier: Burnet, *Own Time* I, 219, 265, 266.
85. The first exchange is printed entire with speeches from both Lauderdale and Middleton in T. Brown, *Miscellanea Aulica* (London, 1702), 206-36. Burnet, *Own Time* I, 359; Nicoll, *Diary*, 393; Row, *Life of Blair*, 436, 461.
86. *LP* I, 191; Nicoll, *Diary*, 405, 407.
87. Row, *Life of Blair*, 438.
88. NLS Ms 573 f.77.
89. *SHS Miscellany* V (Edinburgh, 1933), 157.
90. Burnet, *Own Time* I, 260, 263, 264, 265-6.
91. Mackenzie, *Memoirs*, 9; Kirkton, *History*, 96.
92. For Fletcher's career see G. W. T. Omond, *The Lord Advocates of Scotland*, 2 vols. (Edinburgh, 1883) I, 171-86; Nicoll, *Diary*, 418; Row, *Life of Blair*, 462-3, 469, 472-3; Kirkton, *History*, 205.
93. BM Add Ms 23121 f.51.
94. RPC I, 314.
95. *Ibid.*, I, 338-9.
96. *Ibid.*, I, 350.
97. NLS Ms 597 f.129; Turner, *Memoirs*, 139-40.
98. RPC I, 354-5.
99. *Ibid.*, I, 357-9.
100. *Ibid.*, I, 359.
101. Row, *Life of Blair*, 437-8.
102. BM Add Ms 23119 f.26, 27.
103. NLS Ms 597 f.95.
104. *LP* I, 175, 181, 184.
105. BM Add Ms 23121 f.17; HMC Laing I, 339.

106.   *LP* I, 170-1.

107.   NLS 2512 f.13; Burnet, *Own Time* I, 266. Burnet's account of the incident, *ibid.*, I, 360-1, seems quite wrong. See also *SHS Miscellany* I (Edinburgh, 1893), 252-3.

108.   NLS Ms 2512 f.17.

109.   Row, *Life of Blair,* 433-4.

110.   APS VII, 455.

111..   Burnet, *Own Time* I, 365-6.

112.   BM Add Ms 23119 f.86. See also *LP* I, 154-5, 157, 162; Burnet, *Own Time* I, 366.

113.   Nicoll, *Diary,* 395-6.

114.   RPC I, 403-4.

115.   BM Add Ms 23121 *passim;* HMC Laing I, 342-3; NLS Ms 2512 f.29, 33.

116.   See the letter to be conveyed to the king: *LP* I, 154-5. The private arrangements between Moray and Lauderdale concerning what was for the king's eyes and what was not are described in *LP* I, 137. These indicate that this letter was written for the king's benefit. See also *LP* I, 169, 'Privat instructions', para. 2; Burnet, *Own Time* I, 368 and n.

117.   Burnet, *Own Time* I, 369.

118.   *SHS Miscellany* I, 254; NLS Ms 2512 f.19; *LP* I, 191-3 indicate the close links between Lauderdale, Rothes and Sharp and their sense of the opposition to them from a party in Edinburgh.

119.   Nicoll, *Diary,* 408-11 for the text.

120.   Burnet, *Own Time* I, 369 suggests that control of the Privy Council was the objective.

121.   *LP* I, 149, 169; NLS Ms 597 f.110.

122.   *Correspondence of Sir R. Kerr,* 2 vols. (Edinburgh, 1875), II, 474-5.

123.   BM Add Ms 23120 f.118.

124.   BM Add Ms 23122 f.116.

125.   BM Add Ms 23121 f.17.

126.   *LP* II, App. A ii.

127.   NLS Ms 2512 f.29; NLS Ms 2512 f.33.

128.   BM Add Ms 23122 f.37; Nicoll, *Diary,* 413.

Chapter 5

1.   He set off for London in February: *LP* I, 129; NLS Ms 2512 f.17.

2.   M. Lee, *The Cabal* (University of Illinois Press, Urbana, 1965), 12-13.

3.   *Ibid.,* 20.

4.   *LP* II, App. A.

5.   *LP* I, 155.

6.   *Ibid.,* I, 157.

7.   NLS Ms 2512 f.19.

8.   Rev. J. A. Lamb, 'Archbishop Alexander Burnet, 1614-1684' (*RSCHS* XI 1951-3), 134-5.

9.   Row, *Life of Blair,* 468. See also Burnet, *Own Time* I, 371.

10.   BM Add Ms 23121 f.11.

11.   Kirkton, *History,* 205ff.

12.   Text, Wodrow I, 404.

13.   BM Add Ms 23122 f.11.

14.   *LP* I, 196-8; Row, *Life of Blair,* 466-8 describes the follow-up to the sentences. Kirkton, *History,* 207-8.

15.   RPC I, 529.

16.   BM Add Ms 23122 f.87.

17.   NLS Ms 2512 f.29, 7 March 1664. Row, *Life of Blair,* 464, gives a contradictory and less trustworthy account.

18.   NLS Ms 2512 f.29.

19.   NLS Ms 2512 f.29. See also *LP* I, 198.

20.   NLS Ms 2512 f.29. See also *LP* II, App. A iii-iv. Row, *Life of Blair,* 456-7.

21. NLS Ms 2512 f.29, 35.
22. HMC Laing I, 316-7.
23. *LP* II, App. A iii.
24. *Ibid.,* I, 198; NLS Ms 2512 f.38, 42.
25. NLS Ms 2512 f.27, 31, 38.
26. *Ibid.,* f.33; *LP* II, App. A iv.
27. NLS Ms 2512 f.38, 56.
28. *Ibid.,* f.40.
29. *Ibid.*
30. For example, NLS Ms 2512 f.48, 52.
31. *SHS Miscellany* I, 259.
32. NLS Ms 2512 f.54.
33. Burnet, *Own Time* I, 369.
34. NLS Ms 2512 f.56, 58, 60.
35. HMC Laing I, 342.
36. *LP* II, App. A xi, also vi, viii.
37. NLS Ms 7023 f.4; NLS Ms 597 f.116.
38. APS VII, 465; Burnet, *Own Time* I, 367.
39. NLS Ms 7023 f.4.
40. D. Ogg, *England in the Reign of Charles II,* 2nd ed. (London, 1967), 283-4.
41. *LP* App. A v-ix; NLS Ms 2512 f.44, 46.
42. NLS Ms 7023 f.4; Row, *Life of Blair,* 473; Kirkton, *History,* 208.
43. BM Add Ms 23122 f.183.
44. BM Add Ms 35125 f.101.
45. *LP* I, 202. Seconded by his wife: *ibid.,* I, 203. See *ibid.,* I, 225 for evidence of Sharp's hostility.
46. A correspondence begins about October 1664.
47. BM Add Ms 23122 f.232.
48. *LP* II, App. A xiii; Burnet, *Own Time* I, 373, 378.
49. Nicoll, *Diary,* 421.
50. *LP* I, 204. Airy is wrong in his note; see Omond, *Lord Advocates* I, 186. See also Sir John Gilmour's opposition on legal grounds to a sentence passed by the Commission: Kirkton, *History,* 210; Burnet, *Own Time* I, 376-7.
51. *LP* II, App A xvii.
52. NLS Ms 2512 f.68, 70; *LP* I, 209.
53. *LP* I, 208-9. *Ibid.,* II, App. A xvii suggests this was on the advice of Sharp and Burnet.
54. NLS Ms 2512 f.66, 68; *LP* I, 192; II, App. A xvii, xx.
55. NLS Ms 2512 f.72; *LP* I, 210-1, 215.
56. NLS Ms 2512 f.64, 68; *LP* I, 206-7, 211.
57. NLS Ms 2512 f.68; *LP* I, 211.
58. HMC Hamilton (Supp), 82; *LP* I, 214, 217, 222; II, App. A xviii, xxi.
59. *LP* I, 216.
60. *LP* I, 220, 226.
61. *LP* I, 225, 226; NLS Ms 2512 f.80.
62. NLS Ms 2512 f.74.
63. *Ibid.,* f.76, 78.
64. *LP* I, 223-4.
65. Kirkton, *History,* 211, 218.
66. The clearest demonstration of this will be found in RPC I, xxi and RPC II, xviii. See also Row, *Life of Blair,* 475.
67. *LP* II, App. A xxiv-xxviii.
68. *LP* II, App. A xxviii-xxix; NLS Ms 2512 f.82, 84.
69. NLS Ms 2512 f.82; *LP* I, 233.
70. For an outline of these developments see Ogg, *Charles II,* 283-97.
71. *LP* II, App. A xxx.

72. *LP* II, App. A xxxi.
73. Turner, *Memoirs,* 142ff; *LP* I, 235-6.
74. *LP* II, App. A xxv-vi.
75. NLS Ms 3420 f.170; HMC Laing I, 352-4.
76. NLS Ms 3136 f.18; *LP* I, 237-8; Burnet, *Own Time* I, 383-4.
77. BM Add Ms 23125 f. 56, 66; *LP* I, 239.
78. HMC Laing I, 354.
79. *LP* I, 242; BM Add Ms 23125 f. 145.
80. RPC II, 202-4.
81. C. S. Terry. *The Pentland Rising,* gives the most detailed and useful account of the rising and reproduces many of the documents. Descriptions of the actual battle are to be found in *LP* I. Additional material can be found in BM Add Ms 35125 ff. 145-6, Add Ms 23125 f. 194ff., NLS Ms 2512 ff. 91-2, NLS Ms 7033 ff. 68-9, NLS Ms 597 ff. 136, 140, 143, HMC 72 Laing I, 354-5.
82. The sequel has been described by Ian Cowan, *The Scottish Covenanters, 1660-1688* (London, 1976).

Chapter 6
1. HMC Laing I, 360.
2. Burnet, *Own Time* I, 382.
3. *LP* I, 240-5; Burnet, *Own Time* I, 381-2.
4. *LP* II, 93: 'dis-service to the Church, as some would have to be beleeved.'
5. *LP* I, 269, 274, 274-5, 276; II, 10, 28-30.
6. Burnet, *Own Time* I, 428; *LP* I, 269 and n; II, App. A xliv, xlv; HMC Laing I, 355-6; Row, *Life of Blair,* 510.
7. NLS Yester Box 130, folder 3: King's letter to Sharp; see also *LP* II, 93; HMC 3rd report, 423.
8. *LP* II, 1-7; HMC Laing I, 358; Kirkton, *History,* 261; Burnet, *Own Time* I, 431, 433.
9. *LP* I, 240 and n.
10. *Ibid.,* I, 241-2.
11. Fanned by Bellenden: *LP* I, 281; see also *LP* II, 13.
12. *LP* I, 254-5; see also his conduct after Rullion Green: Burnet, *Own Time* I, 423.
13. *LP* I, 274. See also *LP* I, 278; II, 7, 12.
14. J. M. Buckroyd, 'The Dismissal of Archbishop Alexander Burnet 1669' (*RSCHS* XVIII, 1973), 149-55.
15. Kirkton, *History,* 260; Burnet, *Own Time* I, 427, 439.
16. Nicoll, *Diary,* 414.
17. Burnet, *Own Time* I, 439; Kirkton, *History,* 261.
18. Burnet, *Own Time* I, 378.
19. Robertson, *Robert Moray,* chapters I-VI.
20. Burnet, *Own Time* I, 376, 427.
21. Robertson, *Moray,* 102.
22. See the correspondence between them: NLS Mss 5049, 5050.
23. *LP* I, 228-33; Stephen, *Sharp,* 307-18.
24. NLS Ms 5050 f.147.
25. Burnet, *Own Time* I, 443.
26. Burnet, *Own Time* I, 256; Row, *Life of Blair,* 408-9.
27. Burnet, *Own Time* I, 382-3.
28. RPC II, 294.
29. *Ibid.*
30. RPC II, 343.
31. Ogg, *Charles* II, 313.
32. HMC Laing I, 363; *LP* II, 22-3, 33; NLS Ms 7023 f.72; Kirkton, *History,* 262-3.
33. *LP* II, 8, 10, 13, 15, 17, 32-3.

34. *Ibid.,* II, 22, 31.
35. Burnet, *Own Time* I, 248-9.
36. Texts Butler, *Leighton,* 403-13.
37. *LP* II, App A xlviii-ix.
38. NLS Ms 7024 f.43.
39. *LP* II, 43-4.
40. NLS Ms 2512 f.116.
41. NLS Ms 7024 f.43; *LP* II, 34-5.
42. HMC Laing I, 356; *LP* II, 9; Kirkton, *History,* 258-60.
43. *LP* II, 14; see also *LP* II, 6, 12-14, 19, 21, 23-4; NLS Ms 3112 f.5; Row, *Life of Blair,* 512; Burnet, *Own Time* I, 433.
44. BM Add Ms 23127 f.20.
45. *LP* I, 271, 275, 281; II, 6-7, 34; NLS Ms 573 f.66; NLS Ms 2521 f.89; BM Add Ms 23125 f.161; 23126 f.205, 206; HMC Laing I, 362; Row, *Life of Blair,* 508; Burnet, *Own Time* I, 429.
46. *LP* II, 8.
47. *LP* II, App. A xliv.
48. NLS Ms 7023 f.34; Kirkton, *History,* 259; Burnet, *Own Time* I, 430-1.
49. NLS Ms 7023 f.60, 72; Kirkton, *History,* 272-3; Burnet, *Own Time* I, 433-4.
50. BM Add Ms 23127 f.128, 132; *LP* II, 33.
51. *LP* II, 22-3, 32; BM Add Ms 23127 f.152; Burnet, *Own Time* I, 434-5.
52. BM Add Ms 23127 f.152; *LP* II, 32; Burnet, *Own Time* I, 434-5.
53. NLS Ms 7023 f.88.
54. *LP* II, 51; App. A xlix.
55. *LP* II, 59-61.
56. *LP* II, 52-9; Row, *Life of Blair,* 513; Burnet, *Own Time* I, 433.
57. *LP* II, 70.
58. *SHS Miscellany* I, 263.
59. NLS Ms 7023 f.100.
60. RPC II, 348.
61. *Ibid.,* II, 353; *LP* II, 72-3.
62. *LP* II, 86.
63. NLS Ms 7024 f.64, 74, 77, 81.
64. *Ibid.,* f.67; Row, *Life of Blair,* 515; Burnet, *Own Time* I, 440-1.
65. *LP* II, 86; NLS Ms 2512 f.104, 110.
66. NLS Ms 2512 f.106.
67. *LP* II, App. A liii-lvii.
68. NLS Yester Box 130, folder 3.
69. RPC II, 390.
70. NLS Ms 2512 f.114; *LP* II, 93-4.
71. NLS Ms 7023 f.162, 164.
72. NLS Ms 2512 f.116; Row, *Life of Blair,* 521.
73. NLS Ms 3136 f.31; 7023 f.155; Yester Box 5, folder 4; Burnet, *Own Time* I, 439-40.
74. *LP* II, 101-2.
75. NLS Ms 3136 f.28, 30, 31, 35, 37; 7023 f.121; Yester Box 5, folder 4.
76. *LP* II, 103-4.
77. NLS Ms 7023 f.165; Kirkton, *History,* 276; Row, *Life of Blair,* 518.
78. *LP* II, 105, 106, 107-8; NLS Ms 7023 f.170, 173.
79. NLS 7023 f.179; *LP* II, 109.
80. *LP* II, 109.
81. NLS Yester Box 5, folder 5; 7023 f.182; *LP* II, 109-12.
82. NLS Ms 7024 f.102, 103, 107, 110.
83. NLS Ms 7023 f.184, 187, 189.
84. NLS Ms 7024 f.107, 110.
85. *LP* II, 118.

86. *Ibid.*, II, 118-9; NLS Ms 7024 f.110, 116.
87. NLS Ms 3136 f.44.
88. *LP* II, 113-4.
89. NLS Ms 7024 f.116.
90. NLS Ms 7024 f.118; HMC Laing I, 370-1; *LP* II, 119-20.
91. *LP* II, App. A lxiii; Row, *Life of Blair,* 517.
92. NLS Ms 3136 f.44; Burnet, *Own Time* I, 441.
93. NLS Ms 7024 f.147.
94. *Ibid;* Burnet, *Own Time* I, 441.
95. The earliest report seems to date from about Feb. 1668: NLS Yester Box 130, folder 3.
96. NLS Ms 7024 f.150.
97. NLS Ms 3830 f.63; Kirkton, *History,* 287; NLS Yester Box 5, folder 4.
98. Burnet, *Own Time* I, 506.
99. NLS Yester Box 130, folder 3.
100. NLS Ms 3136 f.107; Kirkton, *History,* 288.
101. NLS Ms 7024 f.153. I have not been able to find the paper itself.
102. NLS Ms 3136 f.102.
103. NLS Yester Box 5, folder 5. There is an indication in a letter from Sir James Lockhart of Lee of yet another petition at the end of April which does not seem to have been presented.
104. *SHS Miscellany* II (Edinburgh, 1904), 335-40 for the elder Burnet's statement on the subject.
105. For these biographical details see T. E. S. Clarke and H. C. Foxcroft, *A Life of Gilbert Burnet* (Cambridge, 1907), chapters I-III.
106. Text *SHS Miscellany* II, 340-58; Burnet, *Own Time* I, 387-9.
107. NLS Ms 3136 f.107.
108. RPC III, 38-40.
109. *Ibid.*, III, 47, 62, 70, 77, 104, 106, 130, 149.
110. NLS Ms 7024 f.161; *LP* II, 196.
111. NLS Ms 7023 f.219.
112. *Ibid.*, f.220.
113. Burnet, *Own Time* I, 503.
114. NLS Ms 7023 f.189.
115. NLS Ms 7024 f.152, 153; Yester Box 5, folder 5; Row, *Life of Blair,* 521-2. For developments in England see N. Sykes, *From Sheldon to Secker* (Cambridge, 1959), 71-5.
116. NLS Ms 3136 f.100.
117. NLS Ms 2512 f.118.
118. RPC II, 488, 501-2, 572-3.
119. NLS Ms 7024 f.103; RPC II, 518-9, 522-3.
120. RPC II, 491 ff., Burnet, *Own Time* I, 503.
121. NLS Ms 7023 f.183.
122. RPC II, 500.
123. *Ibid.*
124. *Ibid.*, II, 602.
125. *Ibid.*, II, 618-21; NLS Ms 7024 f.150.
126. RPC III, 3; Burnet, *Own Time* I, 503.
127. RPC III, 61-2.

Chapter 7
1. *LP* II, 189-90.
2. HMC Laing I, 372.
3. APS VI, 372-4.
4. Burnet, *Own Time* I, 509.
5. HMC Laing I, 373.

6. BM Add Ms 35125 f.214; NLS Ms 2512 f.126.
7. NLS Ms 3136 f.115.
8. NLS Yester Box 130, folder 3.
9. RPC III, 35.
10. NLS Ms 7024 f.171; *LP* II, 195.
11. NLS Yester Box 5, folder 4.
12. NLS Ms 3136 f.116.
13. NLS Ms 7024 f.171, 176; Burnet, *Own Time* I, 513.
14. NLS Ms 7024 f.185; Mackenzie, *Memoirs,* 159; Row, *Life of Blair,* 528.
15. *LP* II, 152.
16. *Ibid.,* 152-3.
17. NLS Ms 7024 f.189; *LP* II, 153; Mackenzie, *Memoirs,* 159-60.
18. *LP* II, 153; Burnet, *Own Time* I, 512.
19. NLS Ms 7024 f.192. Episcopal disaffection was noted by Lauder: 'This procedure startled all our Bishops extremely': Sir John Lauder of Fountainhall, *Journals,*(Edinburgh, 1900), 230.
20. NLS Ms 7024 f.186.
21. *LP* II, 121, 146.
22. *Ibid.,* II, 190.
23. *Ibid.,* II, 195.
24. *Ibid.,* 195.
25. *Ibid.,* II, 191.
26. *Ibid.,* II, 199.
27. NLS Yester Box 5, folder 4.
28. For the details of this episode see NLS Ms 7024 f.177, 180; NLS Ms 7003 f.166; *LP* II, 137-9, 141; RPC III, 77-8, 82, 84, 116; Mackenzie, *Memoirs,* 157-8.
29. Text *LP* II App A lxiv-vii; Burnet, *Own Time* I, 510.
30. NLS Ms 7024 f.180. Robert Law, *Memorialls,* ed. C. K. Sharpe (Edinburgh, 1819), 21: 'the draught of the paper looking imperious lyke . . . did exceedingly displease them'.
31. NLS Ms 7024 f.180.
32. Burnet, *Own Time* I, 510-1.
33. NLS Ms 7024 f.183.
34. *LP* II, 165, 166-7.
35. NLS Ms 7024 f.198; Mackenzie, *Memoirs,* 158; Row, *Life of Blair,* 529.
36. *LP* II, 175.
37. NLS Ms 3136 f.112, 113.
38. *LP* II, 193; NLS Ms 3136 f.115.
39. NLS Ms 7024 f.170. See Kirkton, *History,* 289-91 for disputes among the dissenters.
40. *LP* II, 193-4.
41. *LP* II, 194-5, 198; HMC Laing I, 375.
42. *LP* II, 198.
43. NLS Ms 7003 f.157.
44. NLS Ms 7024 f.179. I have not been able to find this document.
45. NLS Ms 7024 f.181.
46. RPC III, 70, since 2 September.
47. NLS Ms 7024 f.187.
48. *Ibid.,* 7024 f.191.
49. *Ibid.,* f.186.
50. NLS Ms 7024 f.191, 195; Mackenzie, *Memoirs,* 161.
51. *LP* II, 165-6, 169, 171, 173.
52. NLS Ms 7025 f.2.
53. NLS Yester Box 5, folder 5. This letter is undated, but it belongs to the first four months of 1670.
54. NLS Ms 7121 f.5. It is evident from the few that survive that others had been sent: Burnet, *Own Time* I, 516-7.

L

55. Clarke and Foxcroft, *Burnet,* 78.
56. NLS Ms 7121 f.3; Row, *Life of Blair,* 532.
57. NLS Ms 7025 f.4; RPC III, 123; Kirkton, *History,* 291.
58. RPC III, 124.
59. NLS Ms 7025 f.4.
60. *Ibid.*
61. NLS Yester Box 5, folder 4.
62. NLS Ms 7025 f.17.
63. NLS Yester Box 5, folder 5.
64. *LP* II, 181-3. Butler takes these documents to be an acceptance: *Leighton,* 434.
65. NLS Ms 7004 f.48, 57; this last resort had been planned in January: NLS Ms 7025 f.2, 3. See also Burnet, *Own Time* I, 518.
66. NLS Ms 7004 f.97.
67. *Ibid.,* f.109.
68. NLS Ms 7121 f.3.
69. NLS Ms 7025 f.8, 10; Ms 7024 f.9; Burnet, *Own Time* I, 517.
70. RPC III, 130.
71. NLS Ms 7025 f.11.
72. NLS Ms 7121 f.6, 8; Burnet, *Own Time* I, 517.
73. RPC III, 156, 157-9; Kirkton, *History,* 291-2; Row, *Life of Blair,* 534.
74. NLS Ms 7004 f.33, 39, 41, 44, 48, 57; Ms 7034 f.3.
75. NLS Ms 7004 f.27, 35, 37, 101; RPC III, 161.
76. NLS Yester Box 5, folder 4, 5; Ms 7004 f.83, 91, 97, 105, 107, 109, 112, 115, 117, 118, 119; Ms 2512 f.134; Row, *Life of Blair,* 535.
77. NLS Ms 7004 f.74, 103.
78. *Ibid.,* f.44, 48.
79. NLS Yester Box 5, folder 5; NLS Ms 2512 f.132, 134.

Chapter 8
1. See Wodrow's comments II, 166ff; Burnet, *Own Time* I, 523; Row, *Life of Blair,* 536-7; Kirkton, *History,* 305-6; Mackenzie, *Memoirs,* 189-90.
2. APS VIII, 7.
3. *Ibid.,* VIII, 8-9.
4. *Ibid.,* VIII, 9-10.
5. *Ibid.,* VIII, 10.
6. *Ibid.,* VIII, 11-12.
7. That was Airy's view: *LP* II, 184n.
8. NLS Ms 7004 f.47.
9. For its membership see RPC III, 158.
10. NLS Ms 7004 f.48.
11. *Ibid.,* f.74, 107.
12. *Ibid.,* f.103.
13. NLS Ms 7121 f.3.
14. Burnet, *Own Time* I, 524.
15. NLS Ms 7004 f.107, 112, 115, 117, 118, 119, 125, 129; Wodrow II, 156-8n; Burnet, *Own Time* I, 522-3.
16. NLS Ms 3136 f.128.
17. NLS Ms 7004 f.115.
18. *Ibid.,* f.119.
19. *Ibid.,* f.125.
20. *Ibid.,* f.91.
21. APS VIII, 12.
22. *LP* II, 166, 168, 176; NLS Ms 7025 f.13; 'my morall friend' is Sheldon.

23. *LP* II, 172, 174.
24. See his letter *ibid.,* II, App A lxviii.
25. Sykes, *Sheldon to Secker,* 73-5.
26. *LP* II, 184, 185.
27. Burnet, *Own Time* I, 438-9.
28. NLS Ms 7004 f.9.
29. APS VIII, 10.
30. *LP* II, 187.
31. Burnet, *Own Time* I, 518-9; Row, *Life of Blair,* 536.
32. Burnet, *Own Time* I, 499-500.
33. Sykes, *Sheldon to Secker,* 68-75.
34. *LP* II, 170.
35. RPC III, 221-2; Kirkton, *History,* 291-2.
36. NLS Yester Box 5, folder 5.
37. NLS Ms 3136 f.135.
38. NLS Ms 7025 f.41; Kirkton, *History,* 295-6.
39. Burnet, *Own Time* I, 524-5; Kirkton, *History,* 293-4; Law, *Memorialls,* 32.
40. NLS Ms 7025 f.26.
41. NLS Ms 3136 f.135; Yester Box 5, folder 5.
42. Burnet, *Own Time* I, 520-1; Kirkton, *History,* 296-7; *LP* II, 200. See Wodrow II, 178 for the form in which the dissenters discussed the proposals. Law, *Memorialls,* 32-3.
43. *LP* II, 200; BM Add Ms 23134 f.96.
44. NLS Ms 7004 f.138.
45. BM Add Ms 23134 f.118.
46. *LP* II, 204-7.
47. NLS Yester Box 5, folder 5.
48. *LP* II, 205.
49. *Letters from Lady Margaret Kennedy to John, Duke of Lauderdale* (Edinburgh, 1828), 11, 14, 15, 16, 19, 27, 29.
50. Burnet, *Own Time* I, 527.
51. *LP* II, 208-9. R. K. Marshall, 'The House of Hamilton . . . in the seventeenth century: with a calendar of the correspondence . . . to 1712'. PhD Edinburgh, 1970. 'Calendar' II, 411, no.6102.
52. NLS Ms 7004 f.168a; Ms 7023 f.247.
53. NLS Yester Box 5, folder 5.
54. *Ibid.;* BM Add Ms 23134 f.138.
55. Burnet, *Own Time* I, 519.
56. *Ibid.,* I, 527. For the text of Leighton's proposals at this meeting see Wodrow II, 181n.
57. NLS Yester Box 5, folder 5.
58. *Ibid.*
59. NLS Ms 7025 f.35.
60. *Ibid.,* f.72.
61. *Ibid.,* f.36.
62. Burnet, *Own Time* I, 529-31.
63. NLS Ms 7025 f.41; Yester Box 5, folder 5. For Leighton's account of what passed at the meetings in January see Butler, *Leighton,* 444-50; Burnet, *Own Time* I, 529-30.
64. NLS Ms 7025 f.6.
65. NLS Ms 7023 f.259.
66. See Wodrow's comments II, 182, 184; NLS Ms 7025 f.6; NLS Ms 7023 f.259.
67. NLS Ms 7025 f.42.
68. NLS Ms 7023 f.261.
69. *LP* II, 214; HMC Laing I, 381; NLS Ms 7025 f.62.
70. NLS Ms 7025 f.62; NLS Ms 3648 f.9; *SHS Miscellany* II, 358.

71. NLS Ms 7023 f.282.
72. *LP* II, 215, 221; RPC IV, 285.
73. NLS Ms 7025 f.42.
74. RPC III, 277.
75. NLS Ms 7023 f.261.
76. RPC III, 347.
77. HMC Laing I, 381.
78. NLS Ms 7005 f.30, 34; NLS Ms 7025 f.53.
79. NLS Yester Box 5, folder 5.
80. NLS Ms 3648 f.9.
81. Burnet, *Own Time* I, 534-5.
82. NLS Ms 7025 f.42.
83. NLS Ms 7023 f.261.
84. RPC III, 311-2.
85. *LP* II, 187.
86. RPC III, 347.
87. NLS Ms 7005 f.30.
88. HMC Hamilton (Supp), 84.
89. *Ibid.,* 85.
90. *Ibid.,* 84-5.
91. *SHS Miscellany* II, 358.
92. NLS Ms 3648 f.9.
93. Burnet, *Own Time* I, 534-5.
94. BM Add Ms 23135 f.143; HMC Hamilton (Supp), 85-6.
95. Text Wodrow II, 202; F. Bate, *The Declaration of Indulgence 1672* (London, 1908).
96. NLS Ms 7005 f.126, 130.
97. RPC III, 586-90.
98. BM Add Ms 23134 f.185.
99. NLS Ms 7025 f.6.
100. RPC III, 300-1.
101. *LP* II, 212; NLS Ms 7023 f.263.
102. RPC III, 308.
103. BM Add Ms 23135 f.17.
104. RPC III, 312. This order was repeated in October: *ibid.,* III, 393.
105. BM Add Ms 23135 f.75.
106. RPC III, 340-1. See *ibid.,* III, 392-3 for a similar order to parish clerks in October.
107. *Ibid.,* 441, 442-5.
108. *Ibid.,* III, 463-4.
109. *Ibid.,* III, 545-51, 555, 558-61 give further evidence of continued conventicling.
110. APS VIII, 71; Mackenzie, *Memoirs,* 220.
111. APS VIII, 72-3.
112. *Ibid.,* VIII, 73.
113. *Ibid.,* VIII, 89.
114. BM Add Ms 23135 f.168, 175; *LP* II, 224.
115. Burnet, *Own Time* I, 439; Mackenzie, *Memoirs,* 217-8.
116. *LP* II, 211-2 and n. Airy is wrong in suggesting that this marked the end of the relationship, although it certainly indicated its trend. In April 1672 a letter to Tweeddale (NLS Ms 7005 f.130) indicates that he was still discussing Scottish affairs with Lauderdale. Burnet suggests, however, (*Own Time* I, 533) that by late 1671 there was no longer any friendship between them.
117. Burnet, *Own Time* I, 438, 519, 534; Kirkton, *History,* 315-6; Mackenzie, *Memoirs,* 212-3.
118. Burnet, *Own Time* I, 534.
119. This issue is discussed in NLS Yester *passim*.
120. Mackenzie, *Memoirs,* 218. See also Mackenzie's account of Tweeddale's political alliances: *ibid.,* 179-81.

121. Kirkton, *History,* 316-7.
122. NLS Ms 7023 f.259 January 1671; *SHS Miscellany* I, 265.
123. NLS Ms 7023 f.263 February 1671.
124. HMC Hamilton, 142 [August] 1671.
125. BM Add Ms 23135 f.175 June 1672, Lauderdale's speech to Parliament.
126. APS VIII, 57.
127. HMC Hamilton, 141-2; BM Add Ms 23134, 23135 *passim.*
128. HMC Laing I, 381.
129. HMC Hamilton (Supp), 85.
130. NLS Ms 3648 f.9.
131. BM Add Ms 23135 f.135.
132. *Ibid.,* f.143.
133. HMC Hamilton (Supp), 86.
134. *Ibid.*
135. *LP* II, 214.
136. *Ibid.,* II, 215; NLS Ms 2512 f.148.
137. BM Add Ms 23134 f.216.
138. NLS Ms 2512 f.136; 7005 f.34; 7025 f.**42,** 53, 62; 3648 f.9; Yester Box 5, folder 5; *SHS Miscellany* I, 266-7; BM Add Ms 23134 f.216; **23135** f.17; *LP* II, 218-20.
139. NLS Ms 7005 f.64.
140. *LP* II, 216-7.

Chapter 9
1. RPC III, 586-90.
2. Wodrow II, 203; Kirkton, *History,* 327-30.
3. Wodrow II, 206-10. Text *ibid.,* II, 207-9, n; Kirkton, *History,* 330-4. See also Hamilton's account of these developments: HMC Hamilton, 142.
4. Kirkton, *History,* 335-6; Law, *Memorialls,* 51.
5. Kirkton, *History,* 337; RPC IV, 34-5, 56-7, 98-9, 104-5, 108-9.
6. HMC Hamilton, 142, 144.
7. *Ibid.,* 145.
8. *Ibid.,* (Supp), 86.
9. *Ibid.,* 86-7.
10. HMC Hamilton, 147, 148.
11. For further details of Hamilton's opposition to Lauderdale on other grounds see John Patrick, 'The origins of the opposition to Lauderdale in the Scottish Parliament of 1673' (*SHR* LIII, 1974), 1-21.
12. *LP* II, 241-7, III, 1-6, 15-17.
13. BM Add Ms 23136 f.37.
14. For this and what follows see William Cobbett, *Cobbett's Parliamentary History,* 36 vols., (London, 1806-20) IV, 625, 662; Kirkton, *History,* 341; *LP* III, 6-15, 18-20, 21-34, 35-7; Mackenzie, *Lauderdale,* ch. xxi; Mackenzie, *Memoirs,* 264; Ogg, *Charles II,* 382-6.
15. *LP* III, 38-41.
16. RPC III, 593; IV, 35, 78, 126-7, 178-9; for additional descriptions of these events see HMC Hamilton 142-3; *LP* II, 233.
17. RPC III, 605-6; BM Add Ms 23135 f.207, 253. Note the Council's evasion of any statement on the subject: RPC IV, 4-5.
18. RPC IV, 30-1.
19. *Ibid.,* IV, 31, 37-8, 40, 47, 48, 58-9, 64, 72-3, 87, 93-4, 97-8, 140-1, 180; Kirkton, *History,* 342.
20. RPC IV, 35-6, 40-1, 52-3.
21. *Ibid.,* IV, 57-8, 71-2; Kirkton, *History,* 337-8.
22. NLS Ms 7034 f.55; 7121 f.10, 12; HMC Hamilton, 148. Text Wodrow II, 263-4.

23. Burnet, *Own Time* II, 55.
24. HMC Hamilton, 148-9. This paper dates from May 1674. Events had already shown by that date, however, that Burnet had cherished these views for some time: see also NLS Ms 7121 f.10.
25. NLS Ms 7034 f.55.
26. *LP* III, 57.
27. NLS Ms 7121 f.12 gives Burnet's own account.
28. BM Add Ms 23136 f.153.
29. HMC Laing I, 401.
30. BM Add Ms 23136 f.144.
31. NLS Ms 7034 f.56.
32. *LP* III, 42, 53.
33. The account of this meeting is in BM Add Ms 23136 f.135 and *LP* III, 42-4. No trace of the momentous discussions appears for that day in RPC IV, 178.
34. Text NLS Ms 7034 f.57.
35. BM Add Ms 23136 f.153; *LP* III, 46-7; NLS Ms 2512 f.159. It seems likely that the Bishop of Brechin was initially also involved, but lost courage: Kirkton, *History,* 348.
36. BM Add Ms 23136 f.153.
37. *LP* III, 46-7; BM Add Ms 23136 f.144. Wodrow II, 300-1.
38. BM Add Ms 23136 f.145.
39. For Ramsay's own account of this see HMC Laing I, 397-9; BM Add Ms 23136 f.182. For a very different account from the Dean of Edinburgh see BM Add Ms 23136 f.178. See also Marshall, 'Calendar' II, 441, No. 2745; Row, *Life of Blair,* 547.
40. *LP* III, 52.
41. Clarke and Foxcroft, *Burnet,* 72-4, 78, 97-8.
42. *Ibid.,* 102, 106-7, 117.
43. *Ibid.,* 119-21; *LP* II, 244; III, 10; Law, *Memorialls,* 69.
44. Scott, *Fasti* III, 259.
45. HMC Laing I, 392.
46. NLS Ms 7025 f.106.
47. *LP* II, 231-2.
48. Text Butler, *Leighton,* 477.
49. Quoted *ibid.,* 464.
50. HMC Hamilton, 147.
51. *LP* II, 238-9.
52. HMC Hamilton, 149. See also Lauderdale's instructions *LP* II, 235.
53. Yester Box 5, folder 5; NLS Ms 7121 f.12.
54. *LP* III, 55-9.
55. *Ibid.,* III, 62.
56. *Ibid.,* III, 75-6.
57. For Sheldon's realliance with the king see V. S. Sutch, *Gilbert Sheldon* (The Hague, 1973), 125-7.
58. Bodleian Ms Add C 34 f.156. A copy of this in the SRO, Register House, Edinburgh is endorsed as a forgery, but I see no reason to doubt its authenticity. See also *SHS Miscellany* I, 286-7; in April 1674 Hatton thanks Sharp for a recommendation to the English bishops.
59. Burnet, *Own Time* II, 66-7; Mackenzie, *Memoirs,* 314-5.
60. *SHS Miscellany* I, 269-72.
61. BM Add Ms 23136 f.153.
62. NLS Ms 2512 f.159; Row, *Life of Blair,* 541-2.
63. RPC IV, 220.
64. *LP* III, 63-4; BM Add Ms 23136 f.173.
65. RPC IV, 248-9; BM Add Ms 23136 f.183.
66. RPC IV, 248-9. Note also the action against the Bishop of Brechin.
67. Clarke and Foxcroft, *Burnet,* 125-6; Burnet, *Own Time* II, 58-61.

68. RPC IV, 265. See also *sederunt, ibid.,* IV, 263. Row, *Life of Blair,* 549; the contest was probably not as close as Row asserts.
69. HMC Hamilton, 150. See also Marshall, 'Calendar' II, 441-6 for evidence of the close interest of the Hamilton family in Ramsay's case in the summer of 1674.
70. Texts Wodrow II, 304-8.
71. BM Add Ms 23137 f.62.
72. RPC IV, 577. NLS Ms 2512 f.181, 183; Wodrow II, 308-16; BM Add Ms 23137 f.86.
73. NLS Ms 7121 f.10; HMC Hamilton, 148; Burnet, *Own Time* II, 53.
74. RPC IV, 167-8.
75. *LP* III, 54. Contemporary moves against dissent in England must also have influenced Lauderdale: Sutch, *Sheldon,* 127.
76. D. R. Lacey, *Dissent and Parliamentary Politics in England 1661-89* (New Brunswick, N.J., 1969), ch. v.
77. NLS Ms 2512 f.157.
78. *Ibid.,* f.159.
79. *Ibid.*
80. *Ibid.*
81. Mackenzie, *Memoirs,* 273; Kirkton, *History,* 344-5; RPC IV, 258-61; Row, *Life of Blair,* 538-9.
82. *SHS Miscellany* I, 279.
83. *Ibid.,* I, 269-72.
84. RPC IV, 186-7; Row, *Life of Blair,* 538; Kirkton, *History,* 343.
85. *Ibid.*
85. RPC IV, 190-1.
86. *Ibid.,* IV, 197-200; *LP* III, 48-9.
87. For a convenient summary see RPC IV, xvi; Row, *Life of Blair,* 538-41, 545-51; Kirkton, *History,* 348-53.
88. Row, *Life of Blair,* 551.
89. Lamb, 'Alexander Burnet', 142.
90. NLS Ms 7023 f.261.
91. RPC IV, 285-6.
92. NLS Ms 2512 f.142.
93. RPC IV, 307.
94. Keith, *Scottish Bishops,* 282; Row, *Life of Blair,* 552.
95. Burnet, *Own Time* II, 73-4; Cobbett, *Parliamentary History* IV, 683-7; Mackenzie, *Memoirs,* 315-6; Mackenzie, *Lauderdale,* ch. xxi.
96. Cobbett, *Parliamentary History* IV, 699.
97. HMC Hamilton (Supp), 89; HMC Laing I, 402; Marshall, 'Calendar' II, Nos. 2839, 2920; Law, *Memorialls,* 77.
98. See HMC Laing I, 403-4, 406, for the expression of Burnet's identification with Lauderdale's political fortunes.

Chapter 10
1. HMC Laing I, 403-4, 406; NLS Ms 2512 f.176.
2. RPC IV, 412-3.
3. *Ibid.,* IV, 425-7. See also notes of a discussion on this subject: SRO GD 157/1846.
4. RPC IV, 428-9.
5. *Ibid.,* IV, 438-9.
6. Sutch, *Sheldon,* 125-7.
7. RPC IV, 473. It seems, however, that the garrisons were disbanded during the winter: *ibid.,* IV, 486, 498-500; NLS Ms 7025 f.131.
8. RPC IV, 492-3.
9. *Ibid.,* IV, 493-4.

10. *Ibid.,* IV, 135.

11. *Ibid.,* IV, 152.

12. *Ibid.,* IV, 172.

13. *Ibid.,* IV, 494.

14. *Ibid.,* IV, 500-1, 509; Wodrow, II, 455-8.

15. RPC V, 198.

16. *Ibid.,* IV, 547-9.

17. *Ibid.,* IV, 550.

18. *Ibid.,* IV, 551.

19. *Ibid.,* IV, 578.

20. *Ibid.,* IV, 581.

21. Wodrow II, 273-8 for documents relating to this meeting and subsequent regional meetings.

22. NLS Ms 2512 f.203.

23. The tone of NLS Ms 2512 f.181, 183, indicates the solidarity of this triumvirate.

24. NLS Ms 2512 f.181, 187, 189, 197, 199. In June 1676 Rothes was cautiously sounding Hamilton: HMC Hamilton (Supp.) 92.

25. NLS Ms 2512 f.181 See also HMC Hamilton, 152; NLS Ms 2512 f.195, 201.

26. NLS Ms 2512 f.187. There were others busy at the same time in an attempt to break up the party: *LP* III, 78-9; HMC Hamilton, 151, 154.

27. HMC Hamilton (Supp), 89-91.

28. HMC Hamilton, 153; Law, *Memorialls,* 87; Row, *Life of Blair,* 565.

29. *LP* III, 80-1; NLS Ms 2512 f.191, 195. These are the events described by Turner, in his account of Burnet's role, to Hamilton in May 1677: Turner, *Memoirs,* 259-61.

30. NLS Ms 2512 f.195.

31. HMC Hamilton (Supp), 91-2; HMC Hamilton, 154, 155; NLS Ms 2512 f.193.

32. HMC Hamilton, 151, 153.

33. NLS Ms 2512 f.197, 199.

34. Scott, *Fasti* II, 159.

35. RPC III, 586-8.

36. *Ibid.,* IV, 34.

37. *Ibid.,* IV, 108.

38. *Ibid.,* IV, 193, 203.

39. *Ibid.,* IV, 238-9.

40. *Ibid.,* IV, 399-402.

41. *Ibid.,* IV, 435-6.

42. Kirkton, *History,* 367-9; Burnet, *Own Time* II, 113-4.

43. RPC V, 2, 10, 18, 21, 34, 72.

44. Kirkton, *History,* 370; Mackenzie, *Memoirs,* 317; Burnet, *Own Time* II, 114.

45. *LP* III, 83-5; NLS Ms 2512 f.201; Mackenzie, *Memoirs,* 317.

46. RPC V, 6-7 for the new membership. Law, *Memorialls,* 97; Kirkton, *History,* 370.

47. NLS Ms 2512 f.201.

48. HMC Hamilton, 155; RPC V, 85-6. See also the party's discomfiture: *SHS Miscellany* I, 285.

49. RPC V, 233.

50. *SHS Miscellany* I, 274.

51. According to Kirkton, *History,* 371, Kirkton and others did give Lauderdale their version, but after the reconstitution of the Council.

52. CSPD 1677, 443-4; Law, *Memorialls,* 134-5; Row, *Life of Blair,* 566-7; Kirkton, *History,* 375; Mackenzie, *Memoirs,* 321-2.

53. HMC Drumlanrig I, 223.

54. *Ibid.,* I, 224.

55. *Ibid.,* I, 225.

56. *Ibid.,* I, 226, 227.

57. *Ibid.*, I, 226: 'the bishops good opinion for L[auderdale] decays'. Kirkton, *History,* 376.
58. BM Landsdowne Ms 988 f.142; HMC Portland II, 37; Mackenzie, *Memoirs* 322. For more on Hickes see W. B. Gardner, 'The Later Years of John Maitland, Second Earl and First Duke of Lauderdale' *(Journal of Modern History* XX, 1948), 113-22.
59. HMC Portland II, 37-8.
60. HMC Drumlanrig I, 223-4, 224-5, 225-6, 227.
61. RPC V, 206-9.
62. *Ibid.*, V, 213-6.
63. HMC Drumlanrig I, 223. See also Burnet's account of its poor reception, *Own Time* II, 144.
64. RPC V, 255-6.
65. J. R. Elder, *The Highland Host of 1678* (Glasgow, 1914).
66. NLS Ms 597 f.270.
67. HMC Drumlanrig I, 230.
68. *Ibid.*, I, 229-30. See also Kirkton, *History,* 390.
69. HMC Portland II, 45.
70. NLS Ms 3134 f.119. Mackenzie, *Memoirs,* 322 hints at the same story.
71. RPC V, 272-3; *LP* III, 89-91.
72. *LP* III, 89. For instructions see RPC V, 320-4.
73. Law, *Memorialls,* 137.
74. RPC V, 270-1.
75. *Ibid.*, V, 279-80; Law, *Memorialls,* 136.
76. *LP* III, 89.
77. RPC V, 296-8; *LP* III, 91.
78. HMC Drumlanrig I, 233.
79. BM Lansdowne Ms 988 f.148, 149.
80. I have not been able to find the document. It is referred to by Hickes in BM Lansdowne Ms 988 f.149.
81. BM Lansdowne Ms 988 f.149.
82. *LP* III, 95-8.
83. RPC V, 320-4.
84. HMC Hamilton, 164. According to Marshall, 'Calendar' II, 499 No. 9214, wrongly attributed to the Earl of Perth.
85. HMC Drumlanrig I, 229.
86. RPC V, 304-5.
87. *Ibid.*, V, 305-6.
88. HMC Hamilton, 156.
89. HMC Portland II, 44. J. R. Jones, 'The Scottish Constitutional Opposition in 1679' (*SHR* XXXVII, 1958), 37-41 gives a document indicating these links and a considerable degree of organisation in the party.
90. For further detail of the whole campaign see Elder, *Highland Host* and the appendix on the Committee for the West in RPC V.
91. RPC V, 354-5.
92. Burnet, *Own Time* II, 145.
93. Wodrow II, 372.
94. Quoted *ibid.,* n; Burnet, *Own Time* II, 147.
95. BM Lansdowne Ms 988 f.154.
96. RPC V, 268; Mackenzie, *Memoirs,* 327-9.
97. *Collection of State Trials,* 2nd. ed., 8 vols. (London, 1730-57); John Lauder of Fountainhall, *Historical Notices,* 2 vols. (Edinburgh, 1848) I, 183-6.
98. Burnet, *Own Time* II, 136-43.
99. Kirkton, *History,* 383-5.
100. *LP* III, 99-102. On this occasion the Earl of Cassillis had given his account of what had happened: SRO GD 157/1659; RPC V, 419-22, 425-32. Note also the defensive tone of the Council's letter to the king on 16 March: RPC V, 395-6.

101. Burnet, *Own Time* II, 146-7; Law, *Memorialls,* 137.

102. HMC Portland II, 49.

103. RPC V, 407, 444-5.

104. HMC Portland II, 50. He took with him a letter from Sharp and the bishops: NLS Ms 7034 f.84, printed in Wodrow II, 412.

105. HMC Portland II, 50: 'which my Lord, who is privy to every line in it, is well satisfied with'.

106. George Hickes, *Ravillac Redivivus* (London, 1678).

107. RPC V, 438, text Wodrow II, 442-6.

108. *LP* III, 103-53, 241-6; HMC Hamilton, 160-2; Hamilton (Supp), 94-9; HMC Drumlanrig I, 235-6; Burnet, *Own Time* II, 146-8; NLS Ms 2512 f.207; Kirkton, *History,* 392-3.

109. See the king's letter of 26 March, RPC V, 413-4, and his mention of 'great misfortunes that followed latly upon the lyke beginnings'.

110. The letter does not appear in RPC. Text Wodrow II, 451.

111. RPC V, 413-4.

112. Bodleian Ms Eng. Hist. b.2 f.72, despite RPC V, 406-7. Quoted by Yould.

113. For the instructions: CSPD Add., 1678, 221; Burnet, *Own Time* II, 149.

114. APS VIII, 218-9.

115. Hamilton attempted to influence elections to the Convention: Marshall, 'Calendar' II, 503 nos. 8095, 2965. Lauderdale did the same, but more successfully, Law, *Memorialls,* 138.

116. *LP* III, 154-60, 247-56; NLS Ms 2512 f.211; HMC Drumlanrig I, 237; HMC Portland II, 50-1; CSPD Add., 1678, 244, 274, 292, Law, *Memorialls,* 138-9.

117. *Letters . . . to Sancroft,* ed. W. N. Clarke [hereafter Clarke] (London 1848), 1-2.

118. SRO GD 157/1847.

119. NLS Ms 2512 f.215.

120. *Ibid.* See also the letter from Sharp to the Bishop of Galloway in April 1679, emphasising the connection between the fate of the church in England and that in Scotland: *SHS Miscellany* III (Edinburgh, 1919), 'The Bishop of Galloway's Correspondence', 74-5.

121. RPC VI, 91, 97-9, 124.

122. CSPD 1678, Addenda 468, 483. For Hamilton's impression of his victory, see HMC Drumlanrig I, 238.

123. For the information on English politics which follows I have used J. R. Jones, *The First Whigs* (London, 1966) and K. H. D. Haley, *The First Earl of Shaftesbury* (Oxford, 1968), chapters xxiii and xxiv.

124. Cobbett, *Parliamentary History* IV, 1116-8, 1130.

125. *LP* III, 162-4; RPC VI, 160-3, 166-7, 174-8.

126. RPC VI, 180.

127. *Ibid.,* VI, 207-8.

128. HMC Hamilton (Supp), 99.

129. *Ibid.,* 99-100 for a paper presented by Hamilton to the king. A number of the Privy Council had been summoned to London to give an account of their proceedings on this occasion: RPC VI, 194-5. For further details of this conference, see Wodrow III, 168-9; Burnet, *Own Time* II, 234-5.

130. RPC VI, 270-2.

131. *Ibid.,* 218-9. For Burnet's suspicion of this report, *Own Time* II, 238. The course of the rising and its eventual culmination at Bothwell Brig are described in Cowan, *Scottish Covenanters,* 96-9.

132. RPC VI, 239.

133. CSPD 1679, 178. The supplication of the nonconformists to Monmouth, text Wodrow III, 105, indicated that clemency was expected from him. See also *ibid.,* III, 147-9; HMC Hamilton, 162; HMC Hamilton (Supp), 100-1; Burnet, *Own Time* II, 239; Law, *Memorialls,* 150.

134. RPC VI, 264-5, 278. Burnet asserted it was Monmouth's own desire, *Own Time* II, 240-1, but CSPD 1679, 175 suggests Monmouth's instructions were drawn up by Lauderdale.

135. Butler, *Leighton,* 506 for text.

136. For this case see Wodrow III, 6-9; RPC VI, 290, 297.
137. RPC VI, 293.
138. *Ibid.,* VI, 280-1
139. *Ibid.,* VI, 301-4.

Chapter 11
1. *LP* III, 181-2.
2. *Ibid.,* III, 182-3; James's reply, *ibid.,* III, 184-5 perhaps indicates by its tone his suspicion of Lauderdale's motives.
3. RPC VI, 344.
4. 'Things are very quiet,' reported James in January: HMC Dartmouth I, 44, 47, 49.
5. Burnet, *Own Time* II, 247.
6. *LP* III, 174-5.
7. NLS Ms 2512 f.217, 219.
8. Clarke, 5.
9. RPC VI, 273.
10. *Ibid.,* VI, 393.
11. HMC Hamilton (Supp), 89-91. There are also rumours of poor relations between Lauderdale and James in that year: Marshall, 'Calendar' II, 460 No. 2844.
12. HMC Dartmouth I, 41. For James's desire not to appear arbitrary, see *LP* III, 192.
13. NLS Ms 2512 f.222.
14. *Ibid.,* f.224; BM Add Ms 23245 f.92 for the letter which the Bishop of Edinburgh took with him, in the same vein.
15. NLS Ms 2512 f.224.
16. For assessments of English politics at this juncture, see F. C. Turner, *James II* (London, 1948), 177; Jones, *The First Whigs,* 89-92.
17. For details of the negotiations, see Row, *Life of Blair,* 570-1.
18. RPC VI, 452-3.
19. *Ibid.,* VI, 459-62.
20. Clarke, 13.
21. Wodrow III, 182.
22. *Ibid.,* III, 89-111.
23. HMC Dartmouth, I, 45, but this may date from 1681.
24. RPC VI, 429.
25. *Ibid.,* VI, 432-6, 444.
26. In November 1680 the Scottish bishops recalled the good offices done by James in 'blunting the edge of the late indulgence . . . when he went to wait on the King' (Clarke, 24). It was in February 1680 that James went south, long before the disturbances of the spring and summer.
27. Wodrow III, 202-32; RPC VI, 481.
28. *LP* III, 210.
29. Clarke, 19; *LP* III, 212.
30. Sir John Dalrymple, *Memoirs of Great Britain and Ireland,* new ed., 3 vols. (London, 1790) II, 12 (Part I, Book I).
31. This period is discussed by Cowan, *Scottish Covenanters,* 103-37.

Bibliography

BIBLIOGRAPHICAL NOTE

THIS book attempts to analyse the evolution of the government's ecclesiastical policy in Scotland from 1660 to 1681. Its purpose is to reveal as far as possible the motives of that policy and the pressures that created it. That such a study should not previously have been attempted is in itself curious. The explanation is to be found in a consideration of the historiography of the subject.

The Restoration government in Scotland operated a system of censorship which ensured that the official view of dissent should be made public. In November 1661 the Privy Council passed resolutions prohibiting the publication of any material without prior submission to the Council. This method was not entirely successful in preventing the circulation of the dissenters' own view of their cause; books were printed abroad and smuggled into the country. Contraband literature, however, was liable to confiscation, and its possession was punishable. Correspondingly, at the Restoration when presbyterian dissenters were endowed with instant respectability, there was a strong urge for them to provide their account of the period during which they had been silenced. This task was accomplished in the 1720s by Robert Wodrow in his *Sufferings of the Church of Scotland from the Restoration to the Revolution.*[1]

Wodrow's fundamental purpose was to establish that dissenters during that period had been persecuted solely for their innocent nonconformity. He categorically rejected the assertions of the Restoration government that dissent was merely a means to cover political sedition with the gloss of conscientious objection to episcopacy. Thus by extension Wodrow implied that the government, in taking action against dissenters, was inspired by malice, and that those who suffered were martyrs for their religious beliefs.

Wodrow had ample personal and political reason to argue as he did. His father was born in 1637[2] and thus came to maturity at the very beginning of the Restoration, a firmly convinced presbyterian and Covenanter brought up after the days of the moderate episcopalian compromise of 1610-38. He was sympathetic to those presbyterian ministers outed from their parishes in the

---

[1] Complete references to works cited in this Note will be found in the Bibliography. For more on Wodrow, see A. M. Starkey, 'Robert Wodrow and *The History of the Sufferings of the Church of Scotland*' (*Church History* XLIII, 1974), 488-98.

[2] The information on Wodrow's family background is taken from Robert Wodrow, *Life of James Wodrow* (Edinburgh, 1828), 1-71 *passim*.

1660s, and was licensed to preach in 1673 by an illegally constituted presbytery formed of such ministers. As a conventicle preacher he was intercommuned and forced to go into hiding, and during the last years of the Stuart regime he was obliged to retire altogether from public life and live in a remote part of the west of Scotland. Robert Wodrow, his son, was therefore born and brought up in a pro-Covenanting community which had personal experience and recollection of the ways of Restoration government. He was furthermore writing as a Whig, grateful for the benefits that the Glorious Revolution had brought to his co-religionists. He wrote moreover at a time when the Jacobite risings had demonstrated the necessity for the restatement of the crimes of the Stuarts and the advantages of their successors.

His work, however, is not to be dismissed as that of a vulgar partisan and propagandist. Although he selected his material to exclude matter discreditable to the dissenters or creditable to the government, yet at a time when Scottish documents were mostly unpublished and disordered, he went to some lengths to substantiate his argument with documentary evidence. Furthermore, it embodied a well worked out and consistent account of the period. It was a period, he asserted, during which there was a ruthless persecution for religion by the government in Scotland. The intention was to destroy the presbyterian church and this aim was furthered by the introduction of an erastian episcopate who urged on the persecution of the presbyterians. It was allowed by those who hated the Reformation, and were at bottom profane and atheistical. The persecution entailed the illegal assumption of power and the flouting of the laws of the land so that both civil and religious liberties were destroyed, but it brought incidental benefits to the persecutors. The presbyterians thus harassed had done no wrong but were innocent nonconformists and therefore necessarily falsely accused of sedition and disloyalty. Their sufferings, said Wodrow, were for no crime but for religion, and therefore they were to be seen as martyrs and heroes whose eventual reluctant recourse to arms was taken in self-defence.

This view of the Restoration has proved utterly compelling to the large majority of Scottish historians ever since, and is the source from which virtually all accounts derive, or against which they react. Within the ranks of Wodrow's heirs, however, various schools can be discerned. The one which has had the most influence, and which has shaped the popular view of the Restoration down to the present day, is that of Wodrow's close followers and sympathisers.

During the eighteenth century three major works drew heavily on Wodrow for their form and content. Although Wodrow's methods were as scholarly as he could make them and involved extensive quotation from documentary sources, yet in essence his history consisted of an immense catalogue of individual cases and biographies, for which his information was to a considerable extent hearsay and personal reminiscence. The martyrology in Wodrow was set in the framework of his more reasoned judgments of the nature of the Restoration government, but in his followers that framework was lacking. Moreover, Wodrow had confined his sympathies to those dissenters who had accepted the settlement of the church offered to them by William of Orange. He had little patience for the Cameronians, followers of Richard Cameron, who rejected the settlement as an erastian imposition.

Patrick Walker, in six lives of Cameronians published in the 1720s, was concerned to vindicate his heroes from any stain imputed to them by Wodrow, as he asserted in his address 'To the Reader'. Nevertheless, his work was a series of corrections and expansions of Wodrow, and its principal effect was to confirm and promote the biographical and hagiographical tendencies in Wodrow.

The charm of these very features for readers of Wodrow and those who sympathised with his account of the Restoration was further demonstrated in the middle of the eighteenth century by William Crookshank. In his *History of the State and Sufferings of the Church of Scotland, from the Restoration to the Revolution* he provided an abbreviated version of Wodrow by the simple omission of the documentary material. Thus Wodrow's volumes were reduced to a list of cases.

This trend was yet further established towards the end of the century by the work of John Howie. He, like Walker, had Cameronian sympathies and edited an earlier biographical compilation by Michael Shields, *Faithful Contendings Displayed,* which had strong Cameronian sentiments. In his *Biographia Scoticana,* however, he depended very heavily on Wodrow for his information, as a comparison, for example, of the lives of Argyll, Guthrie, Hackston of Rathillet and others shows.

By the advent of the nineteenth century, therefore, a tradition had been established whereby Wodrow's closest and most ardent disciples abandoned the more rational, serious and coherent elements of his work in favour of hagiography. For reasons which are obscure, this approach proved particularly congenial in nineteenth and early twentieth-century Scotland, and numerous biographical studies were published based on Wodrow. Thomas M'Crie the elder found it incumbent upon him to correct Walter Scott's view of the Covenanters in *Old Mortality* because it did not conform exactly to information in Wodrow. James Anderson produced a particularly dreadful example of the genre in *Ladies of the Covenant.* Alexander Smellie's *Men of the Covenant* was superior to the general level of such works, but W. H. Carslaw's *Heroes of the Covenant* and D. Beaton's *Scottish Heroines of the Faith* were not distinguished works.

The tendency to martyrology continued at a more moderate rate into relatively modern times. James Barr, a distinguished minister of the Free Church of Scotland, produced *The Scottish Covenanters* as late as 1946. Much the greater part of this book is taken up with biographies of individual dissenters derived from Wodrow, and the sentimental and emotional nature of their appeal is underlined by the quotation of bad commemorative verse.

The effect of this long-term popularisation of those parts of Wodrow's work which were in the first place based on less than perfectly reliable sources has been to create a gallery of folk heroes who in popular estimation resisted arbitrary power and contended for freedom. It seems quite certain that a revaluation of Restoration dissenters such as that attempted by Ian Cowan in 'The Covenanters: A Revision Article' in 1968 had been long delayed by the strength of this tradition.

Wodrow, however, has had heirs and successors who were extremely unsympathetic to his point of view. Nevertheless, so strong has his influence been that his opponents have largely confined themselves to attempting to discredit him on his own terms. As Wodrow had asserted that the government during the Restoration was maliciously intent on the extirpation of innocent nonconformists, so his opponents countered that a law-abiding administration had been unwarrantably attacked by seditious rebels masquerading under the cloak of religion. This had been the tenor of government self-justification during the Restoration, and was as much Stuart propaganda as that of Wodrow was Hanoverian.

Thus in 1723 there appeared *A True and Impartial Account of the Life of the most Reverend Father in God, Dr James Sharp.* Much of the book took the form of an attempt to discredit Wodrow's extremely unfavourable view of Sharp. It gave an extravagant account of Sharp as saint and martyr of the holy cause of the God-given ordinance of episcopacy, and followed this with a bitter condemnation of the Covenanters as seditious rebels against duly constituted authority.

There appear to have been no other major attacks on Wodrow during the eighteenth century. The reason for this is most likely to be found in contemporary politics. The Stuarts had shown some unwillingness to lie down and die, and the Jacobite risings and rumours of risings had made any attempt to vindicate Stuart government a hazardous proceeding. Moreover, Wodrow had been awarded the seal of Hanoverian approval with a gift of 100 guineas from George I. Further attempts to discredit Wodrow, therefore, had to await times more politically congenial.

In 1839 Thomas Stephen modelled his *Life and Times of Archbishop Sharp* on the *True and Impartial Account;* he frequently uses and quotes it, although not always with acknowledgement. Stephen's aim was identical: he wanted to show Sharp as a saint and martyr, the Restoration government as blameless and the Covenanters as seditious rebels. Like the author of the *True and Impartial Account* before him, Stephen was explicitly concerned to refute Wodrow:

As his [Wodrow's] object throughout his work is to blacken and defame Mr Sharp's character, and his leaning is too obvious towards the protestors, his opinions in all cases are to be received with great caution.

The best example of an attack on Wodrow is, however, to be found in the notorious debate between Mark Napier and Archibald Stewart in the 1860s. The debate centres on an event described by Wodrow in which two women were alleged to have been put to death by drowning for their nonconformity.

Napier alleged the punishment had never been carried out, and Stewart asserted it had. The real basis of the confrontation, however, was the amount of confidence that could be placed in Wodrow.

Napier initiated the debate in 1863 in the preface to *The Case for the Crown in re The Wigtown Martyrs proved to be Myths:*

> Close research has led me to the conviction, that not a single individual was unjustly put to death for rebellion, or high treason, in Scotland, by the Governments of the Restoration. Unless fanatical assertion be the equivalent to truth and justice, there are no sufficient materials for a Martyrology of Scotland during that period. That which we have from Wodrow is a calumnious tissue of monstrous fables. It has poisoned the History of Scotland to an extent that is now, perhaps, irremediable. He has misled all our historians of mark from David Hume to Lord Macaulay, who have blindly followed him, and lazily, or lovingly submitted to his rubbish, without an attempt at investigation. And thus it is that the national character of Scotland has been defamed by a mock and mythical martyrology of the lowest stamp, and her soil desecrated by fanatical monuments, not to commemorate the martyrs but to perpetuate the calumny.

Napier's design in his *Case for the Crown* was to prove that the so-called Wigtown Martyrs had not in fact been put to death, and his intention thereby was to discredit Wodrow and his view of the Restoration. He was answered by Archibald Stewart in *History Vindicated in the Case of the Wigtown Martyrs,* in which Wodrow was defended:

> If he [the author] has succeeded in collecting and exhibiting such evidence as shall settle the controversy on the question at issue, and at the same time vindicate Wodrow's credibility as a *narrator of facts* he shall have no occasion to regret the trouble (not inconsiderable) which he has had in doing so.

Napier again took up the cudgels in *History Rescued in Answer to 'History Vindicated' being a Recapitulation of the 'Case for the Crown' and Reviewers Reviewed in re The Wigtown Martyrs,* in which his case against Wodrow was repeated and enlarged. The debate was, of course, inconclusive, but it demonstrates the enormous continuing influence of Wodrow and the way in which that influence limited and inhibited historical discussion.

Just as Wodrow's supporters have continued into the twentieth century, so have his detractors. M. E. M. Donaldson, in *Scotland's Suppressed History,* returns to the tradition of contradicting Wodrow. For her too the nonconformists were justly executed for civil rebellion, and she takes the opportunity to assert alternative biographies - much less flattering - of Wodrow's heroes.

The combined effect of these two schools of Wodrow's successors has been to restrict the discussion of Restoration ecclesiastical history in such a way that it has been reduced to the assertion of mutually irreconcilable mythologies. There has, however, been a third school, largely composed of non-Scots, who thereby achieve a measure of detachment from their theme. By the early twentieth century these writers were approaching the point from which an understanding of Restoration ecclesiastical history might have been achieved, had not other factors intervened.

David Hume was a man infinitely more sophisticated than Wodrow. His treatment of Restoration Scotland in his *History of Great Britain* goes some way to a more mature view of events. Like Wodrow, however, he starts as a good Hanoverian from the principle that Restoration government was arbitrary. Thus, by extension, those who resisted that power were defenders of liberty, martyred in the cause. Such a preconception prevented Hume from enquiring into the motivations of government policy and laid him open to the temptation of following Wodrow's account of the Pentland Rising. On the other hand, Hume could see the difficulty that faced the government in attempting to placate an irreconcilable minority who would neither accept nor extend toleration. These two attitudes could not be reconciled, and on the whole Hume was content to see Lauderdale's later career in Wodrow's terms. Nevertheless he had sown seeds which would mature in the nineteenth century.

When H. T. Buckle published his volume *On Scotland and the Scotch Intellect* in the mid-nineteenth century, he made no major advance. He was the first historian of the Scottish Restoration since Wodrow to attempt to support his argument by reference to original works, but nevertheless his principal source for the Restoration was Wodrow and sources Wodrow had incorporated, and consequently his account was a few pages of synopsis of that author in which the heroism of nonconformists figures largely.

Buckle, however, was the last historian to whom the principal documents of the period were not readily available. When Peter Hume Brown wrote his *History of Scotland,* the *Lauderdale Papers,* edited by Osmund Airy, were available to him, and he himself had edited the *Registers of the Privy Council.* The long tradition of following Wodrow still had an influence on him, and consequently he produced an account of the Restoration that was fundamentally incoherent, but his work nevertheless marked a great advance. In the first place his account of Scotland was given from the point of view of the government and not from that of the dissenters. To that date Scottish Restoration ecclesiastical history had been discussed solely in terms of its effect upon nonconformists. That had inevitably distorted any understanding of government policy. Hume Brown attempted to account in some measure for the actions of the administration. His sympathy - derived from Wodrow - for a prisoner executed after Rullion Green and Hackston of Rathillet as 'martyrs', and his view of the 1669 Indulgence as a 'temptation' to outed ministers is, however, not integrated with his parallel attempts at historical understanding.

William Law Mathieson was a more sophisticated exponent of the same line of argument. Like Hume Brown, he made the great transition from giving an account of the Restoration from the point of view of a minority to relating events from the point of view of central government. He was, moreover, conscious of some difficulties posed to the government by dissent. His work, *Politics and Religion,* is the first attempt to give a coherent account of changes in government ecclesiastical policy, although he had only a limited understanding of why they came about, and no notion of how.

M

In almost three quarters of a century since then, very little advance has been made. The outline of government ecclesiastical policy has been known, and that is all. Partly this is to be explained by the almost total lapse of interest in Scottish history from the late 1920s until after the second war. The major journal of the subject, the *Scottish Historical Review,* ceased publication. After 1928 no further issues were published until 1947. Secondly, after a revival of interest in the subject, ecclesiastical history was felt to be an outmoded study. G. S. Pryde, in *Scotland from 1603 to the Present Day,* gave expression to this belief:

> An attempt has been made to interpret the past in a way that is in keeping with historical atti-
> tudes today . . . and one marked tendency nowadays is to attach as much importance to con-
> stitutional, economic and 'cultural' studies as to political and diplomatic, military and eccles-
> iastical. This newer approach . . . is, I hope, apparent in the chapters that follow.

This attitude has been modified since, particularly with regard to the Scottish Reformation. Nevertheless, one of the best of modern Scottish historians, and himself an ecclesiastical historian, Gordon Donaldson, in his review of Scottish history, *James V to James VII,* has been obliged to give an account of Restoration ecclesiastical history which differs little from that of William Law Mathieson.

More recently, in an article in the *Scottish Historical Review* for 1968, Ian Cowan urged a reconsideration of the whole subject of the motivations and intentions of Scottish presbyterians in the seventeenth century and suggested economic and sociological factors which might help to explain their actions. Clearly this is the direction in which research into ecclesiastical history ought to be moving, but there are few signs as yet that it has done so.

Finally William Ferguson, in a provocative and exciting book, *Scotland's Relations with England: a Survey to 1707,* has made an attempt to relate Scottish ecclesiastical policy in the Restoration to English political developments and Scottish political ambitions. Although Ferguson's conclusions are not those adopted in this book, his methodology and approach are very similar.

While this state of affairs exists in the historiography of the Scottish Restoration, historians of the Restoration period in England have developed their ideas on ecclesiastical policy a great deal further. They have explored the idea that ecclesiastical policy had relatively little to·do with religion, and was often simply another factor in political struggles for power; they have analysed its evolution and concluded that political forces moulded and changed its form.

R. S. Bosher, in *The Making of the Restoration Settlement,* was one of the first to unravel the strands in the evolution of English ecclesiastical policy. He alleged that Clarendon and Sheldon between them were obliged, by the necessity of retaining the political support of the presbyterians, to defer implementing their designs for an erastian episcopal establishment until 1662 and 1663. V. S. Sutch, in *Gilbert Sheldon,* extends Bosher's analysis to suggest that Charles challenged that establishment in his desire for toleration, but that Sheldon got his way by deliberate scaremongering about Catholicism.

This interpretation of events at the Restoration was challenged by G. R. Abernathy in *The English Presbyterians and the Stuart Restoration 1648-1663,* but his alternative viewpoint nevertheless assumes that ecclesiastical policy was simply another element in Restoration political policy. A recent synthesis of work on the ecclesiastical settlement by I. M. Green, *The Re-Establishment of the Church of England 1660-1663,* makes the same assumption.

J. P. Kenyon, in *The Popish Plot,* J. L. Miller, in *Popery and Politics in England,* and J. R. Jones, in *The First Whigs,* have all been concerned to show how real fear of popery was exploited to achieve other and political ends. D. T. Whitcombe, in *Charles II and the Cavalier House of Commons,* and D. R. Lacey, in *Dissent and Parliamentary Politics in England 1661-1689,* have shown how dissent, protestant as well as catholic, was used as a political tool to manipulate parties and functions.

What this book attempts to do, therefore, is to apply some of the insights and perceptions of the function of ecclesiastical policy in England to Scotland, in the hope of creating a more sophisticated understanding of the evolution and purposes of that policy. From this study a picture of Scottish ecclesiastical policy has emerged which gives some ideas of the conflicts within the government and the tensions between ideals and practice.

BIBLIOGRAPHY

Unpublished Primary Sources

Bodleian Ms Add C 34 f.156

British Museum Add Ms 23114
                Add Ms 23115
                Add Ms 23116
                Add Ms 23117
                Add Ms 23119
                Add Ms 23120
                Add Ms 23121
                Add Ms 23122
                Add Ms 23125
                Add Ms 23126
                Add Ms 23127
                Add Ms 23134
                Add Ms 23135
                Add Ms 23136
                Add Ms 23137
                Add Ms 23245
                Add Ms 35125
                Lansdowne Ms 988

Glasgow University Library Ms Gen 210. This manuscript has become separated from the Wodrow Collection, now in the National Library of Scotland, of which it was originally a part. It is Wodrow's transcription of the correspondence now in the Scottish Record Office, Register House, Edinburgh.

Two attempts have been made to publish the correspondence. The first forms the introduction to Volume I of Wodrow's *Sufferings*, where the material is partly published and partly paraphrased. The second attempted to supplement this version by the publication of certain additional extracts in Volume II of the *Consultations of the Ministers of Edinburgh*. Neither of these reductions of the correspondence does anything like full justice to the length and complexity of the material.

National Library of Scotland Ms 573
　　　　　　　　　　　　　Ms 597
　　　　　　　　　　　　　Ms 2512
　　　　　　　　　　　　　Ms 2521
　　　　　　　　　　　　　Ms 3112
　　　　　　　　　　　　　Ms 3136
　　　　　　　　　　　　　Ms 3420
　　　　　　　　　　　　　Ms 3648
　　　　　　　　　　　　　Ms 3830
　　　　　　　　　　　　　Ms 3922
　　　　　　　　　　　　　Ms 5049
　　　　　　　　　　　　　Ms 5050
　　　　　　　　　　　　　Ms 7003
　　　　　　　　　　　　　Ms 7004
　　　　　　　　　　　　　Ms 7005
　　　　　　　　　　　　　Ms 7023
　　　　　　　　　　　　　Ms 7024
　　　　　　　　　　　　　Ms 7025
　　　　　　　　　　　　　Ms 7034
　　　　　　　　　　　　　Ms 7121
　　　　　　　　　　　　　Wodrow Folio LXV
　　　　　　　　　　　　　Wodrow Ms Quarto LXIII: Robert Douglas,
'An Account of the Introduction of Prelacy'.
National Library of Scotland Yester Box 5
　　　　　　　　　　　　　Yester Box 130
St Andrews University Muniments SL 705/1-147
Scottish Record Office GD 157
　　　　　　　　　　　　　Parliamentary Papers
Transcripts of the Records of the Kirk Session of the Parish of Crail.

Published Primary Sources

An Account of Scotland's grievances under Duke Lauderdale tendred to the King, 1679.

Acts of the General Assembly of the Church of Scotland 1638-1642, Edinburgh, 1843.

Acts of the Parliaments of Scotland

Baillie, Robert. *Letters and Journals.* 3 vols. Ed. D. Laing, Edinburgh, 1822.

Brodie, Alexander. *The Diary of Alex. Brodie, 1652-80, and of his son, James Brodie of Brodie, 1680-85.* Ed. D. Laing, Aberdeen, 1863.

Brown, T. *Miscellanea Aulica.* London, 1702.

Burnet, Gilbert. *History of My Own Time.* Ed. Osmund Airy, 2 vols. Oxford, 1897, 1900.

Calendar of State Papers (Domestic Series).

Charles II and Scotland in 1650. Ed. S. R. Gardiner. Edinburgh, 1894.

Clarendon, Edward Hyde, Earl of. *The Continuation of the Life of Edward Earl of Clarendon.* Oxford, 1761.

Collection of State Trials. 2nd. ed. 8 vols. London, 1730-5.

Dalrymple of Stair, Sir John. *Memoirs of Great Britain and Ireland.* New ed. 3 vols. London, 1790.

Extracts from the Records of the Convention of the Royal Burghs of Scotland 1615-1676. Ed. J. D. Marwick. Edinburgh, 1878.

Gordon, J. *History of Scots Affairs.* 3 vols. Aberdeen, 1841.

Hickes, George. *Ravillac Redivivus.* London, 1678.

Historical Manuscripts Commission. *Third Report.*

--------. *Dartmouth* I.

--------. *Drumlanrig* I.

--------. *Hamilton.*

--------. *Hamilton (Supp).*

--------. *Laing* I.

--------. *Portland* II.

The Humble address of the Synod of Aberdeen. [Edinburgh, 1661].

Johnston of Wariston, Sir Archibald, *Diary.* Vol. II 1650-54. Ed. D. H. Fleming, Edinburgh, 1919; Vol. III 1655-1660. Ed. J. D. Ogilvie, Edinburgh, 1940.

Jones, J. R. 'The Scottish Constitutional Opposition in 1679'. *Scottish Historical Review* XXXVII, 1958.

Kerr, Sir R. *Correspondence of Sir R. Kerr, first earl of Ancram and his son William, third earl of Lothian, 1616-67.* Ed. D. Laing. 2 vols. Edinburgh: Roxburghe Club, 1875.

Kirkton, James. *The Secret and True History of the Church of Scotland from the Restoration to the Year 1678.* Ed. C. K. Sharpe. Edinburgh, 1817.

Lamont of Newton, John. *The Diary of Mr John Lamont of Newton.* Ed. G. R. Kinloch. Edinburgh, 1830.

Lauder of Fountainhall, John. *Historical Notices.* 2 vols. Edinburgh, 1848.

--------. *Journals.* Edinburgh, 1900.

Lauderdale Papers. Ed. Osmund Airy. 3 vols. London, 1884-5.

Law, Robert. *Memorialls.* Ed. C. K. Sharpe. Edinburgh, 1819.

Letter addressed by Prelates and Individuals of High Rank in Scotland . . . to Sancroft, Archbishop of Canterbury. Ed. W. N. Clarke. Edinburgh, 1848.

'Letters to the Earl of Lauderdale'. *Camden Miscellany* VIII. London 1883.
Letters from Lady Margaret Kennedy to John, Duke of Lauderdale. Edinburgh, 1828.
The Life of Mr James Sharp, From his Birth to his Instalment in the Archbishopric of St. Andrews . . . With an Appendix Containing an Account of Some of Mr Sharp's Actions, During the Time of his being Archbishop: And the Manner and Circumstances of his Death, by one of the Persons concern'd in it. 1719. [First published without Appendix, 1678.]
The Life of Robert Blair . . . containing his autobiography from 1593 to 1636 with supplement . . . to 1680, by his son in law, Mr William Row. Ed. Thomas M'Crie. Edinburgh, 1848.
Mackenzie of Rosehaugh, Sir George. *Memoirs of the Affairs of Scotland.* Ed. T. Thomson. Edinburgh, 1821.
Mercurius Caledonius.
Nicoll, John. *A Diary of Public Transactions and other occurences, chiefly in Scotland From January 1650 to June 1667.* Edinburgh, 1836.
Particular Matters of Fact relating to the Administration of affairs in Scotland, under the Duke of Lauderdale. 1679.
Paterson, John. *Tandem Bona Causa Triumphat,* Edinburgh, 1661.
Records of the Commissions of the General Assemblies. Ed. A. F. Mitchell and J. Christie. 3 vols. Edinburgh, 1892, 1896, 1909.
Register of the Consultations of the Ministers of Edinburgh and some other Brethren of the Ministry. Ed. Wm. Stephen. 2 vols. Edinburgh, 1921, 1930.
The Registers of the Privy Council of Scotland. Third Series.
Scotland and the Commonwealth. Ed. C. H. Firth. Edinburgh, 1895.
Scotland and the Protectorate. Ed. C. H. Firth. Edinburgh, 1899.
Scottish History Society. *Miscellany* I. Edinburgh, 1893.
--------. *Miscellany* II. Edinburgh, 1904.
--------. *Miscellany* III. Edinburgh, 1919.
--------. *Miscellany* V. Edinburgh, 1933.
Selections from the Minutes of the Presbyteries of St. Andrews and Cupar. Ed. G. R. Kinloch. Edinburgh, 1837.
Some farther matter of Fact relating to the Administration of affairs in Scotland, under the Duke of Lauderdale. 1679.
A Source Book of Scottish History. Vol. III. Ed. W. C. Dickinson and G. Donaldson. 2nd. ed. Edinburgh, 1961.
Spalding, S. J. *History of the Troubles and Memorable Transactions in Scotland 1624-1645.* Aberdeen, 1830.
Selections from the Minutes of the Synod of Fife 1611-1687. Ed. Charles Baxter. Edinburgh, 1837.
A Collection of the State Papers of John Thurloe. Ed. Thomas Birch. 7 vols. London, 1742.
A True and Impartial Account of the Life of the Most Reverend Father in God, Dr James Sharp, Archbishop of St. Andrews. 1723.
Turner, James. *Memoirs of his own Life and Times.* Edinburgh, 1829.
The Writings and Speeches of Oliver Cromwell. Ed. W. C. Abbott. 4 vols. Cambridge, Mass., 1937-47.

Unpublished Secondary Sources

Beattie, Colin. 'The Early Career of John Maitland, Duke of Lauderdale 1637-1651'. M.A., McGill University, 1977.

Dow, F. M. 'The English army and the government of Scotland, 1651-1660'. D. Phil. York. 1976.

McNeill, P. G. B. 'The Jurisdiction of the Scottish Privy Council 1532-1708'. PhD. Glasgow. 1961.

Marshall, R. K. 'The House of Hamilton . . . in the seventeenth century with a calendar of the correspondence . . . to 1712'. PhD. Edinburgh, 1970.

Stevenson, David. 'The Covenanters and the government of Scotland 1637-51'. PhD. Glasgow, 1971.

Yould, Rev. G. M. 'The Duke of Lauderdale's Religious Policy in Scotland 1668-79: the failure of conciliation and the return to coercion'.

Published Secondary Sources

Abernathy, George R. 'The English Presbyterians and the Stuart Restoration, 1648-1663'. *Transactions of the American Philosophical Society* LV, 1965.

Anderson, James. *Ladies of the Covenant*. London, 1851.

Anderson, P. J., ed. *Officers and Graduates of the University and King's College, Aberdeen, 1485-1860*. Aberdeen, 1893.

--------. *Roll of Alumni of the University and King's College*. Aberdeen, 1900.

Barr, James. *The Scottish Covenanters*. Glasgow, 1946.

Bate, F. *The Declaration of Indulgence, 1672*. London, 1908.

Beaton, D. *Scottish Heroines of the Faith*. London, 1909.

Bosher, R. S. *The Making of the Restoration Settlement*. London, 1951.

Brown, Peter Hume. *History of Scotland*, 3 vols. Cambridge, 1908-9.

Buckle, H. T. *On Scotland and the Scotch Intellect*. New ed. London, 1970.

Buckroyd, J. M. 'The Dismissal of Archbishop Alexander Burnet, 1669'. *Records of the Scottish Church History Society* XVIII, 1973, 149-55.

--------. 'Mercurius Caledonius'. *Scottish Historical Review* LIV, 1975, 11-21.

--------. 'The Resolutioners and the Scottish Nobility in the early months of 1660'. *Studies in Church History* XII, 1975, 245-52.

--------. 'Lord Broghill and the Scottish Church 1655-1656'. *Journal of Ecclesiastical History* XXVII, 1976, 359-68.

Butler, D. *The Life and Letters of Robert Leighton*. London, 1903.

Cant, R. G. *The University of St. Andrews*. New ed. Edinburgh, 1970.

Carslaw, W. H. *Heroes of the Covenant*. Paisley, 1900.

Clarke, T. E. S. and H. C. Foxcroft. *A Life of Gilbert Burnet*. Cambridge, 1907.

Cobbett, William. *Parliamentary History*. 36 vols. London, 1806-20.

Cowan, Ian. 'The Covenanters: A Revision Article'. *Scottish Historical Review* XLVII, 1968, 35-52.

--------. *The Scottish Covenanters 1660-1688*. London, 1976.

Cramond, W., ed. *The Annals of Banff*. 2 vols. Aberdeen, 1891-3.

Crookshank, William. *The History of the State and Sufferings of the Church of Scotland, from the Restoration to the Revolution*. 2 vols. London, 1749.

Davies, Godfrey. *The Restoration of Charles II.* London, 1955.
-------- and P. Hardacre. 'The Restoration of the Scottish Episcopacy 1660-1661'. *Journal of British Studies* I, 1960, 32-51.
Defoe, Daniel. *Memoirs of the Church of Scotland.* London, 1717.
Donaldson, Gordon. *James V to James VII.* Edinburgh, 1965.
Donaldson, M. E. M. *Scotland's Suppressed History.* London, 1935.
Elder, J. R. *The Highland Host of 1678.* Glasgow, 1914.
Ferguson, William. *Scotland's Relations with England: a Survey to 1707.* Edinburgh, 1977.
Foster, W. R. *Bishop and Presbytery.* London, 1958.
Gardner, W. B. 'The Later Years of John Maitland, Second Earl and First Duke of Lauderdale'. *Journal of Modern History* XX, 1948, 113-22.
Green, I. M. *The Re-Establishment of the Church of England, 1660-1663.* Oxford, 1978.
Haley, K. H. D. *The First Earl of Shaftesbury.* Oxford, 1968.
Henderson, G. D. *The Burning Bush.* Edinburgh, 1957.
--------. *Religious Life in Seventeenth Century Scotland.* Cambridge, 1937. [Chapter VII, 'Externals of Church Worship and Church Government under Charles II'.]
Howie, James. *Biographia Scoticana or . . . Scots Worthies.* Glasgow, 1775.
Hume, David. *History of Great Britain.* 2 vols. Edinburgh, 1754, 1757.
Jones, G. H. *Charles Middleton.* London, 1967.
Jones, J. R. *The First Whigs: the Politics of the Exclusion Crisis 1678-83.* London, 1961.
Keith, Robert. *An Historical Catalogue of the Scottish Bishops.* New ed. Edinburgh, 1824.
Kenyon, J. P. *The Popish Plot.* London, 1972.
Knox, E. A. *Robert Leighton, Archbishop of Glasgow.* London, 1930.
Lacey, D. R. *Dissent and Parliamentary Politics in England 1661-1689.* New Brunswick, N. J., 1969.
Lamb, J. A. 'Archbishop Alexander Burnet 1614-1684'. *Records of the Scottish Church History Society* XI, 1951-3, 134-45.
Lee, Maurice. *The Cabal.* University of Illinois Press, Urbana, 1965.
--------. *John Maitland of Thirlestane.* Princeton, New Jersey, 1959.
Mackenzie, W. C. *The Life and Times of John Maitland, Duke of Lauderdale, 1616-1682.* London, 1923.
Macray, W. D. and F. T. Routledge *et al.,* eds. *Calendar of the Clarendon State Papers.* 5 vols. Oxford, 1872-1970.
M'Crie, Thomas [the elder]. *Vindication of the Covenanters.* 4th. ed. Edinburgh, 1855.
Mathieson, William Law. *Politics and Religion.* 2 vols. Glasgow, 1902.
Miller, J. L. *Popery and Politics in England.* Cambridge, 1972.
Napier, Mark. *The Case for the Crown in re The Wigtown Martyrs proved to be Myths.* Edinburgh, 1863.
--------. *History Rescued in Answer to 'History Vindicated' being a Recapitulation of the 'Case for the Crown' and the Reviewers Reviewed in re The Wigtown Martyrs.* Edinburgh, 1870.

Ogg, David. *England in the Reign of Charles II.* 2nd. ed. London, 1967.

Ogilvie, J. D. 'The Aberdeen Doctors and the National Covenant'. *Edinburgh Bibliographical Society Publications* XI, 1912-20, 73-86.

--------. 'A Bibliography of the Resolutioner-Protester Controversy 1650-1659'. *Edinburgh Bibliographical Society Publications* XIV, 1928-30, 59-74.

Omond, G. W. T. *The Lord Advocates of Scotland.* 2 vols. Edinburgh, 1883.

Patrick, John. 'The Origins of the Opposition to Lauderdale in the Scottish Parliament of 1673'. *Scottish Historical Review* LIII, 1974, 1-21.

Pryde, G. S. *Scotland from 1603 to the Present Day.* London, 1962.

Robertson, Alexander. *Sir Robert Moray.* London, 1922.

Scott, Hew. *Fasti Ecclesiae Scoticanae.* New ed. Edinburgh, 1920.

Shields, Michael. *Faithful Contendings Displayed.* First published ed. John Howie. Glasgow, 1780.

Smellie, Alexander. *Men of the Covenant.* London, 1903.

Smout, T. C. *Scottish Trade on the Eve of Union.* Edinburgh, 1963.

Snow, W. G. S. *The Times, Life and Thought of Patrick Forbes, Bishop of Aberdeen 1618-1635.* London, 1952.

Starkey, A. M. 'Robert Wodrow and *The History of the Sufferings of the Church of Scotland*'. *Church History* XLIII, 1974, 488-98.

Stephen, Thomas. *The Life and Times of Archbishop Sharp of St. Andrews.* London, 1839.

Stevenson, David. *The Scottish Revolution, 1637-1644: The Triumph of the Covenanters.* Newton Abbot, 1973.

--------. *Revolution and Counter-Revolution in Scotland, 1644-1651.* London, 1977.

Stewart, Archibald. *History Vindicated in the Case of the Wigtown Martyrs.* Edinburgh, 1867.

Sutch, V. S. *Gilbert Sheldon: Architect of Anglican Survival, 1640-1675.* The Hague, 1973.

Sykes, N. *From Sheldon to Secker.* Cambridge, 1959.

Terry, C. S. *The Pentland Rising.* Glasgow, 1905.

Trevor-Roper, H. R. 'Scotland and the Puritan Revolution'. *Historical Essays 1660-1750 presented to David Ogg.* London, 1963, 78-130.

Turner, F. C. *James II.* London, 1948.

Walker, Patrick. *Some remarkable passages of the life and death of Mr Alexander Peden.* Edinburgh, 1724; *Some remarkable passages of the life and death of . . . J. Semple . . . J. Welwood . . . R. Cameron.* Edinburgh, 1727; *Some remarkable passages in the life and death of . . . Mr Daniel Cargill.* Edinburgh, 1732. Edited D. Hay Fleming and republished as *Six Saints of the Covenant,* London, 1901.

Whitcombe, D. T. *Charles II and the Cavalier House of Commons.* New York, 1966.

Wodrow, Robert. *The Life of James Wodrow.* Edinburgh, 1828.

--------. *The Sufferings of the Church of Scotland from the Restoration to the Revolution.* Ed. R. Burne. 4 vols. Glasgow, 1828.

Index